The Forgotten Senator
The Life and Character of
Preston B. Plumb

Johanna D. Wickman

Bellis Perennis Publishing
Casper, Wyoming

Copyright © 2023 by Johanna D. Wickman
All rights reserved. This book or any portion thereof
may not be reproduced or used in any manner whatsoever
without the express written permission of the publisher
except for the use of brief quotations in a book review.

Front cover image author's collection, back cover image of Plumb courtesy Mollus-Mass Photograph Collection, United States Army Heritage and Education Center, Carlisle, PA.

Printed in the United States of America

First Printing, 2023

ISBN 979-8-9878520-0-2

Library of Congress Control Number: 2023903030

Bellis Perennis Publishing
Casper, WY 82604

www.prestonplumb.com

For Preston and Carrie

Contents

Foreword	7
Acknowledgments	11
Introduction	15
Chapter 1: Early Years in Ohio	19
Chapter 2: Kansas Settlement	37
Chapter 3: Founding Emporia	77
Chapter 4: War Breaks Out	97
Chapter 5: Off to War	101
Chapter 6: Battle of Prairie Grove and Aftermath	117
Chapter 7: Quantrill's Raid	127
Chapter 8: Bushwhackers	143
Chapter 9: Price Raid	157
Chapter 10: Headed West	171
Chapter 11: Back to Civilian Life	193
Chapter 12: Mr. Plumb Goes to Washington	205
Chapter 13: A Thorough Kansan	213
Chapter 14: A Big Winning	236
Chapter 15: Greater Influence	243
Chapter 16: Family and Business	266
Chapter 17: Senator of the West	279
Chapter 18: "The Senator"	299

Chapter 19: His Last Campaign	309
Chapter 20: Legacy	328
Notes	343
Bibliography	359

Foreword

By Douglas R. Cubbison

Preston B. Plumb may well be the most important U.S. Senator who you have never heard about. In a time of our nation's history when many of our citizens lived truly remarkable lives, Preston Plumb lived such a remarkable life as to stand out. Yet, he is nearly entirely forgotten today. Casper, Wyoming's Johanna Wickman has finally restored Preston Plumb to his rightful recognition as one of the most significant Kansans in our nation's history.

Born in 1837 in Ohio, as a young man Plumb demonstrated the courage and will to persevere which served as hallmark personal traits, when he survived a fight with a bear at the age of ten, although he would carry the scars from the attack for the remainder of his life. Two years later, at the age of twelve, Plumb attended Kenyon College in Gambier, Kansas. To help his family pay his tuition, Plumb worked at the printing office of the school newspaper, *The Western Episcopalian*–affording him an introduction to and creating a lifelong fascination with journalism. At the age of sixteen, Plumb became the owner, operator and editor of the premier newspaper in Xenia, Ohio- *The Xenia News*. Already, at this early stage in his life, Plumb was also demonstrating the photographic memory which served him well throughout his long and illustrious career.

Plumb moved to "Bloody Kansas" in 1856; and shortly became fully engaged in the virulent strife which then engulfed the territory. Plumb made the acquaintance of fabled abolitionist John Brown, and in August 1856 the nineteen-year transported a large load of 250 Sharps Rifles with ammunition and related military equipment to Brown and other "Free-State" interests. After a year of working for a newspaper in Lawrence, Plumb became one of the founding fathers of the fledgling community of Emporia, and set up the first newspaper–*The Kansas News*–in that town following a perilous trip through Missouri transporting the printing press. He was active in the militia, and was a delegate to the 1858 Kansas Constitutional Convention. Surviving a bout with smallpox in 1858, by 1861 Plumb was an embedded community leader, a member of the first State Legislature and a Kansas Supreme Court reporter.

With the onset of the rebellion, in August, 1862 Plumb raised a company of recruits in Emporia for what would become Company C of the 11th Kansas Volunteer Infantry (subsequently the 11th Kansas Volunteer Cavalry), with Captain Preston B. Plumb their commanding officer. Following their first involvement in the Battle of Cane Hill

(November 28, 1862) Plumb continued his involvement with the press by becoming the publisher and editor of the 11th Kansas's informal regimental newspaper, *The Buck & Ball*. Plumb also fought at the Battle of Prairie Grove, served in the pursuit of Quantrill following his burning of Lawrence (August 1863), fought the dreaded Confederate partisans of Quantrill and "Bloody Bill Anderson" throughout 1863-1864 in western Missouri and eastern Kansas, and then helped repulse the 1864 Missouri counteroffensive of Confederate Major General Sterling Price- particularly earning commendation at the Battle of Westport immediately east of Kansas City.

In January 1865 the 11th Kansas Cavalry was transferred far to the west, to help secure the Overland (Oregon-California) Trail and the paralleling Pacific Telegraph Company line which connected California with the remainder of the Union. His service on the remote and isolated frontier, in which he regularly found himself the senior officer present, resulted in promotion to Lieutenant Colonel of the 11th Kansas Cavalry and frequent post and detachment command responsibilities—which he fulfilled with skill, talent and aplomb.

Discharged on September 13, 1865 he returned to his beloved Emporia, and immediately resumed his promising business and political careers—and got married! By 1867 the newlywed Plumb was re-elected to the State Legislature where he served as Speaker of the House. He became the President of the Emporia National Bank, and his leadership was instrumental in that financial institution weathering the Panic of 1873. Concurrently, Plumb became an Attorney and established the firm of Ruggles & Plumb, which shortly gained the reputation of being the foremost law firm in the state.

Four years later, only 39 years old, he was elected to the United States Senate, and he represented the citizens of Kansas and the interest of his state for the remainder of his life. Plumb served on three of the most important committees in the U.S. Senate- the Military Affairs Committee, the Mines and Mining Committee, and as Chairman of the Committee on Public Lands. Senator Plumb would drive the bill through the Senate creating the Department of Agriculture. Particularly as Chairman of the Senate Committee on Public Lands, Plumb was instrumental in establishing Federal land policies, rules and regulations as the nation completed its occupation and settlement of the western portion of the continent. Plumb argued for twelve-year term limits in the Senate, and helped create Yosemite and Sequoia National Parks in California.

Plumb soon earned a reputation of an exceptionally hard-working Senator, personally answering every piece of correspondence that he received, daily reading every single newspaper printed in the State of Kansas, and championing hundreds of brother veterans' petitions for pensions.

Demonstrating virtues which are far too rarely displayed in the halls of the U.S. Capitol today, Plumb throughout his life carried a sterling reputation for being virtuous, impeccably honest, generous, charitable, incredibly reliable, moral, and deeply religious. He was a passionate abolitionist, deeply committed to achieving equality for Black-Americans of his nation, and endorsed women's suffrage. He, quite literally, worked himself to death in the U.S. Senate, and died unexpectedly in office on December 20, 1891–he was only 54 years of age, but he had packed an incredible amount of living into his lifetime.

Surprisingly, Preston Plumb has only been the subject of a single biography–written by distinguished Kansas Historian William E. Connelly, *The Life of Preston B. Plumb*, in 1913. Although meticulously researched, Connelly's biography is written in a relatively pedantic and dry style–and in any event this biography is now over a century old and is badly dated.

Johanna's biography of Preston Plumb is derived from comprehensive research, in particular benefitting from family letters and Emporia documents never previously perused by scholars. What makes this biography particularly valuable is that Johanna's exhaustive research enables her to tell much of Plumb's story in his own words–essentially this is very much Plumb's autobiography which he never compiled, much more than a conventional biography. A considerable portion of the biography is focused upon Plumb's key service as a Senator.

Hopefully this lively, engaging biography will restore Preston B. Plumb to his well-deserved position in history. I highly recommend this biography to Civil War buffs, scholars studying the antebellum period in Kansas and the history of the US Senate in the late 19th Century, any citizen of Kansas and Wyoming–the two states with which he was intimately involved–and to anybody attempting to comprehend the growth and development of mining, mineral, property and land rights and ownership in the western states of our nation–topics which remain highly relevant over a century after Preston Plumb implemented the initial Federal policies.

Preston B. Plumb is unquestionably the most important United States Senator who you have never heard of. This superb biography will, for the first time in over a century, document a life fully and well lived, which directly influenced the growth and development of the western states of our republic.

Douglas R. Cubbison
Curator
U.S. Army Heritage and Education Center
U.S. Army War College
Carlisle Barracks, Pennsylvania

Acknowledgments

Researching and writing a book like this is next to impossible without the help and support of friends and family. Over the past few years, I have been fortunate enough to meet so many wonderful people through this project. I am grateful for the help of my family and friends, as well as for the new friendships writing this book has brought me.

First and foremost, I would like to thank my mother, Martha, for her invaluable help with this book. I scanned thousands of pages of documents in my research and she painstakingly transcribed them for me so that I could organize and sift through them. Without her help, I'd probably still be trying to do all that myself and you might see a Preston B. Plumb biography sometime in the 2030s…She also was very helpful in finding newspaper articles for this book. She spent countless hours perusing online newspaper databases finding all sorts of gems—many of which are included in the book. She proofread, helped me compile notes, edited, and helped with just about everything. Thank you, Mom!

The rest of my family, my father John, and my sisters, Gloria, and Olivia, provided constant counsel and advice as I worked on this project. Gloria's help in proofreading and editing was especially helpful. I could not have done this without her help! Friends John Goss, Craig Lawson, Amy Taucher, and Con Trumbull read through drafts of chapters and listened to countless Plumb stories over the past few years with nothing but support. Thank you, Steven Dacus, for supporting my research on this project and for offering your insights on the illustrations and content in the military chapters.

A special thank you goes to the Fort Caspar Museum for their help and support with this book. Rick Young and Michelle Bahe have also been listening to Plumb stories for years–thank you for supporting this!

I would especially like to thank the members of the Plumb family who have not only supported this project but also shared their family archives and history with me. I am forever grateful to you Jody Wolf, Carrie Clarke, and Amanda Plumb Eberly. And many thanks to John Meredith for your photographs.

This book would not have been possible without the help of many Kansans who offered research materials, advice, and even opened their homes to a virtual stranger from Wyoming. I am extremely thankful for the help, support, and friendship of Rob and Lesa Reves who have done all of those things to help me finish this book.

I would also like to thank the staff of the Lyon County History Center for all of their support for this project. I scanned thousands of pages of archival material there and had an absolute blast doing it. Many thanks to William Boyer, Lisa Soller, and Greg Jordan.

I would also like to thank Michael Halleran for working with me to try to track down as much as possible about Preston Plumb's Masonic history. Bob and Jane Symmonds were kind enough to allow me to stay at their home while I was researching in Emporia. Kevin Johnson and Matt Mulheran shared a large amount of 11th Kansas resources with me.

Special thanks to Lisa Keyes at the Kansas State Historical Society for all of her help within their archives. She located and scanned a large amount of material for me throughout this project.

This book features custom artwork done by Andy Robbins and Maria Rose Wimmer. Their incredible artistic talents helped illustrate key moments in Plumb's life and added another layer of depth to his story. I am very appreciative of their hard work!

Many of the images featured in this book required editing and "polishing" in order to make them suitable for print. Vince Crolla was kind enough to lend his expertise to that work, and it's made all the difference in the world with those pictures.

Special thanks to Douglas R. Cubbison for contributing the Forward to this book.

I also wish to thank an extraordinary group of friends who stood by me throughout this project. This was by far the most difficult and life-changing thing I've ever done. I could not have finished it without their support and guidance. My heartfelt thanks to Monica Faust, Sarah Lemos-Aune, Kendra Mateo, and Amy Taucher. Also, thank you, Con Trumbull, for "keeping it real."

The vast majority of source material for this book comes from a series of interviews conducted between 1910 and 1913 by Kansas historian William Elsey Connelley. Although our two books on the life of Preston B. Plumb differ greatly, his thorough research laid the groundwork for my book, which would not have been possible without it. I would especially like to thank Carrie Plumb and the Plumb family (Mary, Dale, Ruth, Caroline, and Preston Jr.) for hiring Connelley to write his biography, and therefore funding his research that has led to this book. Carrie and Dale were especially involved in his research and left behind a tremendous amount of information that was very useful. Sifting through the thousands of pages of Connelley's interviews would have been a chore had they not been typed and indexed by Mabel Plumb Edwards over a century ago. I am very grateful for all of the work done by Connelley and the Plumb family.

Last but certainly not least, I wish to thank those who pre-ordered this book well over a year ago. Your confidence in my ability to write this book and your support allowed me to travel to Kansas to complete the research needed to create this book. Thank you for believing in me and this project! Tristan Birkemeier, Douglas R. Cubbison, Steven Dacus, Gina and Shawn Holden, Craig Lawson, Dob Wallace, John and Martha Wickman, Gloria Wickman, and Olivia Wickman.

I hope you enjoy the story of Preston B. Plumb.

Introduction

I first discovered Preston B. Plumb while performing research for my master's thesis in 2013. I did some cursory research on him and the more I began to dig, the more I became fascinated by him and disappointed that such an interesting and remarkable human being had essentially been lost to history. I found that there were remnants of him left in Emporia, Kansas, but for many, the meaning behind the Plumb name and its association with him and his significance, had been lost. I told myself then, that someone needed to write a biography of him, I just never anticipated that that "someone" would be me.

In 2017 I was fortunate to receive two research grants from the Wyoming State Historical Society (Lola Homsher Research Grant) and the Kansas State Historical Society (Edward N. Tihen Research Grant) to travel to Topeka, Kansas to the Kansas State Historical Society's archives to review material relating to the 11th Kansas Volunteer Cavalry and their time stationed at Fort Halleck in present-day Wyoming in 1865. Unfortunately, I did not uncover much information on that short research visit of their military service, but I did discover a motherlode of firsthand accounts of Preston B. Plumb in the form of research materials left behind by William Elsey Connelley.

Connelley was hired by the Plumb family in 1910 to write a biography on Preston B. Plumb which was later published in 1913. The book is now long out of print and although it contains a wealth of information, it requires an intense dedication to Senator Plumb to read it in its entirety. Dry as Connelley's book may be, the research he left behind is priceless. He corresponded with and interviewed hundreds of people who personally knew Plumb. To have so many firsthand stories about the man is incredible.

In the summer of 2021, I traveled to Emporia, Kansas, and scanned thousands of pages of interviews and newspaper articles Connelley had collected. I made another trip to Topeka that same year to scan more of Connelley's materials along with other sources. Those trips along with a few others scattered around Kansas comprise the bulk of this book.

I began writing my biography as Connelley had written his—a traditional academic-style history book. My original goal was to update the language and style for more modern audiences and place more of an emphasis on who Plumb was as a person—not just an inflated resume. As I began to write, I slowly started to see the charm and personality of Plumb fade from the page. I couldn't understand why, because I had loved reading the stories about him, but somehow when I paraphrased them onto the page they lost something. It was then that I realized I was going to write a somewhat unusual history book.

You will notice as you read this book that this is a biography of Preston B. Plumb as told by those who knew him. This is not your typical academic history book, this is a compilation of stories in the words of those who actually knew the man—or in many cases, the words of Connelley as he summarized the information that they gave him during those interviews. For that reason, those interviews are largely unedited. I have made a few edits here and there for ease of reading, but those have been very minimal. Most books do not use such long quotations, and I deliberately chose to incorporate as many as I could into this book so that readers could hear these stories as close to how they were originally told as possible.

I wanted the stories to remain as colorful as they were over 100 years ago when these folks told them to Connelley, and I wanted their names to be involved in this book too. Plumb didn't live in a vacuum. Friends, family, fellow soldiers, senators, and homesteaders—all of these people shaped him and made him into the man he was, and I thought it important to keep them and their names in his story, because they were a part of his life story.

There are already a number of books on the subject of Bleeding Kansas, the Price Raid, Quantrill's Raid, and many of the other historic events Plumb put himself in. In the interest of keeping the focus of this title on the stories of those who knew Plumb, I did not delve into those topics at any great depth. Nor did I go through his military record with the aim to critique any of his judgments, or tear his Senate record apart through a contemporary lens. My aim in writing this was not to introduce you to a man largely forgotten by the history books only to nitpick him, or to argue one way or the other using him as a tool to that end. My goal was simply to introduce you to him by way of those who knew him best, and let that speak for itself.

My hope is that for those reading this book, they'll see a boy who essentially came from nothing, persevered, and grew into the man who founded a town, started a newspaper, served his country as a soldier, risked his life to help those less fortunate, became a lawyer, served in the state legislature, rose to become one of the most popular senators in the history of Kansas, and who above all, was a devoted family man who cherished his wife and children. And that, like all of us, he, too, was flawed. He was a human being who showed that all of us, great or small, can succeed in this life if we have the same fierce drive and compassion he showed throughout his.

Chapter 1

Early Years in Ohio

Born October 12, 1837, in Berkshire, Ohio, Preston Plumb was the eldest of eight children born to David and Hannah (Bierce) Plumb. Little is known of his early life aside from some anecdotes relating to his personality and penchant for being a hard worker—traits that followed him his entire life.

Plumb was a quick study at whatever he threw his attention at and began his schooling at the young age of four. His father was a wagon maker of modest means, and young Plumb often found himself helping with daily chores.

Around the age of six, he learned how to chop wood and was quite proud of his new skill. He quickly grabbed his sister, Ellen, and said, "Ellen! Come out here! I can chop wood!" Ellen recalled that she came out of the house and stood near where he was chopping wood. The heavy axe was too difficult for young Plumb to control and it slipped and came down on the arch of Ellen's foot. She made a full recovery but had difficulty walking for the rest of her life.

Plumb had his own encounter with serious injury at the age of ten. He and some friends had gone into the woods to play in a neighbor's barn that had swings installed in it. Also in the barn, was a pair of chained pet bears. While Plumb was pushing the girls on the swing, he slipped and fell within reach of one of the bears which immediately grabbed him and began mauling him. Frightened, the other children ran and left him. As one bear was mauling him, the two bears began to fight, allowing him a chance to roll away and crawl to safety. He was seriously injured on his right leg and abdomen and doctors feared that he would not survive. The incident occurred near the Fourth of July, and it was very hot in Ohio, which hampered his recovery. The doctors bandaged him up and the family hoped for the best. While he was recovering, he taught himself how to knit and once joked that he knitted a pair of socks "tight enough to hold water." He also occupied his time reading, a habit that would become a lifelong passion. He eventually made a full recovery, although he carried the scars from that vicious attack for the rest of his life.

By 1849, Plumb had attended all of the schools in Marysville, Ohio (where the family had lived since 1843) and was eager to continue his schooling elsewhere. It was the wish of both his parents that their children pursue other careers than the family wagon-making business. Although he was not yet 12 years old, Plumb left to attend Kenyon College in Gambier, Ohio. The family could not afford the tuition or boarding costs, so it was arranged for Plumb to work in the printing office of the school newspaper, *The Western Episcopalian*. Annual tuition at the school was $30.00, equating to roughly $1,100 in 2023 values. Certainly a low tuition rate, but out of reach for the humble Plumb family.

Kenyon College had a reputation as a strict school, often using corporal punishment and placing an emphasis on manual labor in the fields or working on the roads surrounding the college. The college may have been difficult to endure, but it also produced some distinguished alumni including Rutherford B. Hayes (19th President of the United States) and Edwin M. Stanton (Secretary of War under President Abraham Lincoln). It is not known exactly how long Plumb attended the school, but most estimates seem to agree on around three years. He did not graduate with a degree, and it is not known why he left the school to return home. He did, however, discover a love of printing and the newspaper trade, which he put to great use in the future. His wife, Carrie Plumb, later recalled, "While at Gambier working in the office of the Episcopal Publishing Company, they put him at work on some type,–I think it was a Bible,–that was so fine he could not stand it, it was so hard on his eyes."

On his return to Marysville, Ohio, Plumb began work at the *Tribune* as a compositor and apprentice. The compositor's job was to arrange and format the text in a newspaper for printing. It was tedious and detailed work to avoid the dreaded "typos." Plumb worked for J.W. Dumble in the *Tribune* office who remarked, "He manifested a wonderful tact at the labor of typesetting, and soon became an expert." Although he did not remain continuously employed at the office, he was able to introduce his younger brother, Josephus, to the trade as an apprentice.

Not long after Plumb began working at the Tribune, a rival newspaper opened in Marysville. This newspaper quickly folded, leaving behind a slew of printing equipment. Plumb approached Dumble and encouraged him to contact the editor of the *Tribune*, C.S. Hamilton, to purchase the dormant equipment. Hamilton had no interest in seeing the competing newspaper revived, and was not keen on seeing Plumb and Dumble leave to work on it—at least in Marysville. He finally agreed to offer the boys $100 towards the purchase price, if they would move the equipment and set up their newspaper elsewhere. Both Plumb and Dumble had little funds to put towards their endeavor, so Plumb spoke to his parents. The Plumbs mortgaged their home to raise the funds, and Plumb and Dumble purchased the printing equipment and settled in Xenia, Ohio to open their newspaper. Xenia is located about 64 miles to the northeast of Cincinnati and at that time had roughly 5,000 residents.

The first issue of the *Xenia News* was published on February 24, 1854. Preston Plumb was now the editor and owner of a newspaper, and had only just turned 16 years old.

Xenia News

It is important to consider the politics of 1854 to put Plumb's newspaper and actions into perspective. The Kansas-Nebraska Act became law in May of that year, and triggered the "Bleeding Kansas" period as abolitionist and proslavery forces flooded into Kansas and Missouri in an attempt to swing votes in the Kansas and Nebraska territories. This also created the Republican Party (as well as other smaller parties), of which Plumb would become a powerful member. Plumb himself was a staunch abolitionist like the rest of his family. Also at this time, Plumb added the middle initial of "B." to his name, becoming Preston B. Plumb as opposed to simply Preston Plumb, his birth name. The "B." itself did not stand for anything and was only an initial. He remarked to a friend that he did it, "just because it makes a better signature."

By all accounts, *The Xenia News* was a popular and successful newspaper, due in large part to Plumb's energetic personality. One of his partners wrote, "He did everything about the paper; set type, ran the hand-presses, gathered news; anything there was to be done; was quick to arrive at conclusions; very positive; at times quick of temper, but soon over it." Plumb not only covered national news but also dedicated space to local events and happenings. His ability to understand what people would be interested in reading, and providing that content, enabled him to build a successful newspaper. Always present in the paper were editorials denouncing slavery. Some were written by Plumb himself, and others were written by J.D. Liggett, a popular minister in the area.

This photograph of Preston B. Plumb was taken about the time that he started The Xenia News around the age of sixteen. Image courtesy Kenneth Spencer Research Library, University of Kansas.

Plumb quickly earned the reputation of a hard and tireless worker. Liggett described the following story illustrating that point:

> He [Plumb] was a good printer, i.e., was a rapid and accurate typesetter and pressman. All the press work on country papers was done by hand power. Mr. Plumb was, for his age, unusually mature and manly, intelligent, energetic, and industrious…There was an election of county officers and neither political party had made any nominations. There was a free fight for all the offices. The big prize was the office of treasurer, for which there were sixteen candidates, one of whom was the editor of the other paper of the town, and as a consequence, the printing of all the tickets, with their almost endless combinations, came to our office. Plumb was the only pressman, and for several days he ran that press almost day and night, and the result was a felon [painful bacterial infection] on the middle finger of his right hand, but he never let up on his job. I pleaded with him in vain to quit and let the tickets alone. About sundown of the day before the election the last order for tickets was filled, when one of the candidates for treasurer came into the front room where I was and said he wanted ten thousand more tickets, printed different from what he had. I said it could not be done in our office for any amount of money, as our only pressman had a felon on his right hand and should not do any more. Plumb overheard the conversation and spoke right out, "O pshaw, take the order; I'll print the tickets." I protested in vain. He took the job and finished it at one o'clock the next morning.

In 1856 Dumble sold his interest in the paper to Plumb, and he in turn sold that interest to Liggett. During this time, Plumb also boarded at Liggett's home. Liggett recalled, "He was never idle. When he came to his meals he always had some book at hand to read if he was detained, and his reading was always of standard authors. He read rapidly and remembered well what he read."

In March of 1856, Jacob Stotler answered an advertisement Plumb had placed in his paper to hire a foreman for his office. Other printers tried to discourage Stotler from applying, telling him that Plumb was difficult to please and hard to work for. Despite their warnings, Stotler accepted the position and became lifelong friends with Plumb. He found

Plumb to be "exacting, but fair and just—that he hated a lazy man or a shirk—and that it was an easy matter to get along with him."

While Plumb was busy as the editor of his newspaper and tirelessly fulfilling printing contracts, he was also studying law. Even as a teenager, Plumb felt pulled towards doing more than simply operating a newspaper.

The Sacking of Lawrence

On May 21, 1856, the city of Lawrence in the Kansas territory was sacked by proslavery forces. The town of Lawrence had been founded by anti-slavery settlers from the east coast and members of the Free-State movement. Two newspapers, the *Kansas Free State* and *Herald of Freedom* were utterly destroyed in the attack. The papers were Free-State newspapers encouraging further settlement in the area by abolitionists. Their offices were ransacked, and their printing presses and type were destroyed and scattered. The Free State Hotel, known as an informal headquarters for the movement, was razed by cannon fire. While much of the town was looted, only one life was lost in the attack—that of one of the pro-slavery belligerents, killed by a piece of falling debris from the destroyed Free State Hotel.

The result of this affair was to stir the Free-State movement and encourage them to seek help from northern states. As was popular at the time, citizens often gathered to hear orators from other towns and states speaking about the news or causes in their areas. On June 14, 1856, a talented orator by the name of Marcus J. Parrott arrived in Xenia to speak about the attack on Lawrence in the hopes of procuring aid for the Free-State movement. As a newspaper reporter, and ardent abolitionist, Plumb attended the meeting and reported on it in the following issue of the *Xenia News* on June 20th. He wrote:

> He [Parrott] confirmed all the reports of outrage committed by the prowling marauders from Missouri and other states, upon the unoffending people of Kansas, which many self-wise persons affect to deny. Eighteen out of the nineteen election districts in the Territory were overrun by a large body of armed men on the day of the election of members of the legislature, and the elections were carried by the grossest fraud and outrageous violence. After the invaders had thus seized the legislative power, the next step was to disenfranchise all the Free-State men by

requiring them to take the oath to support all the obnoxious laws they had enacted, before they could be permitted to vote. A more bold and tyrannical usurpation than this could not be conceived of. The people were thus driven back upon their original rights, and pursued the justifiable course of establishing a provisional government of their own. But for pursuing this course of policy, the bloodhounds of slavery had been let loose upon them, to murder, rob, burn, steal and otherwise destroy their property. The people of the Territory are poor and cannot hold out for a long time, unless speedy and efficient aid is afforded them. Mr. Parrott's object was to solicit such aid for his suffering brethren in Kansas."

It is impossible to fully detail the impact this had on Plumb, except to say that it thoroughly moved him to action. As many would characterize him later in life, once he seized upon something, he was tenacious to the end with it. His mind was made up, and he was going to Kansas to help. He went to his former partner Dumble and said, "Joe, I am going to Kansas and help fight this outrage down, or die with the Free-State men." Dumble attempted to talk him out of it, as he had no real plan except to go, but Plumb was stubborn and thoroughly invested in the cause, and would not hear of it.

Plumb wasted no time and left at once. His newspaper account of Parrott's speech was printed on June 20th, and by the 24th he had arrived in St. Louis, Missouri. During this trip to Missouri, Plumb took careful notes and studied each of the towns, and became familiar with their politics. He wrote several articles for the *Xenia News* acting as a correspondent for the paper. These reports provide excellent firsthand accounts of the situation at the time, and also offer a glimpse into Plumb's personality. For that reason, they are included in their entirety below. Plumb's letter dated July 6th, 1856 reads as follows:

THE XENIA NEWS.
Friday, July 18, 1856 [Published]
Interesting Correspondence from Kansas.
Lawrence, K.T., July 6th, 1856 [Written]

The Pacific Railroad

I left St. Louis on Tuesday last, the 1st inst., at ½ past 1 o'clock P.M., on the Pacific Railroad, on my way to Kansas. This railroad is finished to Jefferson City, on the Missouri river, a distance of 125 miles from St. Louis. The building of this road to Jefferson cost an enormous amount of money, being built through a very rocky, hilly range of country, requiring a great deal of tunneling and excavation through a mass of solid rocks, and running, as it does, through a very sparsely settled portion of country, with not a single town for over 75 miles; on the upper end of it the money had principally all to be furnished by St. Louis. This is, I believe, the Bentonian route to the Pacific. At Franklin, on the Missouri River, about 40 miles from St. Louis, on this road, a branch has been commenced which is called the "Southwestern Branch," and which is intended to connect with the Texas Road to the Pacific. But little work is being done on either route, at present.

The Gasconade Bridge

After leaving Franklin, the car in which I was seated was nearly empty, and what few passengers were in it, were in a drowsy mood, and many of them soon were fast asleep. I could not withstand such influences. The "drowsy god" beckoned me and soon I was fast locked in the loving embrace of Morpheus, in which condition I remained until a friend seated behind me touched my arm saying, "We are approaching the Gasconade Bridge." I woke with a shudder! The memory of the fearful disaster which happened at this place in October last, came fresh to my mind; in fancy I pictured to myself that fearful scene. It was the occasion of an excursion from St. Louis to Jefferson, where was to be a celebration in joy of the event of the completion of the road to that point; the train was a large one, and the cars were crowded with the excursionists; it was growing late, and the engineer of the train was driving the locomotive at a high rate of speed, in order to arrive at Jefferson City in time for the celebration; they approached the bridge, situated in a lovely dell, where, at times, ran a stream called the Gasconade, but which was now almost dried up; the heavens were cloudy, and the falling rain pattered against the windows of the cars, while the wind went howling by, all combining to give additional horror to the heart-rending scene which was to follow; the train swept onto the bridge, (if such could be called the fixture which had been erected for the occasion,) at a rapid rate; the timbers which had not been fastened, and which had been rendered slippery by the rain, are suddenly displaced, and hundreds of human beings precipitated into the chasm below, in which fortunately there is little or no water. Hundreds of persons from the surrounding country had collected to see the cars cross; and they who should have rendered assistance to the wounded and dying, commenced the work of robbing the unfortunates! But night soon throws her sable pall over this scene of misery and shame. Many were the hearthstones made sorrowful by this disaster; a nation felt the shock. We cross the bridge very slowly–scarcely at a man's pace,–seemingly as if there was still danger, although the bridge is perfectly safe; on arriving at the other side there can still be seen fragments of the cars which were broken at the time of the great disaster.

Jefferson City
A few miles from Jefferson we cross the Osage River, which is a considerable stream, and navigable for several hundred miles from its mouth. About half-past 8 o'clock P.M. we arrived in Jefferson City, which is the capital of Missouri. It is a place of about 2000 inhabitants, contains the State House, Penitentiary and other public buildings, but is not a place of much business.

Missouri River, Lexington and Kansas City
At this point we go on board the steamer "Cataract" which runs to Weston, Missouri, in connection with the Pacific R.R., and which leaves Jefferson about 10 o'clock every Tuesday night. On the way up we pass many nice towns situated on either bank of the river, but none of "newspaperial celebrity" in Missouri, excepting Lexington and Kansas City. The former place interested me more than the other at present, on account of the circumstance of the Chicago emigrants being disarmed at this point, of which I suppose you have had full particulars long

since; but as we passed it in the night, I did not get a "sight at it."

Slavery's Defences

At Liberty, on the right bank of the Missouri, which we passed on Thursday, there were stationed two pieces of brass six-pounders, pointed toward the river, in order to blow out of the water any boat which was suspected of having on board "damned Abolitionists," and which refused to land. I saw upwards of twenty pieces of cannon, of different sizes, stationed along the river bank, in Missouri, at different points, and all of them had been posted there for the same avowed object—that of preventing companies of "abolitionists" from going into the territory of Kansas. At Liberty, we encountered a boat going down from which we learned that a company of Illinois emigrants, eighteen in number, had been disarmed at Leavenworth City, and sent back, and that it was the intention of the "border ruffians" to search every boat going up the river at that point, and send back all the Abolitionists they could find. This news created a little fluttering on board, and in consequence a couple of men from New Hampshire concluded to go back, and at the next landing they got off the boat to wait until they could get on board of a boat going downstream. There were several armed Missourians aboard who were going up to Leavenworth to "stay until after the election" in the Territory.

P.B. Plumb

THE XENIA NEWS
Friday, July 25, 1856
Interesting Correspondence from Kansas
Lawrence, July 6th, 1856

Leavenworth City

About 6 o'clock in the evening of Thursday we arrived at Kansas City, which is about half a mile from the line between Missouri and Kansas, on the Missouri river, and about 40 miles from Leavenworth. It is a place of about 500 inhabitants, and is quite a pleasant looking place. On the land are lying a large number of large iron ornaments, and other articles intended for the new State House, at Lecompton, K.T. We here got on board quite a number of Missourians who were going to Kansas, armed to the teeth; and certainly a "harder" looking set I have seldom seen.— The night was quite dark and our progress was so slow that we did not arrive in Leavenworth City until about 4 o'clock the next morning, which was the morning of the "Glorious Fourth." A guard was stationed on the levee who had been keeping watch during the night, and watched closely all who landed at that point, and also searched the boat for Sharps rifles, &c. If it had not been for the "good crowd" of armed Missourians who landed at the same time, I expect an attempt would have been made to search me, as I was carrying in addition to my carpet sack, a suspicious looking bundle which had been entrusted to my care by a gentleman at St. Louis, to be delivered at Leavenworth. The first thing that attracted my attention was the fact that every person I met was armed with a "colt." After taking my "traps" to the hotel I started out to see the city! Leavenworth contains about 1,500 inhabitants, and is most beautifully located on the brow and sides of a sloping eminence, which slopes to the water's edge. The scenery back of the town is of surpassing beauty, and such as I cannot do justice to. The Fort is situated about two miles up the river from the town, on an eminence commanding a fine view of the surrounding country. I walked out to the fort on the afternoon of the 4th, to see Uncle Samuel's soldiers. There were but about 40 there at the time, the balance being off at Topeka, to dispose of the Free State Legislature, which met that day, and to quell any disturbance that might occur. There is no fort, properly speaking, as the barracks have been turned into a storehouse for provisions &c. This is merely intended as a supply station for the forts west of this. The Government have under cultivation over 5,000 acres of land, which, however, does not furnish one-third enough provisions for the soldiers and their animals. By the time I got back to Leavenworth City, the inhabitants, and the bands which had been collecting there for a few days past, began to come in from the various barbecues which had been held in the neighborhood, and I had a chance to observe of what kind of material the army that was to subdue Kansas, was made. Several members of Col. Buford's company were there, and about one-half of a company of 150 Georgians who had come into the Territory a few days previous to the 4th, also, and a large number of the "law and order" citizens of Leavenworth; in all some 300 armed persons, and a rougher looking set, I certainly never saw. They were about half drunk, and made the air "hideous" with their blasphemy, and imprecations.

The Illinois Emigrants

The Illinois company which was disarmed and sent back at this place, came up Wednesday on the Steamer Arabia. Their rifles and revolvers were stowed away in sacks and boxes, and they were not armed at all, themselves; but the moment they were landed the boxes and sacks were broken open and the arms were taken out. Their carpet sacks and trunks were also opened and searched, and a sum of money taken. About 60 blankets, a large lot of plows, axes, hoes, and other agricultural implements were also taken and not returned. After having taken everything they could lay hands upon, they were put on board a boat which was going down to St. Louis, and ordered never to return to the Territory under the pains and penalties of death! Before they were sent away, however, they were taken before the Mayor of the town, and tried for treason against the United States! A messenger had been dispatched to the Fort, for United States troops to protect the emigrants; but did not arrive until they had been sent away. Four of them escaped at Leavenworth and another of them managed to get aboard another boat, after proceeding down the river about 300 miles, and came back there on Saturday morning, and went over to Lawrence, immediately.

Political Opinions of the People

I became acquainted with several gentlemen residents of Leavenworth, who were pro-slavery in their sentiments who assured me that if a fair expression of the opinion of the people of the Territory could be had at the polls, Kansas would be free! One of these men is the owner of 4 negros; another of them is receiver at this place, an office which he holds under the government. He asked me what Buchanan's chances were in the North. I told him that I believed he would be beaten.—"Then," said he, "may God bless the people that beat him." He laid all the evils that the people of Kansas are suffering, at the door of the President, and a man pledged to carry out those measures which created these difficulties he wanted to see beaten.

There are two papers published in Leavenworth City. One, the *Herald*, the proslavery paper, and the other, the *Journal*, an advocate of peace, and also of Millard Fillmore. A few days since the mob threatened to throw the Journal press and type in the river for not approving of all they had done. If they do it they will have a good time. The editor is Mr. S.S. Goode, of Ohio. All men there are regarded as abolitionists and traitors who do not go for Buchanan and Breckenridge, by these Georgia bullies. There are many other incidents connected with my visit to Leavenworth, which I shall have to omit at present, for want of room.—On Saturday morning I left Leavenworth for this place, where I arrived about 3 o'clock the same day. It is a live place, and has some lively inhabitants. I shall write again in a few days.

Yours,
P.B. Plumb

THE XENIA NEWS
Friday, July 25, 1856
Lecompton, K.T.
July 9, 1856

Kansas is at present quiet, but I am afraid it is but the calm which precedes a storm.

After leaving Lawrence, I visited Messrs. H. and G.W. Cosley, formerly of Xenia, at their residences about 4 miles west of Lawrence. I found themselves and families in good health and spirits, notwithstanding the unfavorable circumstances which have occurred since their arrival in Kansas to mar their happiness and prosperity. The neighborhood in which they are settled is strongly "Free State," and in an object of particular hatred among the "Law and Order" party, as they well know that it would be useless to attempt to enforce a single one of their bogus laws upon the FREEMEN of this neighborhood. After remaining in this neighborhood a day or two, I came to Lecompton, the Pro-Slavery capital of Kansas Territory, and the centre from which emanates all the proclamations, indictments, &c., which have been promulgated by Gov. Shannon, Marshal Donaldson, Sheriff Jones, and others, assisted by a corrupt Grand Jury. Lecompton is pleasantly situated on the north bend of the Kansas river, and contains about 300 inhabitants, including about 100 armed loafers that are used as a posse to enforce the behests of a drunken n—r-driving crew of officials, who are sucking the life-blood of a free people, under the sanction and patronage of the Executive of this "Great and Glorious Republic." One would think, to take a view of matters from this Territory, that the United States Government existed for the special purpose of propagating Slavery. Gov. Shannon's life has been in danger from both the Pro-Slavery and Free State parties ever since his arrival in the Territory. The Pro-Slaveryites will not brook anything but the most abject submission, and when Shannon has shown any "compunctious visitations," they have threatened his life until at last, he has sold himself "body and soul," and to drown his remorse has taken to drinking, and can be found under the influence of liquor at almost any hour of the day. This is pro-slavery testimony, which is considered good amongst a certain class in the North. I arrived at Lecompton on Tuesday afternoon, and learning that Jones was in town went to see him at this office. I found him engaged with the books of the new State House, which is being erected at Lecompton, and of which he is Architect and builder, having under his control the fifty thousand dollars appropriated by Congress for that purpose at the time of the passage of the Nebraska and Kansas bill. Privately he is very much of a gentleman, but publicly, he is just as much of a scoundrel; and although admitting, as he does, that a majority of the bona fide settlers of Kansas are in favor of making it a Free State, he declares that Kansas shall be a Slave State, although the price of it be the Dissolution of the Union!

And that the war would most certainly commence again before long, and continue until the question was definitely settled. He read to me passages of letters which he had received from various parts of the South, in which were promised "men and money" in abundance. Thus it is—the South work while the North blusters; and so long as such a state of things continues to exist, there can be no doubt of the result. Men who have starvation for themselves and families looking them in the face, cannot fight with a good heart; and starvation it will be, if something is not done soon to relieve them. The difficulties prevented them from getting in their crops in time, and as a consequence what little grain has been planted will turn out but poorly. A majority of them have sworn to leave their bones in Kansas rather than be driven out by these "border ruffians"; and dying will look Heavenward, with confidence in the justness of their cause, which will rob death of its terrors.

On every hand, I see evidences of the devastation and ruin which has visited this beautiful country and rendered families houseless, and hearthstones desolate, under the cover of "Law," and in a vile and infamous attempt to fasten upon the settlers of Kansas a blighting institution which lives upon the degradation and slavery of the white laborer, and the degeneration of our white races. The "half has not been told" of the suffering and ruin that has taken place here. The border ruffian cutthroats, boast of outrages which, for the sake of humanity, I could wish were not true; but which are oftentimes worse than they represent them to be. And the Government which should protect citizens in the exercise of their rights, pays for the commission of these outrages out of the National Treasury! If a pro-slavery man wishes to commit a depredation, he goes to Jones, who is Deputy U.S. Marshal, and gets a commission as a Deputy, summons his posse from among the herds of Southern cut-throats who are always around, and proceeds to the commission of his outrages against Free State settlers; and as they are under orders from a U.S. Deputy Marshal, of course the Government has to pay for it.

At the time of the passage of the Kansas-Nebraska act, an appropriation of fifty thousand dollars was made by Congress for the purpose of erecting a State House, and twenty-five thousand dollars for the purpose of paying the per diem of members of the Legislature, salaries of Judges and Governor, and other expenses of the Territorial Government. The cost of the State House which is now being built is estimated at $80,000, the $25,000 appropriation is almost gone, there having been an enormous drain upon it of late for marshal's fees &c., and there is no hope of getting any appropriation from the present Congress. In this dilemma, the Slaveocracy have determined to tax the people of the territory to pay the expenses of this bogus Legislature, and pay such men as Jones, Shannon, Donaldson, LeCompte, Atchison, and Stringfellow, for oppressing them. But the people will not suffer taxation for that purpose. They will die first! A short time before the election last fall, this omnipresent Jones went out into the Territory and demanded of each settler the sum of one dollar for the privilege of voting! Not a man would pay him. The matter was then dropped until after both elections had been held, when another attempt was made to collect it which also failed. And so will all attempts to collect any tax ordered by the present government. Although there is no killing going on at present, the stealing has by no means ceased. Almost any night horses and cattle are stolen from Free State men; and I have it on unquestionable authority that Clark, an Indian agent in the Territory, and one of the murderers of Barber, are now paying an expert thief ten dollars a head for horses and mules stolen and delivered to the Indian Mission. These things have been represented to the government; but no note is ever taken of any outrages committed on Free State men; and such being the case, the time for making reprisals has come, and for every man killed on the Free State side two will die on the other; and for every horse stolen from the Free State men, the slaveryites will suffer in like proportion. And let Gov. Shannon himself beware! I have conversed with the settlers of Kansas at the plow, and at the hearthstone, and have shared their homely fare, and although men of peace, they know their rights, and knowing, will maintain them. And if Shannon will get drunk and insult defenceless women he will not live to repeat the cowardly act. Many of the settlers from the North look upon themselves as deserted by their brethren, and having forborne until forbearance has ceased to be a virtue, are only anxious to die as becomes men, with their faces to their foes and their arms in their hands.

During my conversation with Jones, I mentioned that it was my desire to see the prisoners, Robinson, Smith, and others, who are under a guard of U.S. Soldiers in a camp about 3 miles from Lecompton. He informed me that the captain's orders were very strict concerning the prisoners, and that he had instructions not to admit any person to see them except on business, unless a "pass" was given from Marshall. Although I could not plead "business," Jones gave me a "pass" of admittance, and I walked into the camp and gave it to Capt. Sackett, who immediately remarked that it was not needed, and that any friend of the prisoners would be admitted to see them. I walked into the tent occupied by the traitors and introduced myself as being from Ohio, which was a sure passport to their goodwill. They are all in good health and spirits, and seem to enjoy themselves as well as circumstances will admit. Until within a few days past, letters and papers have been stopped, and they have not received them at all. Now, however, it is different; Capt. Sackett is a man of honor, and able to distinguish between justice and tyranny. Their friends are allowed to visit them, and they are allowed to receive their correspondence. Mrs. Robinson is sharing her husband's captivity, solacing the hours of his confinement, and doing all in her power to render the prisoners comfortable. She is a brave and beautiful little woman and worthy of her Spartan husband. I regard Gov. Robinson as one of the clearest headed men I have ever seen. He is not a brilliant man, but he is just the man for this emergency—The pro-slaveryites know that in him they have an enemy who is in himself a "tower of strength," and Shannon and his master Jones, as well as the balance of the crew, have sworn that he shall be condemned and hung! A traitor! To his country! Because he was rash and bold enough to think and act as if the government of that country was formed to protect American citizens in the exercise of their rights.

The event of the last few days was the assembling of the Free State Legislature at Topeka on the 4th inst., and its dispersion by Col. Sumner, in accordance with the proclamation of the President. The Legislature convened at 10, the roll was called, and Col. Sumner came into the Hall amid much confusion, and ordered them to disperse, which they did immediately. There were about 2,000 Free State citizens of Kansas in attendance at Topeka, a large number of whom were armed, on account of the report that the pro-slavery men would attempt violence. All went off peaceably and in good order. The citizens returned to their homes as they came, satisfied that in obeying the commands of a regularly authorized U.S. officer, rested with full powers they had done wisely.

The Free State party here looked upon the nomination of Fremont by the Republican convention as a good omen of the future, as he was their first choice.
The weather has been extremely hot here for some weeks and the crops are suffering badly.

I shall leave here for Topeka to-morrow, and will write to you from there. There is, however, no certainty in the mails, as they are closely inspected before they leave the Territory, and if anything suspicious is found it is opened.

Kansas is beautiful, beautiful beyond description! The breezes that sweep over her fair and fertile plains are health-giving and redolent with the perfume of thousands of sweet scented flowers; but in the midst of all these, there is one name that is sweeter than all; a name that brings a thousand fond recollections to my mind—a name of which I am proud—the name of my native State, Ohio.

P.B. Plumb

Chapter 2

Kansas Settlement

After traveling around the settled areas of the eastern side of Kansas, Plumb chose to make Kansas his permanent home. But rather than simply moving to Kansas, he decided to further the Free-State cause first.

While attending a Free-State convention in Iowa, Plumb was tasked with smuggling weapons from Iowa into Kansas. His cargo consisted of one cannon (dismantled), Bowie knives, Sharps rifles, and thousands of rounds of ammunition. Although only 18 years old at the time, Plumb was put in charge of the dangerous mission and recruited a small group of men to accompany him.

The story below was told by Captain A.C. Pierce, one the men recruited by Plumb, to historian and biographer William Connelly.

> Pierce arrived at Iowa City in August 1856, about the first of the month. It was necessary for him to work, for his money was low. He secured a place as a copyist in the law office of Penn Clark. About the first of September, he went into a barber's shop to be shaved. There he met a tall slim young man, who had come in for the same purpose. Neither of them had much beard, but both "were getting slicked up a little," as Captain Pierce put it. That young man was Preston B. Plumb, who was there from Lawrence, Kansas, to aid in the transportation of arms to aid the Free State Settlers there to maintain themselves against the border ruffians. Plumb inquired of Pierce what he was engaged in at Iowa City, and when told Pierce added that he was going on to Kansas as soon as he got a chance. Plumb said he was going to Kansas and that Pierce could go with him. Pierce replied that he would be glad to go. Pierce says that Plumb was then a confiding, captivating fellow that got close to one, that is, deeply impressed anyone he talked with.
>
> Plumb had three teams and three wagons. These teams were horses—a span of horses to each wagon. He had gone to Kansas from Ohio in the spring of that year, but Pierce does not know whether at this time he was just up from Lawrence or had been home and was returning to Kansas from Ohio.

Plumb was in Iowa City to take arms into Kansas. One of his wagons was loaded with supplies – provisions for men and horses on the journey to Kansas. One wagon was loaded with Sharps rifles, revolvers, Bowie knives, and ammunition. There were two hundred and fifty (250) Sharps rifles, the same number of revolvers, and the same number of Bowie knives. There were several boxes of cartridges for the rifles. There were also a brass cannon and its carriage. This cannon and its carriage were put into one of the wagons and boarded up so that no one could see them. The arms and ammunition were put into one wagon – perhaps a small portion in the wagon which carried the cannon. Pierce thinks the cannon was a ten-pounder, and that it was taken by the Militia of Shawnee County to repel the Price raid invasion of Kansas and was captured by the rebels at Westport and recaptured at the battle of Mine Creek.

In Plumb's party were ten men. Pierce thinks he picked them up about Iowa City in something of the same way in which he was recruited. McClung was coming from Ohio. So far as Pierce can remember the men were: Preston B. Plumb, Alfred C. Pierce, ___ Curtis, O.A. Curtis joined the party at Winterset, Iowa–no relation to this Curtis. [Leigh] McClung, ___Eldridge, (not of the Lawrence Eldridges), ___Pellette, ___Smith, (the cook for the party and was from Boston), ___ Johns, Samuel F. Tappan, and a man named Walker–does not remember his given name. (Walker went on to Oregon later and there got rich. Another man–the drill master was in the party. Pierce is not certain but that Tappan joined the party at Nebraska City, with James Redpath, Richardson, and others, but will not say he did not join the original party at Iowa City.)

Plumb was elected Captain of the company and had entire charge and direction of it until it reached Topeka. The company left Iowa City about four o'clock in the afternoon on the third day of September 1856, and drove out five to eight miles, then camped for the night.

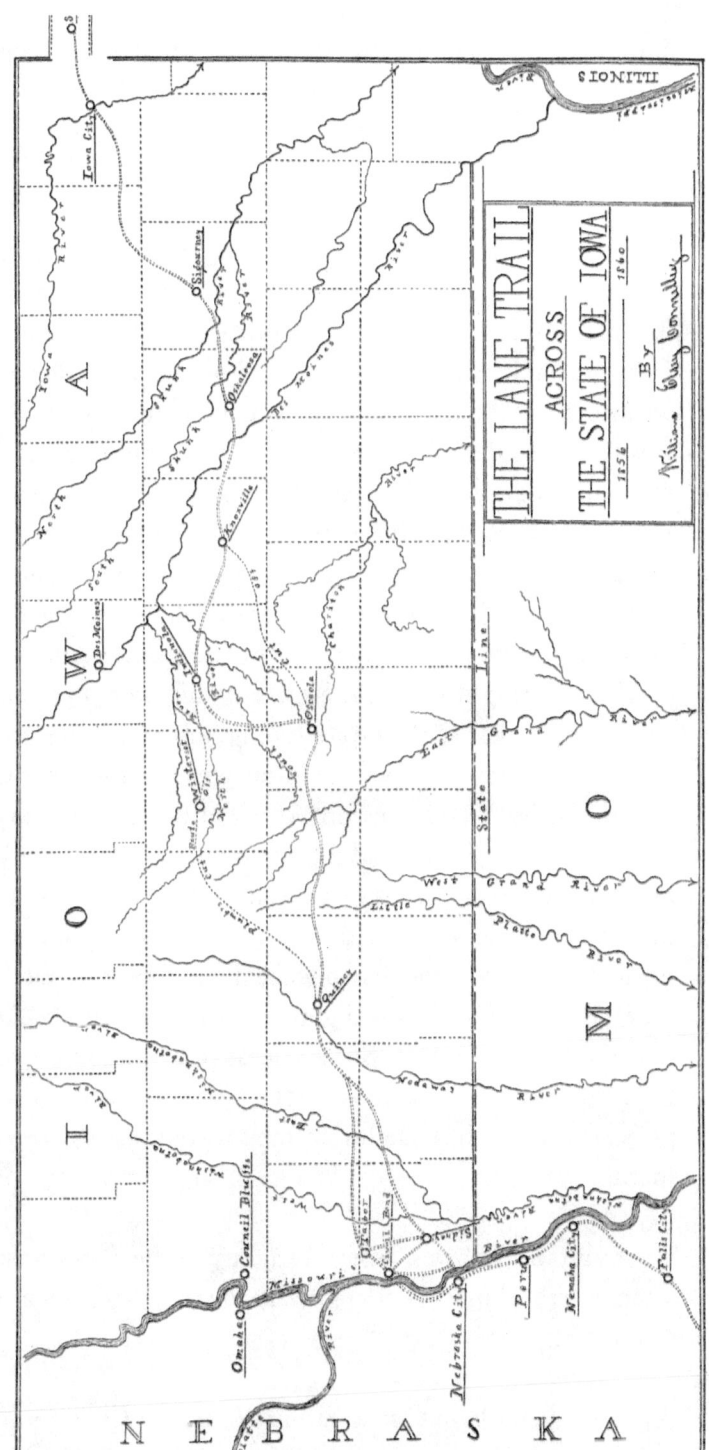

The map above shows the route Plumb and his party traveled across Iowa. For Plumb, this journey was largely on foot, and often times barefoot. Image courtesy Kansas Historical Collections Vol. XIII.

Iowa City was then the capitol of Iowa. There were many people there who favored the South, and Plumb was in more danger of having his lading captured and taken from him there than most any other place in Iowa.

Pierce does not recall many incidents of this journey through Iowa. While crossing Skunk River they saw a man drowning. The party had, in fact, crossed the river and got some distance from the bank, when someone called out for help. Pierce was walking barefooted and bareheaded, with an umbrella over him. It was in the afternoon. Pierce ran back to the river and found the people dazed and helpless. The man had gone down for the last time. Pierce was advised not to plunge into the stream while hot and perspiring, but this he disregarded. He dived into the deep water and in swimming under there touched the drowning man with his foot. This gave him the location, and he then dived down and brought him to the surface, and swam to the shore with him. He left as they were rolling him on a barrel to get the water out of him and does not know whether they revived him or not. The party had gone on. At Sigourney, he went to a hotel for the night, but as he had not put on dry clothing the keeper refused to allow him to stay. The party had gone on about three miles west of Sigourney and camped. In coming up with the teams at the camp Pierce had walked barefooted about five miles. But he remained at Sigourney overnight and walked out to camp in the morning. Some cheese had been purchased at Sigourney, which made most of the party very sick and a physician had to be called from the town in the night to attend them.

The trail ran southwest from Iowa City to the Tabor post office. There were not many settlers in the country then. It was all a new country.

At Winterset, Orrin Curtis, father of Senator Curtis, joined the party. (Curtis says he was a traveling salesman then). There was a feeling against Kansas at Winterset, in fact, some feeling all over the North. Many northern people believed in non-interference with slavery. Just met Curtis there. Does not know how the meeting occurred. Pierce remembers that Curtis was a very enthusiastic recruit and that he would make speeches about Kansas from the wagons. His diction was very poor and his language very poor, but this was remedied to some extent by enormous lung power and a raucous voice–altogether poor but earnest speeches.

The company drilled, every day, more or less. All expected to have to fight border ruffians as soon as they got to Kansas. Pierce does not remember the name of the drill-master. He was one of the original party, and later he was killed around Fort Scott. He was a small man.

At Tabor, the citizens gave a dinner in honor of the arrival of the party, which laid over there one day. Pierce and Plumb had walked most of the time. Plumb was very tall and very slender and he had not the vitality that Pierce had, but he had an indomitable will. The party had rushed until Tabor was reached because of the imprisonment of Governor Robinson and others at Lecompton. At Tabor, the party heard that Robinson had been released, and after that, the party took more time.

At the dinner, the people made much of the young men and encouraged them. Most of the Tabor people then were from the Western Reserve, Ohio.

The party crossed the Missouri River at Nebraska City. There they met [James] Lane, who made a speech. Pierce did not hear him, but some of the party did hear him. He was just from the fight at Hickory Point (now in Jefferson County). He made a good speech. From Nebraska City, he went on east and at Chicago made the great and famous Chicago speech.
At Brownsville, Nebraska, the party came up with a larger party bound for Kansas. In this party were Albert D. Richardson, James Redpath, and one of the sons of Old John Brown–Pierce does not remember which one. A Mr. _____ Parsons, who afterwards settled at Ogden (Kansas), was in the party. Pierce

called Brown's son "Brown" after he met him, and was requested to call him by some assumed name, which Pierce has forgotten. Most of the Kansans had assumed names, the better to conceal their movements and mystify the border ruffians.

The party came by Holton, Kansas, and camped there. The town consisted of a cabin or two and some rifle-pits. There had been a skirmish there between the Free State men and the border ruffians, and Pierce thinks "Bullet-hole Ellis" had been wounded there. Not far from Holton, the party saw some Pawnee Indians, but at first supposed they were border ruffians. When it was found that Indians were in front of them the teams were corralled and the men made ready to fight. In fact, the preparations were made to fight while it was still believed the enemy were border ruffians.

North of Topeka, perhaps halfway between Topeka and Holton, some of the party, two of them, one the first Curtis (not O.A. Curtis, the Senator's father) and another whose name is not remembered now, one evening refused to go on to the camping place which had been selected by Plumb. They wished to camp back from the crowd. Plumb would not permit this. Pistols were drawn, but Plumb prevailed and the whole party went on to the creek and camped on the site selected by Plumb. What the mutineers intended to do was never known, but their course afterwards in Kansas was not good.

The night before the party got to Topeka the cannon was hidden in brush. The cannon was mounted on wheels, and must have been at ten-pounder (12-pounder, Tappan says). It and its accompaniments made a good load for a fine gray team which hauled it from Iowa City. It was hidden in the timber. Pierce did not see this piece of artillery again until the Price raid. It was in the battle of the Blue and was captured by Price's men—and it was recaptured at the battle of Mine Creek. On the trip from Iowa City, the cannon had been boarded up, covered, and hidden from view so that people along the road would not know what it was.

Pierce thinks the Sharps rifles, or a portion of them, had been left at Tabor, Iowa, and perhaps the Bowie knives.

On the north bank of the Kansas River at Topeka, Colonel Sumner with his command searched the wagons. The company had camped at Indianola the previous night. Perhaps the cannon had been buried the night before. The soldiers made a search for Samuel F. Tappan, but he escaped. Houses in Topeka were searched for him. He had been in the Kansas troubles and perhaps arrested before and imprisoned with Robinson and others and had escaped, but Pierce does not know.

On the trip across Iowa Plumb was dressed usually in trousers and a shirt. He wore high-heeled boots–poor footwear for hard walking. He did not drive a team. Plumb and Pierce walked together much of the time. They generally walked ahead of the teams, especially when the roads were dusty.
The cannon, Sharps rifles, Bowie knives, and ammunition were furnished by the Emigrant Aid Company through Eli Thayer.

On the trip across Iowa Plumb talked about the Fremont campaign. He was strongly for Fremont. Tappan had a copy of Whittier's poems. The company would often sing the Kansas song: "We cross the prairies as our fathers crossed the sea."

After delivering his cargo of weapons in Topeka, Plumb went on to Lawrence to find work. He was also interested in founding a town, but would need money, supplies, and manpower to accomplish that task. He wandered around the unsettled areas of Kansas and soon found a location for a town that he felt would have great potential. He named it Mariposa, and it was located somewhere in the vicinity of present-day Salina. Captain Pierce was also involved with this and told Connelley about Mariposa:

> The party remained in Topeka some days—perhaps a week—when Plumb, who was looking out for a place to found a town, started with it up the Kansas River. The party was the same,

except for Orrin Curtis and Tappan. Orrin Curtis went to work for Papan on the ferry over the Kansas River and afterwards married a Miss Papan. Plumb had bought an ox team in Southwestern Iowa. When the party started up the Kansas River it had two of the horse teams and the ox team.

Plumb had bought tools—axes, broad-axes, saws, augers, and other tools such as pioneers might need in erecting buildings in the wilderness. These were carried along.

The party camped at Juniata, four miles above Manhattan. From here parties went out to explore for a location. Pierce, Johns, and Curtis went up the Blue River. They were followed by three border ruffians who intended to kill them. An old man named Garrison lived where the town of Garrison now is. The exploring party stopped overnight with Garrison. The three border ruffians came to Garrison and asked permission to come in and kill Pierce and his companions, but Garrison, himself, pro-slavery, refused, saying that if they were killed in his house revenge would be taken on him and he would likely be killed. He warned the Free State men of what was threatened against them, and one of them remained on guard all night. They were armed with Sharps rifles and revolvers. They went on the next morning to the house of a man named Randolph, where the town of Randolph now is. There they turned back and came again to Juniata. Pierce had concluded that the first railroad would be built up the Kansas River and not up the Blue River, and that their settlement ought to be on the Kansas River. The party had figured that a railroad would penetrate that region in ten years. And it was, though the Civil War intervened.

Plumb and four others of the company went on up the Kansas River. He took two teams with him—the ox team and one of the horse teams. He went about fifty miles west of where Salina now is, to the bridge across the Smoky Hill River. This bridge had been built by McIlvane & Sawyer, Government Contractors. This and other bridges had been built the year before—across the Blue, Chapman Creek, Mud Creek, and the Salina River. A bridge had been built across the Republican at Fort Riley in 1855, as had the bridge across the Blue.

When Pierce and his party came back from their exploration up the Blue started up the Kansas River. They met Plumb at Chapman's Creek. He had elected the site for their town where they afterward laid out Mariposa. Pierce thought the town ought to be built where Junction City now is, but Plumb objected because of the proximity of Fort Riley, then a pro-slavery headquarters. The officers were all pro-slavery and would have liked to shoot all the Free State men. Robert Wilson, post sutler there and postmaster wanted to disarm Plumb as he had gone up the river. Plumb told him to stand back and mind his own affairs – that he could not have his gun but might get the contents of it. The post office was in a saloon.

At Chapman's Creek, the party had a good dinner–buffalo meat, new potatoes, rice, etc. Plumb and party had killed the buffaloes. Plumb made a fine report of the country to the West. It was agreed that Plumb should go back to Ohio to get people to come out and settle in the town of Mariposa.
Pierce and the others went on and laid out the town of Mariposa. Pierce was a surveyor. He had a pocket compass, and for a surveyor's chain, he used a lariat. The town was about a mile from the present site of Salina. They built a substantial log house there. The logs were well-hewed, and the house was about 26 feet by 18 feet in size. McClung remained there awhile.

Plumb continued his submissions to the *Xenia News* telling of the events in Kansas and his adventures within the territory. These letters provide an excellent glimpse into his experiences during such a turbulent time in the territory's history.

THE XENIA NEWS
Friday, Oct. 24, 1856
Kansas Correspondence
In Camp, near Juniata, K.T.
Friday Night, October 3d, 1856

Westward: Still Westward
"No pause nor rest, save where the streams
That feed the Kansas run!"

You may be surprised that your Correspondent who wasn't exactly "raised in the woods" should be so suddenly struck with that fatal disease commonly known as the "Western Fever." But it is even so, and the poet above quoted has not half expressed the intensity of the fever which now possesses me.

It is not my desire to give you any account of the journey to this "new Canaan of our Israel," as it has been so long passed that it would be stale and uninteresting; nor of any little adventures that took place—some of them quite interesting and exciting to those participating in them but utterly devoid of all interest to others when recited by a less than ordinary newspaper correspondent. Suffice it to say that after numerous "hair-breadth escapes" and "adventures by flood and field," we arrived at Topeka, K.T., on Friday, Sept. 26, "safe and sound." As you know, we found everything comparatively quiet,--no excitement, except in regard to the action of the governor of which, I suppose your readers have been fully advised ere this, whose course has created considerable talk and astonishment. Things look quiet now, but I am of the opinion that it is but the calm which precedes a storm of great violence. Not wishing to be absent from the Territory in case troubles should again break out, I came to the conclusion to spend the winter here, and as I have determined, some time since, to make Kansas my home, I concluded the best plan would be to "take a claim" and build me a cabin. I can assure your numerous readers that such an operation, to me, contains full as much of the real as of the romantic, and is what I consider quite an undertaking. I am not alone, however, as I am but one of a company of ten young men who are now seeking "elbow room" for the purpose of laying out a town, and selecting suitable claims for farming purposes. The business is new to all of us, and we have nothing but strong arms and willing hearts with which to carry through the enterprise;

yet we have high hopes and expectations. Whether or not they will ever be realized, is for the future to unfold. I have become so captivated with out-door life, that it is quite doubtful if I ever shall live under any other canopy than that which it is the privilege of the meanest to enjoy. I feel the strengthening influences of an entire out-door existence already, and each and every day lends a new charm to this rough mode of living.

I should like much to say a few words in regard to the new order of things in the Territory, but as it is now late, and I shall be off in the morning on a Buffalo hunt, to be gone until our exploring committee return, I shall defer it until another opportunity.

I have seen some portions of Nebraska, and of Iowa, and I admire both very much, but Kansas far surpasses either. The soil is richer, the water better, the timber equally as good, and Kansas abounds in mineral wealth. The future Kansas, if consecrated to Freedom, will be glorious. The same breezes that have wafted the story of her wrongs to the people of the North, have also carried the news of the unexampled fertility of her soil, and its complete adaptation to the wants of all classes of people, and henceforth "Kansas!" will be the Western emigrant's watch-word. It will soon realize the poet's description of the future of the West:

"Broad on either hand
The golden wheat-fields glimmered in the sun,
And the tall maize its yellow tassels spun
Smooth highways set with hedge-row of living green,
With steepled towns, through shaded vistas seen,
The school-houses murmuring with its hive-like swarm,
The brook-bank whitening in the grist mill's storm,
The painted farm house shining through the leaves
Of fruited orchards bending at its eaves,
Where live again, around the Western hearth,
The homely old time-virtues of the North;

Like varying strophes of the same sweet hymn
From many a prairie's swell and river's brim,

A thousand church-spires sanctify the air
Of the calm Sabbath with their sign of prayer."
Let the laboring men of the North come to Kansas immediately, and assist in making it a Free State, and the above description will be more than realized, and they will, of course, reap corresponding benefits from its prosperity.
More anon.

P.B. Plumb

THE XENIA NEWS
Friday, Nov. 14, 1856
Kansas Correspondence
Buffalo Region, K.T.
Oct. 20, 1856

Dear News: The impetus which the novelty and excitement of our nomadic existence of the past few weeks had given to us, was so great that it was with reluctance that we yielded to the superior attractions and advantages of the country around us, and concluded here to make a final halt. For the past two or three days previous to our arrival here, we had been traveling over the broad and trackless prairie, with the sun for our guide; and as the distance between the habitations of men and ourselves increased, the stronger grew our desire to see more of that "Far West" so famed in "Song and Story," and whose border we had just crossed, until at last we had begun to discuss the propriety of continuing our "Tramp" to New Mexico or Utah! But Kansas was our watchword; and here, in the most beautiful and fertile portion of the Territory we have "squatted" and here we intend remaining, having commenced the necessary preparations for the Winter, in the shape of Cabins, &c. We are all in excellent health and spirits.

Our nearest neighbors are the soldiers at Fort Riley, fifty miles distant. We are far enough from them to feel secure in the exercise of our rights! The officers at the Fort are all pro-slavery, and in order to make Whitfield's vote as large as possible, to correspond with that of last year, they sent all the soldiers that could be spared from the Fort on the day of the bogus election, a la Missouri, down to the little town of Ogden, six miles distant, to vote, which was a gross and flagrant violation not only of the Organic Act of the Territory, but also of the Bogus Laws! Thus "out-Heroding even Herod!" himself. This shows that the pro-slavery men are bound to recognize no law but the law of might! When officers of the Government who are given power to enforce obedience to the law, and protect the citizens in the rights guaranteed to them by the Constitution of that Government, can commit such outrages, what can be expected of the Southern Rabble? Being fifty miles from the Fort, the probabilities are that we shall be allowed to regulate our own affairs without the assistance of their surplus voters. I hope so, at least.

There is one attraction, other than the beauty and fertility of the country around us, which had its influence in arresting our wandering steps, which is the abundance of all kinds of Game, such as Buffalo, Elk, Antelopes, Turkeys, &c., and a "small sprinkling" of Wolves. These last are mostly of the smaller kind, denominated "Prairie Wolves," although there is a large number of the large "Gray Wolves," some of which are three feet high, and quite ferocious. We relished exceedingly the excitement of a "Buffalo Hunt" or "Wolf Chase," and entered into it with all the ardor we were capable of.

I do not think the advantages of our location can be overrated. In point of beauty and fertility, it exceeds any portion of Kansas I have yet seen, which is saying considerable. The timber is also full as plenty as in other portions of the Territory. We are about 200 miles from the Missouri River, on the Kansas [River]; but we have an excellent market at Fort Riley, and as we are on the new route to Santa Fe, and California, which has just been opened and bridged by Government, the advantages of our location for a market will be increased.

The last news we have from the lower portion of the Territory does not materially change the aspect of things since we were there. Gov. Geary was imprisoning all the Free State men that he could get hold of, who had been participants in the late struggle, and in this he had been quite successful, having under arrest about 125 of them, but as yet His Excellency has not arrested any pro-slavery men, but on the contrary, had taken a great number of them into his service, on soldier's pay, and have given to them the position of guarding the Free State men who are under arrest awaiting their trial for robbery, murder, arson, &c., which is the title given to the act of defending one's own hearthstone, from fiends in human shape! Many of the Free State men had left the Territory to avoid arrest; as resistance would be madness and folly, as the whole United States force in the Territory is there to back the Governor up in all that he undertakes. I visited Lecompton a few days before we started for this part of the country. The town has not changed very materially since my visit to it last summer, with the exception of 6 or 7 whiskey shops, which were imperatively necessary to supply the increased demand for liquor consequent upon the addition of "Geary's Guard" to the population. These men are from all the Southern States, and certainly exceed in brutality and profanity any set of men I ever saw.

The prisoners are confined in a long wooden building, which is but partially enclosed, with an inadequacy of both provision and bedding. They are not allowed any liberty whatever, and the orders of the guard are to shoot down the first one who tries to escape. Scarcely any of their friends are allowed to visit them, and they are even denied the amount of water necessary to cleanse their bodies! I learned a few days since that three of them have died from disease inoculated by the unwholesomeness of their situation, and several others were ill from the same cause. The prisoners are insulted and abused with impunity, by those who are guarding them; and this is done under the very eyes of the Governor, whose dwelling is not over fifty yards from where they are confined.
The people of the Territory manifest an interest in the Presidential election. They look upon the election of Fremont as their only hope for peace. The pro-slavery leaders, Jones, Titus,

Donaldson, and others of their ilk, proclaim loud-mouthed, that Buchanan is pledged to make Kansas a Slave State, in the event of his election. But whether they "speak from the record" or not, I have, of course, no means of knowing; but of one thing I am certain, and that is, that the pro-slaverites here and in Missouri look forward to the election of Mr. Buchanan as the realization of all their hopes in regard to Kansas. I hope they may be disappointed.

There will be considerable suffering during the coming winter amongst the Free State settlers for want of an adequate supply of provisions, unless something is done to prevent it. Money is very scarce in the Territory, and provisions very high. Many families are now living almost entirely on vegetables, and who will be obliged to leave the Territory very soon, as hundreds of families have already done, if aid is not given to them in some shape or other immediately. There has been a considerable amount of money placed in the hands of the "Kansas Central Committee" from time to time; but it is distributed unfairly. They seem to be of the impression that Lawrence and the immediate vicinity, is Kansas entire, and consequently, the other portions of the Territory do not come in for a share of the money. The money, or a great portion of it, I have good reason to believe, has not been given to relieve the most needy, and the result has been, that hundreds of families have left the Territory who, with a very [small] assistance, would have been able to remain. Many of them were amongst the best citizens of Kansas, who could withstand invasion, robbery &c., but could not withstand starvation, which was staring them in the face. It is a notorious fact, that certain individuals who have taken a prominent part in raising funds for the aid of Kansas, have made it a "paying" operation while others who have stayed on the ground and taken part in all the trials and troubles that have taken place here, and who have been consistent advocates of the rights of the people, have lost all their means, and are now suffering for the necessaries of life. I could mention names in both cases, but the cause is in so precarious a condition that it would be poor policy to create ill feeling in our own ranks when there is such an urgent necessity for union and concert of action.

Thousands of dollars have been squandered in as many foolish ways, and there have been many exhibitions of that "cheap philanthropy" which will work great zeal for the success of a principle so long as the money lasts, and no longer! Rifles are well enough in their place, and if the hopes of the pro-slavery party are realized in the pending Presidential election, they may be needed. But at present provisions are more needed than munitions of war. If the Free State settlers are starved out Kansas will of course become a Slave State, as there will be none to raise a voice against it.—If it is desirable to make Kansas a Free State, it is the true policy to endeavor to place in the hands of the settlers here, the means of keeping themselves until they can raise a crop on their claims; and if men are sent here, let them be men of families, and have them bring their families with them, or young men who come to settle in good faith, and not just for the excitement and fun of the thing. Five-sixths of all the young men who have come into the Territory in the various companies that have arrived by the northern route have left, and some of them under rather suspicious circumstances, too.

If any of your readers should wish to subscribe to a Kansas newspaper, from which they could learn the true state of things as they occur, I would recommend them to subscribe for the *Kansas Tribune*, published at Topeka, by Mr. W.W. Ross, formerly of Ohio. The terms are $2.00 per annum, in advance. Mr. Ross has published his paper during all the disturbances that have taken place in Kansas, and has not swerved from the line of duty, notwithstanding the threats that have been made against him; and when his services were needed, he did not hesitate to take up arms and fight for the cause which was nearest and dearest to him.

I should be glad if there were more settlers here from Ohio than there are, although I find upon inquiry, that of the number remaining here, by far the greatest number are from the "Bonnie Buckeye State." It is, perhaps, needless to add that, as a class, they, are the most respectable citizens of the Territory, and such as Ohio should be proud of.

But the savor from a choice piece of "Buffalo Hump," which "Old Smith," our eccentric cook, is preparing for supper, has reached my nostrils, warning me that it is time for me to close. I will just add, by way of parenthesis, that it would, most probably, be amusing to the "typos" in the *News* office, who have witnessed my feats in the "art preservative of arts," to see how like a "master" I swing a 4 ½ [pound] axe! I am second to but one out of a dozen athletic fellows!
I am not a "bad hand" in a herd of Buffalo with a Sharps rifle; but as Mac [Leigh McClung] disputes the palm [wins the contest] with me, I will only add that I am a "good shot." I will just say that Mac and myself never looked more unlike ourselves nor felt better or weighed more than at present, and draw my long and desultory letter to a close. More anon.
         Yours truly,
         P.B.P.

By December of 1856, Plumb was back in Lawrence working at the *Herald of Freedom* newspaper. Edward P. Harris worked as a typesetter at the *Herald of Freedom* and became closely acquainted with Plumb during that time.

The first time Harris saw Preston B. Plumb was in December, 1856. He thinks it was towards the end of the month, but will not be positive on that point. But he is positive that it was in the month of December. He was in the bookstore of Otis Wilmarth, in Lawrence. Otis Wilmarth was the father of Wilmarth, the present Chief of the Fire Department of Topeka. In the bookstore, Harris saw a very tall, slim, thin man of singular appearance. He was asking for a book which the proprietor of the store did not have in stock. The stranger directed that it be secured for him, and the proprietor said he would order the volume at once. Harris observed that the stranger possessed peculiar habits of gesture and movement. He would cast up his head, turning it slightly to the right, and seem to be looking at the upper corner of the room in front of him – the right-hand upper corner. He was very erect and his every movement had originality in it. His whole manner denoted a strong individuality of which the young man was unconscious.

Colonel O.E. Learnard also worked at *The Herald of Freedom* and described Plumb as "very tall and slim, intelligent, active, quick. He was good-natured, liberal, optimistic, and enthusiastic. And he was a business fellow–knew what was going on and talked of business mostly. He was never of an exacting or grinding turn, but wanted what he paid for and always expected to deliver whatever he sold – was square himself and expected others to be square. These traits Learnard early observed in Plumb, and he observed them as long as Plumb lived–always the same–always a man to be depended on, "always stood square up to the rack, hay or no hay," said the Colonel."

A day or two after Harris had seen the stranger in the bookstore, G.W. Brown brought a new foreman into the composing room of the *Herald of Freedom* office and introduced him to the workmen there. Harris immediately recognized him as the man he had seen in the bookstore–Preston B. Plumb.

Plumb was foreman in the office until the following March–March 1857. Harris thinks Brown paid Plumb fifteen dollars a week; that was about the wages of a foreman in Kansas at that time. Harris thinks a foreman usually got three dollars a week more than a printer at the case.

In appearance, Plumb was peculiar at that time. He was but nineteen years old, but he had the air and manner of a man of thirty, and of one who had had a long business experience. His conversation had nothing of the youth in it, but was that of a matured business man.

Harris says Plumb was a good printer and a good foreman. He insisted on good work. He had unusual energy and was nervous quick, always moving, saw everything and took note of it, and on the street, walked at a sort of swinging gait that no one could keep up with. He seemed always short of time and in a hurry. He never tired. He seemed not to think as other young fellows did. He took immense interest in passing events, but they did not engross his whole attention. There seemed always something on his mind about the future–something he said nothing about but which he was ever thinking and planning about.

Plumb soon made the acquaintance of every man in Lawrence who had any business enterprise on hand–of every man who seemed to be laboring or planning to set up some business which was to be increased and developed by the growth of Kansas. He was sanguine and enthusiastic about the future of Kansas. He seemed to think the future greatness of Kansas was assured and that in that future there were immense possibilities for himself–and anyone else who would work for them.

G.W. Brown sent his wife East to get money with which to reestablish his paper. She went in the summer of 1856. She told of the sufferings of the Free State settlers in Kansas, and how Lawrence had been burned by the ruffians and the papers destroyed. Mrs. Brown returned with about eight thousand dollars. This money was principally in two-dollar bills but there were many fives and tens. Brown had a round brass rule made, and Plumb had set up in this brass rule the following: "Herald of Freedom, Lawrence, Kansas, G.W. Brown Editor and Proprietor, $2.00 per annum."

All the money brought back by Mrs. Brown was sent into the composing room and Plumb had the above impression put on every bill. This advertised the paper all over the country.

While working at the *Herald of Freedom*, Plumb continued to write letters to be published in the *Xenia News* back in Ohio. These letters were intended to attract settlers to the territory, including his new town of Mariposa. Those letters describing his adventures in Kansas are included below:

THE XENIA NEWS
Friday, Dec. 12, 1856
Change—To the Patrons of the News

With this number, my connection with the *Xenia News* as one of its publishers and proprietors ceases. My successor is Mr. John T. Hogue, well and favorably known to this community, both as a printer and a gentleman; and under whose management, with that of my former partner, Mr. J.D. Liggett, who still retains his connection with the establishment, the *News* will doubtless continue to increase in favor and prosperity with a discriminating public. My own connection with the *News* has been both pleasant and profitable beyond my expectations, and I dissolve it with many regrets. And I shall carry with me to my new home in the Far West the liveliest feelings of gratitude to those kind friends who gave to me, an entire stranger, the encouragement which resulted in the establishment of the News, and whose continued friendship, with others, has enabled it to attain to its present prosperous condition in so short a period of time. The reputation which the *News* has enjoyed as a good paper, is due to the labors of my former partner, Mr. J.D. Liggett; and I cannot let the occasion pass without expressing my approbation of his worth as a man and his disinterestedness of purpose in the advocacy of those great principles of Freedom and Justice which underlie our governmental fabric.
Although my connection with the paper has ceased I still feel as lively interest in its continued success as heretofore, and will volunteer a word of advice to its subscribers and patrons—that the great secret of all well-conducted Newspapers in this or any other country, is prompt-paying patrons, and if you wish the *News* to improve, and wish its publishers to be remunerated according to their deserts, the best thing that can be done is to pay in advance, thus easing your own conscience; affording indubitable evidence of your sanity.

Hoping that a "printer's blessing," which I hereby bestow upon my kind friends in "town and country" may not prove of "doubtful utility" I subscribe myself.

    Yours respectfully,
    P.B. Plumb

THE XENIA NEWS
Friday, Dec. 12, 1856
Gone Again

Our former partner and co-laborer, Mr. P.B. Plumb, having recently returned from Kansas and disposed of his business interests has again gone to the far West with the view of making his future home in Kansas. We wish him success to the full extent of his desires and deserts. But his own energy, ambition, and enterprise will doubtless accrue him a good degree of success anywhere. He does not by any means belong to that class of young men who are apt to fail.

Mr. James Hamill, Robert Hunter, and John Hunter also have gone to Kansas with him, with the view of permanent settlement, and will all make valuable citizens in the new commonwealth now being built up there.

 Plumb wrote the following article specifically to attract settlers to Mariposa. It was published in the *Herald of Freedom* on January 10, 1857 as follows:

"The Smoky Hill"
Up Smoky Hill Fork, Kansas
January 3, 1857

Listen, ye startled denizens of Kansas, while I unfold to you the glories of a location in this fair Territory that shames the desert fertility of all other portions, and offers unheard of advantages, alike to the man of wealth and the poor man. But I will not jostle the world of Kansas from its "primal track" by at once disclosing all the wealth of minerals which lie concealed in the hills, only wanting the touch of capital and energy to convert it into Gold, and compare with which the wealth of "Ormus or of Ind" sinks into insignificance; to say nothing of the numberless claims untaken, and town lots unsold. I will not upset your preconceived notions of beauty in Nature by a minute description of this

> "Green land stretching to the evening star
> Fair rivers skirted by primeval trees,
> And flowers hummed over by the desert bees."

Nor will I excite your speculative propensities by raising visions of "Smoky Hill," Railroad stock, selling at a fabulous percent above par; all of which, however, will be realized in time. My friend Jack Lantern, Journeyman Cordivanier, No. 14, Corhill, Mariposa, K.T., who is supposed to be in spiritual communication with future Railroad Presidents, has confided to me, under the injunctions of the strictest secrecy, that the snort of the "Iron Monster," as he bestrides a great tri-rail track of enormous width, opening with thunder and pomp our country to the wealth of the Indies, and "Marts of far Carthay" will be heard in the "valley of the Smoky Hill," and that an enormous depot, for his especial accommodation, will be speedily erected at the aforesaid Mariposa, where although numberless "corner lots" have went off "like hot cakes" there is, in the language of the auctioneer, "a few more of the same sort left."

Everything must have an end, (circle and California gold excepted, as my friend John Phoenix once facetiously remarked) and I confidently predict that all speculation in Osawatomie, (and all other "wattomies"), will soon end; that Lawrence lots will soon cease being sold at ruinous prices; and that claims ten miles from town will not be longer bought for the purpose of dividing and sub-dividing into "lots to suit purchasers" but that the eyes of all men will be turned upon the above mentioned "valley" as the best place for an investment "ever yet offered to the public", and where to say the least, if a man will come with his family, a stout heart and willing hands; with habits of frugality and temperance, he will be prospered to the full measure of his deserts, and can easily pay for his claim from its products by the time it will be in market; where, if he is behind-hand, he can receive the assistance necessary to enable him to erect a house, and get in a crop; where a higher price is paid for farm products than in any other part of the Territory; where cattle graze twelve (and sometimes thirteen) months in the year on the luxuriant grass of the prairies, where his wife and children will be lulled to sleep by the mellow rumblings of the countless herds of buffaloes and by the soft music of the wolves as they "their nightly vigils around his dwelling keep"; and where sickness comes not (without provocation) to darken his prospects, and "make the strong man tremble."

I might continue to enumerate; but I have said enough to convince the most skeptical that the "Canaan of our New Israel" is to be found in the "valley of the Smoky Hill Fork," forty-five miles southwest of Fort Riley, Kansas Territory, United States of America.

With unbounded respect for everybody that comes here to settle, and supreme contempt for the shallow-minded who don't, I remain yours respectfully,

Plumb

N.B. Please tell the people to come early, as the rush for the unoccupied claims in the Smoky Hill Valley, will doubtless exceed in numbers, the rush of office seekers to the "National Bear Garden," about the 4th of March next. "First come, first serve."

P

Plumb continued his correspondence with the *Xenia News* in an attempt to stir up involvement within the Free-State movement, as well as attract settlers to the territory and Mariposa. The "Bogus Legislature," the common moniker for the proslavery legislature elected after rampant voter fraud, was a frequent object of his ire.

THE XENIA NEWS
Friday, January 23, 1857

Our Kansas Correspondence
Arrest of the Members of the Free State
Legislature—The Weather and Resources of Kansas
Lawrence, Kansas, Jan. 12, 1857

Dear News: The only occurrence which has taken place, since last I wrote you, to jostle the Free State citizens of Kansas, out of that propriety into which they have been gradually settling since the arrival of Gov. Geary, was the arrest of the members of the Free State Legislature, by the U.S. Marshal, at Topeka, on Wednesday last, the 7th inst. the offence alleged was "usurpation of office," in assuming legislative powers, at their session on the 4th of March, last, at which time they met, and elected two U.S. Senators and appointed a committee to draft a code of laws, to be presented to them for their approval at their next regular session which commenced on Tuesday last, the 6th inst. This, of course, did not include those who were elected to fill the several vacancies, which had occurred since their former session. The prisoners were taken to Tecumseh, at which place Judge Cato's court was in session, and were immediately admitted to bail for their appearance at the next session of the court!

This arrest was entirely unexpected. The Legislature had not been in session long enough to transact any business before the Marshal appeared with his warrant. No force was used to enforce this warrant; but it was obeyed with alacrity, and upon their arrival in Tecumseh, a social supper and party were given them by the Free State citizens of that place. The excitement in this place was considerable when the first news was received of the arrest, but when the circumstances following the arrest became known, it quietly subsided.

The weather has been severe for a few days past, the thermometer ranging from 18 degrees above to 5 degrees below zero; but more frequently above than below. We have experienced but very few severe winds thus far, and, at present, the indications are favorable to a change to warmer weather.

The prime want of Kansas, at present, is capital. The natural resources of the country are great, and will require the agency of capital to develop them. Immense coal fields exist here, wanting but the touch of capital to bring their treasures into a ready market. Gypsum, Salt, and Alum, also exist in large quantities.

At present, there is scarcely any capital here, and the field is open for foreign capitalists to realize from. Money can be loaned readily for 40 percent per annum, for speculating purposes. More anon.

Yours respectfully,
PLUMB

THE XENIA NEWS
Friday, Jan. 30, 1857
Our Kansas Correspondence
Lecompton, Kansas, Jan. 16, 1857

Dear News: The most important events of this week were the meeting of the Bogus Legislature at this place, on Monday, the 12th inst.; the meeting of the Pro-Slavery delegate Convention, to consider what was best to be done to save Kansas to them, on Monday evening; and the reception of the Governor's Message by the Legislature, on Tuesday. I will refer to them in the order which they come.

The Bogus Legislature
As a body, the Legislature is a very rough-looking assemblage, and is peculiarly noticeable for the amount of liquor consumed by it. Of course, there are exceptions but they are the fewer number. Those of them who were members of the body last year

are of the most ultra kind; while those who were elected this fall are much more moderate in their views, and seem quite disposed to acquiesce in the will of the majority, fairly expressed. Intellectually, they are very inferior, none of them rising even to mediocrity. Quite a discussion arose on the motion to provide seats for reporters in the Hall irrespective of party, which finally resulted in their being admitted, after some of the members had exhausted their vocabulary of slang in abuse of "abolition traitors."

The Pro-Slavery Convention
Was well attended by delegates, most prominent among whom was Dr. Stringfellow, whose influence was all given in favor of hostile and forcible measures in order to obtain supremacy in Kansas. But with all his influence he could not carry his ultra measures, and the meeting came very near breaking up in a row. No definite plan of action was determined upon, that I can learn. The spring of the pro-slavery men in Kansas is broken, and they will scarcely make another attempt at violence to accomplish their ends. The call for the Convention was issued to the "people of Kansas irrespective of party," who were in favor of Law and Order; but a resolution was introduced by Stringfellow excluding all delegates who were not in favor of making Kansas a slave State, which passed.

The Governor's Message
Was received and read on Tuesday, the 13th inst. It is tolerably lengthy and contains many very important facts and acknowledgments. It recommends several important amendments to the statutes, and the repeal of all those odious enactments which have excited so much indignation. He shows pretty clearly that in a majority of cases, the wants of the people were not studied, and that the enforcement of some of the most insignificant of them would lead to endless litigation; or, in plainer words, that the body that enacted them was a band of conspirators, who met but to conspire against, instead of protect the liberties of a free people. The message is very egotistical. There is, however, one very important acknowledgment

contained in it, which it may be as well to put on record. He acknowledges God as the Great Executive—being one step above even a Governor of Kansas, which is quite an admission for "I, John W. Geary," to make. He takes ground in favor of public improvements and the granting of land by Congress to endow a University.

Lecompton and Whiskey
All visitors agree, that Lecompton has the poorest location of any town in the Territory, and added to this the drunkenness and immorality for which it is characteristic, makes it an object of loathing to all decent men. Whiskey reigns supreme; pro-slaveryism waxes fat and grows rampant, from the effect of deep potations. A Miami Valley Distillery would do a good business here. Light cannot penetrate here; the town will sink from corruption, and there will be no wailings at its departure.

Arrest of Stringfellow and Others
January 17, 1857
Yesterday evening Dr. Stringfellow, and several others were arrested on charge of horse-stealing, and admitted to bail to answer the charge. G.W. Clarke, the murderer of Barber was also arrested, on charge of murder, and also admitted to bail! Who will not deny that Kansas is a great country? The Governor was fiercely "pitched into" in the council yesterday, on the "motion to print" twenty-five hundred copies of his Message. He is in decidedly bad odor with the ultras, which is a good indication.

I neglected to mention the fact that the Free State Legislature before its adjournment, drew up a "Memorial to Congress," the prayer of which, was to be admitted into the Union as a State under their present Constitution.

The object is a good one; but the Memorial itself is a poor piece of composition, very imperfect and committing a great many serious offences against Lindley Murray. Neither the Gov. or Lieut. Governor were present at the session, and great indignation was felt by the members of the Legislature at this dereliction of duty, and a meeting was called to express their sentiments in regard to it; when it was ascertained that Gov. Robinson had resigned and gone East, and that the failure of Lieut. Gov. Roberts to attend was the result of willfulness on his part; whereupon the meeting passed a series of resolutions requesting of them an explanation of their extraordinary conduct, and adjourned.

To-night the Printers of Lawrence hold a Festival in commemoration of the birth-day of Ben. Franklin,

Yours respectfully,
PLUMB

THE XENIA NEWS
Friday, Feb. 20, 1857
Our Kansas Correspondence
Lawrence, Kansas, Feb. 3, 1857

Dear News: On Saturday last, the 24th ult., the ladies of Lawrence turned out en masse, and destroyed all the spirituous liquors that could be found in establishments where it was sold as a beverage, and then retired to their homes in triumph. This is the second time the noble and virtuous ladies of this place have resorted to this summary method of ridding themselves of the influence and presence of the "destroyer." Here, as elsewhere, the women are found first and foremost in all good works, and ever ready to share toils and dangers, rather than sacrifice one iota of a principle which they believe to be a true one. All honor to the brave women of Kansas, who have done much to nerve the arms of the struggling freemen in the hours of trial!

The Monday following the above occurrence, (the 27th ult.,) was the day appointed by the governor of Kansas for an election to fill a vacancy in the Council of the Bogus Legislature, occasioned by the resignation of the member from this District, and early in the morning ex-Sheriff Jones arrived in this city for the purpose of opening the polls. At the election in October last for a delegate to Congress and members of the Legislature, the pro-Slavery party cast a total of but seven votes, and that number has not been materially increased since that time, yet, when the ballots were counted on Monday, it was found that over one hundred and fifty votes had been cast for the two candidates, one of whom was a Free State man! It was plainly evident that Free State men had been found who had so little of principle as thus to endeavor to compromise the lofty and novel stand heretofore taken by their party in Kansas. Such an act of pusillanimity and treachery has not before taken place in Kansas. The principle thus surrendered by those who voted, was all that has ever been asked by Atchison, Stringfellow, and others of the pro-Slavery party—the acknowledgment of the right of Missouri to make laws for the people of Kansas. This is what Free State men have heretofore denied, and against which they have fought. Two, at least, of these traitors were from the great State of Ohio, whose large heart has always beat responsive to the throb of Kansas, and many of whose brave sons have shed their blood for Liberty on this soil.

But worse than all this, is the application of the Associations of several Free State towns to the Bogus Legislature for charters! Prominent among which is that of Wyandotte, which has the name of W.Y. Roberts, the Acting Governor of the Kansas Free State Organization, (who is one of the principal stockholders in that place), attached to its application! When such duplicity is shown by those who have heretofore essayed to lead in the struggle for Freedom, the people who love principle better than present prospects of money-making may well pause to inquire whether this mania for speculation which possesses these men shall be allowed to ignore entirely the question of Freedom and Slavery, which has been considered settled only on the supposition that the Free State party would continue to resist the action of illegally elected bodies, and demand that a chance be given to the bona fide settlers of Kansas to settle their own institutions as best suited their own views, without any interference whatever from abroad.

These events, occurring in such rapid succession, have served to inspire the pro-slavery party with hopes stronger than any they have indulged in since their disappointment occasioned by the liberal policy of Gov. Geary. Already they have taken measures to profit by this truckling spirit shown by members of the Free State party. A bill is now before the Bogus Legislature, and has passed to a third reading, providing for the taking of the census as a preliminary step towards electing delegates to frame a State Constitution, which provides that all the actual inhabitants of the Territory on the first day of April next, shall be included. The bogus Sheriffs or County Judges, where no sheriff is appointed, shall appoint one Deputy for each township and proceed to take the census. The returns are to be made by the 10th of April, to the bogus County or Probate Judges. Two registers shall be made out and posted. The county Court shall sit from the 10th of April to the first of May, as a Court of Adjudicature, to settle all disputes in regard to citizenship and from their decision there shall be no appeal! The County Judges shall then publish a corrected list, and no one can vote, whose name is not on it. One copy of this corrected list shall be sent to the Governor, who shall make an apportionment of Delegates for said District, not to exceed sixty in number. The election of Delegates for the Constitution Convention shall be held on the third Monday in June. The county Judges shall appoint places for holding the election, determine the number, and appoint the Judges of elections, three in number. The Judges of election shall make two copies of the returns—one for Territorial Secretary, and the other for County Court—shall decide in favor of the candidates who receive the highest number of votes; but in cases of tie or contest, the Convention itself shall decide. All the counties along the border and river are considered as Districts, thus giving to the Missourians ample opportunity to flock over and register their names, and thus give to these counties the full number of delegates allowed to larger Districts (sixty), while of the interior counties, containing a larger proportion than the border ones, it takes from three to five to be entitled to the full number of Delegates.

A tax-bill has been passed which authorizes the bogus Sheriffs to assess and collect tax upon all property in their various counties, and give receipts therefor, which receipt is the only evidence which can be given that any person is entitled to be registered as a voter.

It is well known that a large majority of the Free State men in the Territory will refuse to acknowledge the right of the Legislature to assess a tax upon their property; but a small minority, such as those who voted on Monday last, will pay their tax and vote, while the pro-Slavery party, with the help of their Missouri allies, will drive all before them; elect their delegates, from a Pro-Slavery Constitution, which they will claim as the will of the majority of the bona fide residents of Kansas.

If Congress persists in recognizing the Bogus Legislature, and gives countenance to its enactments, there will be difficulty in the future. A complete eradication of the whole Missouri system, and a return to the primary organization of the Territory, is the least that will be accepted. No acknowledgment of the right of Missouri to make laws for Kansas will be made, the treachery of W.Y. Roberts and his fellows to the contrary notwithstanding.

Kagi, the Lecompton correspondent of the Kansas Tribune gives an instance of fast travel, which, as he says, puts "Fremont's Ride" completely in the shade." A new county has lately been organized in the south-west of the Territory, bordering on New Mexico, about five hundred miles from Lecompton, and, according to law, an election was held on the first Monday in October last for Representative, and next day (Tuesday) a man arrived at Lecompton with the returns of the election from that county, from which it appeared that he had received a majority of the votes cast. Of course, upon the meeting of the Legislature, he was admitted to his seat!

By the way, this Kagi, who is an outspoken man, had a difficulty with Judge Elmore, (proslavery) at Tecumseh, a few days since, which resulted in Elmore being shot in the groin and badly wounded, and also in Kagi being wounded in the side. It seems that during Kagi's stay at Lecompton, as reporter for the *Kansas Tribune*, he had occasioned to write some very plain truths in regard to Elmore, which so exasperated the latter that upon his meeting him a few days since, he attempted to cane him, the result of which I have stated above.

If we believe half the accounts which we hear, and the letters which we read, every nook and corner of Kansas will be "taken up" before another twelve-month elapses. The number of emigrants will undoubtedly be enormous, and there is, unquestionably, room for all that will come. Any legitimate business will flourish here as well as in the States. The geographical centre of the United States will someday be the centre of wealth and intelligence.

Already
"I hear the tread of pioneers,
Of nations yet to be;
The first low wash of waves where soon
Shall roll a human sea.

The rudiments of Empire here
Are plastic yet and warm;
The chaos of a might world
Is rounding into form!

Each rude and jostling fragment soon
Its fitting place shall find—
The raw materials of a State.
Its muscles and its mind!"

Persons intending to emigrate to Kansas will consult their own convenience and comfort, by coming by way of the Missouri River. To such, I recommend to bring but very few, if any articles of furniture, as it can be purchased here cheaper than it can be brought from the States. Articles of bedding should be brought, as they will be scarce and dear. Whatever of goods you do bring, should be shipped to "N. McCracken, Leavenworth City, Kansas, care of Simmons & Leadbetter, St. Louis." At Leavenworth, they will be in direct communication with many parts of the Territory, by means of a line of hacks, and with all portions by good roads. Ox teams can be purchased here advantageously. Good oxen will be worth from $60 to $80 per yoke. Horses and mules can also be had in abundance.

Good claims, well timbered and watered, still exist in abundance in many portions of the Territory, although many of the best have been taken by the first comers. Timber is generally a great deal plentier than it is in either Illinois or Iowa; and coal exists in many localities, though in what quantity is not definitely known, as no mines have as yet been worked, which is partly the result of the disturbances, and partly because the government reserves all known salines and mines, and individuals having coal on their claims are desirous of procuring titles for the same before proclaiming that fact.

To those persons who are desirous of obtaining first choice of claims, as good if not a better chance is afforded by settling on the Smoky Hill Fork, back of Fort Riley, than in any portion of the Territory, where there has as yet been but few locations made, and where timber and stone abound in large quantities, and where the soil equals in richness, and the landscape in beauty, that of any portion of Kansas. A town called Mariposa has been laid out within a few weeks, forty-five miles southwest of Fort Riley, in the forks of the Salines and Smoky Hill, on the new government route to Santa Fe, at which point a sawmill and other necessary improvements will be erected early in the coming spring. A petition has also been forwarded to the Post Office Department at Washington, praying for the establishment of a Post office at that point. The location of the town on the Santa Fe road will have the effect of making it the best market in the Territory for farm products, while the fertility of the soil in the neighborhood cannot fail to recommend itself to those who intend its cultivation. The Town Association have displayed the utmost liberality in laying off their town plat, having reserved six different squares for churches, four of the same size for schools, and two large plats in opposite portions of town for the purpose of public parks. The existence of coal mines and salines in the immediate neighborhood, as also of gypsum and chalk, will go far toward inducing emigration to this point as one of the best locations to be found in the Territory. Mechanics of all kinds will be in great demand here in the spring. There is a direct communication between this place and Leavenworth by means of a good military road well bridged.

The Missouri will probably be open about the first of March, when emigrants should be prepared to come immediately. "First come, first served." Respectfully,

PLUMB

THE XENIA NEWS
Friday, March 13, 1857
Our Kansas Correspondence
Lawrence, Kansas, February 26, 1857

Dear News: The bogus concern yclept [by the name] "Legislature," which has been in session in Lecompton for some time past, closed its labors by a grand spree, on Friday night last, at about two o'clock. As one of the results of their labors, I may notice that by their enactments they have made the Statutes passed last winter respectable, which I never expected could be done. The "Census Bill" of which I gave a synopsis in my last, was passed over the veto of the Governor, unanimously. The Governor vetoed it because it did not give him, as the Executive of Kansas, any power whatever, and not because of its manifest unfairness. They passed an act to punish Rebellion against the Territory of Kansas, and defining the same. This is a most complete farce, but it is intended to carry out the "subduing" process, inaugurated by the election of this body, who have been usurping the rights of the people. Rebellion forsooth! As if the people who formed the Government have not a right to remove it when it becomes a nuisance, and ceases to carry out the objects for which it was established! The crime of rebellion is not known in popular governments, where the power rests with the people directly. It is only in despotic governments, where the tyrants are always seeking to strengthen and perpetuate their tyranny. So in Kansas. The Governor signed this bill, and of course, will have to enforce it. They had better be making extensive preparations for hanging and imprisoning the rebels! The punishment is death or imprisonment for twenty years!

The insurrection act is also a precious bit of legislation. It can easily be construed so as to prevent the assemblage of all bodies of the people for the purpose of petition or remonstrance, under the penalty of being arrested as an insurgent.

The first boat-load of emigrants landed at Leavenworth city a few days since. Among them was Mr. John Hammond, of Yellow Springs, Ohio, who will make Kansas his home. There were about 300 emigrants on board. Of this number, about 200 have passed through Lawrence, on their way into Neosho country, which is decidedly the best of Kansas now open, and in reach from this place. New towns have been laid out all along the Cottonwood and Neosho, which are in a thriving condition. One was located in the fork of the Neosho and Cottonwood a few days since, and before 24 hours had elapsed $2500 worth of shares had been disposed of, and a new issue made at higher rates. The secret of this is Yankee enterprise, in establishing steam mills, a printing press, &c., immediately on the ground.

The Land Office will probably be opened in a few weeks. I do not think it will be possible for speculators to get hold of the land here in large quantities. The settlement will be rapid, and most of the land will be preempted by actual settlers.

Yours Respectfully, P.

While Plumb continued to extol the virtues of the Smoky Hill Valley, his settlement of Mariposa was in trouble, as Captain Pierce related to Connelly.

One night when [Pierce's] party was building the house at Mariposa a band of border ruffians came into the tent to drive them off, but the boys showed plainly that they would not be driven away. The ruffians were drinking and wanted a row. They remained in the vicinity several days, always exhibiting an insulting attitude. They pretended to be on a hunting expedition and did do some hunting. They had brought a barrel of whiskey with them and remained until it was consumed, then they went away. They did not molest the Free State men a second time.

The last of the settlers at Mariposa drifted away in the month of March 1857. The last to leave were Pellette and Johns. They starved out. They went hunting, driven thereto by hunger. They found a buffalo bull and were lucky enough to kill it. While Pellette was left to skin and guard the carcass Johns came into the settlement to get the oxen and haul in the meat. Pellette got one side of the buffalo skinned when night and a terrible blizzard descended on the land together. Johns did not return with the oxen. Pellette feared to try to find the settlement in the storm and darkness. But he was freezing to death. In his extremity, he thought to crawl under the hide skinned from the side of the dead buffalo, and here he found a tolerable shelter. But his troubles were not over by any means. No night was too dark or blizzard too cold to keep off hungry wolves when they smell a dead buffalo. They came about Pellette in their snarling yelping, gliding, hair-raising way, and he would crawl from his snug place and shoot at them and frighten them away. Then he would crawl back and by the time he was getting a little thawed out the ghostly murderous pack was sniffing about the carcass of the buffalo and he would have to get out and fire at them again. This was kept up all night. It became a fight for life with these wolves, for they would likely have killed Pellette had they gotten to tearing the carcass of the buffalo; and if he had gone away from it he would have perished in the storm. He said he was never so glad in this world as when he saw Johns coming with the oxen.

Plumb would have made the settlement go if he had had enough money, but he had none after getting on the ground. None of the men blamed Plumb for not going on with the settlement. Fort Riley was a great drawback to that country then. It was all pro-slavery and molded public sentiment. Robert Reynolds was Probate Judge under the bogus laws. He was the head man. Truman L. Pooler was a man who Pierce hauled saw logs for during the winter of 1856-57, and Reynolds asked him about Pierce, saying that Pierce had better leave as he had a Sharps rifle and took the New York Tribune. The saw-logs were of cottonwood and Pierce hauled them over the snow. The lumber was used at Fort Riley. Fred Emery was Register of the Land Office at Ogden. He had commanded the company that had murdered Brown at Eastin, Leavenworth County. Tom Reynolds, son of Robert Reynolds, has hung south of the river by vigilantes for horse-stealing later. Two others of Reynold's sons became highwaymen along the trail up the Smoky Hill and were killed. The best one of these boys was George Reynolds, and he went into the rebel army. Drinking whiskey was the chief pastime of these fellows about Fort Riley.

Plumb returned to Ohio to finish his affairs and make a pitch in the newspaper to attract settlers to Mariposa, but it failed. His brother George described his return to Ohio, "The Company my brother came out to Kansas with first laid out a town called Mariposa a part of what is now Salina. Then he came back to Ohio to our home. I remember when we went home from school one evening there was a stranger at the house, a tall brown fellow with a slouch hat and we did not go very close to him. Finally, Mother said, "Aren't you going to speak to Preston?" He had only been away from Xenia six or seven weeks but we had not seen him for a year and he was so brown from being on the prairies we did not recognize him."

Plumb's family had also become enamored of the Free-State cause and had decided to move to Kansas as well. Preston's father, David, had also been traveling to Kansas. George Plumb described the situation:

> After Preston came back from his first trip my father and Preston both went to Kansas but not together. We did not hear

from either of them for quite a while. There was a big Fremont & Dayton mass meeting in the town. They served free dinner and the town was completely eaten out. I never saw so many people in such a small place. At this meeting, the statement was made by one of the speakers that there was a report that Captain Plumb was killed in Kansas. Soon after this, my father came home but he had not seen Preston. However, he had been taken prisoner on the stage from Lawrence to Leavenworth and we wondered if that was not the foundation for the rumor. My father had been along the Wakarusa and made some friends. After we moved out we used to go by there and stay overnight on our trips back and forth. He met [John] Brown and [James] Lane. He was in Lawrence a good deal; was there at the time it was sacked.

He came home in the summer of '56; times were beginning to get hard. He had mortgaged the home in going security for Preston at the time he bought the printing office at Xenia and the house was sold to satisfy the mortgage.

In early 1857, Plumb received word of a new town company looking for a fifth member to join and help found a town. The buy-in was $1,000 and Plumb's family helped him come up with the large sum of money. He was accepted as a member and a requirement of his membership was to start a newspaper in the new town of Emporia. "When Plumb secured his interest in the Emporia Town Company he urged Harris,"—the typesetter at the *Herald of Freedom*—"to go there with him, saying it was an opportunity to start a fortune." Harris declined, and Plumb set off on his own to start a town.

Drawing of the town of Emporia from 1859. This was done scarcely two years after the founding of the town. Author's collection, History of Lyon County by Jacob Stotler.

This portrait of Preston B. Plumb was taken in late 1856 or early 1857 at about the time Emporia was founded on February 20, 1857. Image courtesy Kenneth Spencer Research Library, University of Kansas.

Chapter 3
Founding Emporia

Until the founding of Emporia, Plumb's life in the territory of Kansas was entirely transient. He had worked in Lawrence, laid out the townsite of Mariposa, and returned to Lawrence to work at the *Herald of Freedom*. The Emporia Town Company provided him with the perfect opportunity to get settled and plant roots.

Plumb was the youngest member of the Emporia Town Company at only 19 years of age. The other members of the company included G.W. Brown (the leader of the company), General G.W. Deitzler (secretary), Lyman Allen, and Columbus Hornsby (both merchants from Lawrence). Plumb was the only member of the company to immediately make the town his home, which was necessary for him to publish a newspaper.

The first buildings erected at the townsite were crude and Plumb had the difficulty of having very little money, no newspaper office–and critically–no printing press. In order to obtain a press, he would have to make a dangerous trip to Cincinnati, Ohio and bring the press back to Emporia through Kansas City.

At that time, Kansas City, Missouri Territory was full of proslavery settlers and businessmen who did not take kindly to the Free-State men. Traveling through the area and being recognized or even deemed an abolitionist would incur the wrath of these "border ruffians," resulting in robbery and possibly even death. Although this was a risky trip for the teenaged Plumb, it had to be done.

West Virginia Senator Stephen Elkins' father, a proslavery settler and future confederate soldier, was aboard the boat that Plumb took at Kansas City. His son described the dangerous trek:

> He took a boat at Kansas City for St. Louis. The border ruffians were at that time patrolling the river and killing Free-State men. Plumb knew the danger he was inviting but it was necessary to get his press into operation as early as possible, and he hoped he would not be recognized. But he was recognized by the ruffians and soon saw that his life was in imminent danger. At Lexington, Missouri he was to be taken from the boat and hung. The father of Stephen B. Elkins was on the boat, going down the

river on business. He was struck with the fine appearance and manly behavior of Plumb when he was assailed by the ruffians and resolved to take his part. He told Plumb that it was quite likely that the threat to hang him at Lexington would be carried out, or an attempt made to carry it out, but that he would stand by him and use his influence to protect him. There was a large crowd of pro-slavery people at the landing when the boat arrived at Lexington, assembled to meet the pro-slavery men on it and do what they directed. Elkins had much trouble and ran some danger in standing off the mob but finally did it and saved Plumb. There was trouble at Arrow-Rock also, but Elkins got him through to St. Louis all right.

While Plumb was off in Cincinnati purchasing a printing press, his family was in the midst of relocating to Kansas, although they weren't sure exactly where in Kansas at the start. Plumb's brother George stated:

He [their father David] did not know how to get money enough to move the family to Kansas but finally succeeded and we started in March of 1857. We went from Marysville to Cincinnati by rail and there took the boat down the Ohio river, to St. Louis. There were a lot of slaves on the packet being brought to Missouri. Their master and mistress were along. The slaves were down on the lower deck and whenever we put in to get wood on the north shore the slaves were shut up so they could not escape and when we got back in midstream again they were let out to get some air.

When we got to St. Louis we had to transfer to the Emma Packet; had to stay in St. Louis several days; finally got everything arranged and ready to start and the boat was pulling out when we saw a man come running down the wharf waving his hat and calling. The captain stopped and went back; the people laughing to think how a passenger had nearly been left. Father went down to look about and discovered the man was Preston. He had been to Cincinnati and bought a printing press from the Cincinnati Type Foundry and wanted to get it on board this boat but was going back east himself. He told father he was going down into the Neosho valley; had gone in with a company that was going to start a town and he was to publish a paper, so we decided to go to the same place. When we landed at Kansas City we bought some ox teams; had one wagon with us which father had made. The printing press was landed over at Wyandotte as it would not have been safe to unload it in Missouri. Preston had sent for [Jacob] Stotler and he was there to come down with the printing outfit. I do not know when or how he got there for he was not on the boat we came on. There was a man named George Gardner a carpenter, who worked along with us. He and father went back to Wyandotte to bring the press down and Stotler and a man by the name of J.H. Holmes were there. They had a long hard trip. Holmes had over 5000 lbs. on his wagon and stalled in every ravine. They had to make a crossing whenever they came to a stream as there were no roads,–just went across the prairie. It was sometime in May when they got here and the first paper was not published till June 6th. They stayed all night at our place out on Plumb Creek and came into town the next day. The hotel where they expected to set up the press had no floor in. I helped several days; they set the press up just back of the hotel.

Preston was back and said we had got to get the paper out and let people know we were down here. After the first issue, there was not another for a week or two. In the meantime, they got a temporary floor in the hotel and the press was set up in the back of the Emporia House. The paper was called *The Kanzas News*.

The spelling of Kansas with a "z" was a deliberate move by Plumb to indicate that the newspaper was Free-State leaning. Being located in Emporia was an advantage for Plumb as it kept him out of direct danger from the border ruffians, and allowed him to have a more tempered perspective on border events as he was not directly impacted by them. The weekly *Kanzas News* was carried throughout the region and as it grew in fame so did Plumb's name—especially within the Free-State organization.

The Plumb family suffered their first tragedy almost immediately after arriving in Emporia. Plumb's brother, Josephus, had injured his leg while working in Xenia at Plumb's newspaper. The injury had rendered him bedridden and he came down with tuberculosis. He insisted on accompanying the family to Kansas rather than staying with relatives in Ohio. Just a few short weeks after arriving in Emporia, Josephus died on April 30, 1857, at the age of 16. He was one of the first burials in Maplewood Cemetery.

Publication of the *Kanzas News* began to attract settlers almost immediately, but the town was still under construction and most amenities were still being built. A concern at the time was finding a reliable source of water. In the very early days, water was hauled into town from the Cottonwood River, but a freshwater well would prove much more efficient. A "water witch" had been hired to divine water with a peach stick to no avail. In mid-May 1858, Plumb was heading to Lawrence and instructed John Hammond on his way out of town to, "dig, dig anywhere, but dig. If you find water, I will come back, and if you don't, I won't." According to Hammond's son, William, who was a boy at the time, his father proceeded to dig on the east side of Mechanic Street between Fifth and Sixth Avenues and struck water. Plumb immediately returned from Lawrence to find Hammond. His son recalled:

> Father and I were crossing Sixth Avenue by Fick's store, and saw Mr. Plumb coming down the stairs on the outside of the News building. He hurried over to father, put his arm about him, and said, 'John Hammond, God bless you. You've saved the town, and the Town Company is going to reward you for it.' He unbuckled his buckskin belt and gave father five twenty-dollar gold pieces. He said it was all the money the Town Company had. In addition, he gave father one share of ten lots anywhere father wanted them. He chose two lots on Commercial between Third and Fourth, and the lots on State where the Major Calvin Hood place was built. The next morning after this incident, I went to work in the News office as a devil [apprentice]. Mr. Plumb said to me, 'Will, I wish I had another good man like your father to help me. We'd soon have a good town here. We'll have more water soon. If we don't, we will pump it from the Cottonwood. Someday we'll have one of the most beautiful cities in Kansas. Your father and I may not live to see it, but I hope you will."

Mrs. Randolph was another early settler to Emporia who arrived in 1858 with her family. Church services were an important social function

Photograph of the Emporia News building taken after Plumb had sold his ownership, but the appearance was the same. Image courtesy author's collection.

at that time, and her family immediately inquired where Sunday services were to be held.

> We stopped in front of the hotel. Billy thought they might be having their 'ceremonies' in the hotel parlor today (they had no fixed place for church meetings, but gathered together where it was convenient.) Billy said he would investigate and soon returned with a tall slender man, his hair was rather long– he had a jerky way of throwing his head as if trying to keep a particular long lock out of his eyes–indeed all of his movements seemed to be abrupt and full of energy. He was dressed in a suit of light gray cloth with a felt hat of the same color–all looked as if they had had a good bit of wear. They must have been made of good stuff for I do not remember him wearing any other suit in those early days. Billy introduced him as P.B. Plumb (of course we knew who P.B. Plumb was) "Certainly we are going to have church, but come in and Billy and I will hustle around and locate the church." After being gone some time he returned saying their meeting today was in a little unfinished dwelling house standing where Jay's Hall does today. It was sided up, had a roof and floor, but no doors or windows.
>
> In taking us out of the house we passed through the office that was full of men who I am sure were not there when we went in. Mr. Plumb paused and began introducing us to them, some of them were from Xenia, Ohio and we claimed them for neighbors. We seemed to be objects of particular attention. We were told afterwards there were twenty-five young gentlemen in Emporia and only two young ladies. No wonder they wanted to so please a family that had two young ladies that they would make their home in Emporia. The whole crowd started for church–Mr. Plumb leading the way, telling us of this beautiful valley, the fertility of the soil, of Emporia's future possibilities and probabilities, emphasizing all he said with quick decisive manner. Boards had been laid on some trestles for seats. We found Mr. and Mrs. Morse and two women there and those who came with us formed the congregation. Mr. Morse preached a good sermon, although he looked as if he had just conquered a chill and was keeping

the fever in subjection until he got home, his grit and perseverance were always a marvel to me.

The "boys" gave us some fine singing–for many years they contributed this part of the church service cheerfully.

Mrs. Randolph also recalled a rather humorous incident involving Plumb's newspaper office and the town dances that were held frequently.

She remembers that when the people were instituting a lodge of Good Templars, she smelled smoke and fire and someone, on looking from a window saw the roof of Plumb's printing office on fire. Someone seized a bucket of water and poured it down the stove pipe. Plumb had been to Lawrence and had just returned and was asleep in a chair by his stove. The water fell down on Plumb completely soaking him. He was angry and used some picturesque language, thinking, perhaps, that it was a practical joke. "Why, man, your office was on fire, and we were putting it out." "Well," said Plumb, "Can't a man have a little bonfire of his own without being wet down with cold water?"

She says that every new house built in Emporia was dedicated with a dance. Plumb attended one of these and danced with Mrs. Randolph, and she remembers that he was not a very graceful dancer, but that he danced with all his might–with head, hands, and feet. But he enjoyed himself as all did. She remembers that he wore a suit of gray and wore it long and until it was worn completely out.

They lived one winter in a house next to a building in which Plumb, Jake Stotler, [Leigh] McClung, and other young men slept. When there was a party or anything going on at night, she could hear the young men discussing their dress. One might say, "Jake, you have to work tonight, Can't I wear your vest tonight?" Or, "Mack, you are not able to go out tonight, can't I wear your coat? It is better than mine." None of them ever asked to wear Plumb's coat, for he rarely took it off. "We had better times then than people have now. We had left the past behind us, and we had the future to make, and we enjoyed the present. We could live in a one-room cabin and have a good time and enjoy life."

Although Plumb was not an admirer of the militant abolitionist John Brown or his violent methods, he did on occasion work with him. George Plumb and L.T. Heritage recalled the following story:

> In the fall, he [John Brown] went to Missouri to get slaves. In December '58, Plumb and someone else went from here to the cabin where John Brown had the slaves which he had captured in Missouri. It was near Mound City, Kansas. They went at the request of someone, probably Brown himself, who had sent out for aid (George Plumb said he did not remember how they got the word). Brown had the slaves at Mr. Adair's house on Pottawatomie Creek and Plumb went to help him get them further away from the border. Brown left Lawrence with eleven slaves going east on January 24th and on March 12th they landed in Canada.

One of the more dramatic incidents in Plumb's life relating to the Free-State Movement was a prison break carried out in December 1858 at Fort Scott, Kansas. A couple of Free-State men had been arrested and were likely to be hanged, which was a situation that many Free-State supporters could not allow to pass. Plumb joined an armed party of extreme Free-State men including John Brown and James Montgomery to effect the release of the prisoners. Alpheus Hiram Tanner described the entire incident as follows:

> Warrants continued to issue from Judge William's court, and the officers, still in need of something to do for a living, continued to make arrests and stir up trouble. Ben Rice, of Bourbon, and John Hudlow, of Linn, were arrested in defiance of the compact made with the governor. They were confined in the old government building at the north corner of the square. This was in the fall. They were chained to the floor, with only old quilts sent in by their friends for bedding. Winter was coming on, and their friends demanded trial or bail. Both were denied.

Excitement grew, and it was the opinion among Free-State men that they should be released by force if necessary. At a public meeting at Rayville, attended by both Linn and Bourbon County people, it was voted to proceed to Fort Scott and release them. So much opposition developed that the project was abandoned. As the prisoners were in the hands of the federal authorities, many declined to take the risk. But cold weather was near, and the situation called for action, and secret meetings were held in both counties to determine the proper course. Montgomery finally decided to call for advice from other parts of the territory. Men were sent to Lawrence and Emporia for advice and assistance, and the leading men concluded to get together a sufficient force and go and do the job. Help came in a small squad from Lawrence, under S.N. Wood; one from Osawatomie, under S.S. Williams; and another from Emporia, which I afterwards learned was headed by P.B. Plumb. They met at Fort Bain, near the head of the Osage in Bourbon County, and were then joined by Montgomery and a band from Mound City. Capt. Sam Stevenson, from the head of the Osage, and Captain Barnes, from farther down towards the state line, joined them at a lone house on the prairie about eight miles northwest of Fort Scott. The whole force, now numbering seventy-five was placed under the command of Montgomery, and I think, contrary to many others, that this was by far the largest force ever placed under his command at any time previous to the war.

Of this force probably thirty lived along the Osage in the north part of Bourbon County. Just before leaving camp for the last start, John Brown came in with four or five men. He wished to take command, and some say a vote was taken to see if he should be chosen to lead. But he was not wanted at all, and he left and refused to take part unless he could command. He wanted to burn Fort Scott, but Montgomery was of a different mind. He promised us that no damage should be done and that it would be a bloodless affair.

I believed then, and still believe, that he had a secret understanding with the guard. I don't know if they were United

States soldiers or a militia posse, but I still think they were our friends and were expecting the raid.

The start from this camp was made to bring the party to Fort Scott at daylight. The Marmaton was crossed at the old military crossing, two or three hundred yards above where the National Avenue Bridge now is. The horses were left near the river, and six or eight men were left there, which may explain the difference in the accounts of the numbers. Most writers give it as sixty-eight, but at the last camp, there were just seventy-five. From here the advance was made in three columns and was very rapid, almost a trot.

The prisoners were kept in the old government building, afterwards occupied by Judge Margrave as a residence, and though built about 1844, it is still standing in very good repair. A man named Cleveland was in the lead and forced the door in with a single push, and there was no resistance from the guards. Their arms were conveniently stacked and were taken possession of at once, and every man in sight was taken prisoner. No one would have been hurt except for the foolhardiness of Deputy Marshal John Little. He kept the old sutler's store and was staying there with George A. Crawford. As the posse passed by his store, he opened the door and fired at short range into the crowd with No. 2 buckshot, wounding Ben Seaman and J.H. Kagi, a German military officer, afterwards hung at Harper's Ferry with John Brown. After the shot, Little went to a side door and looked out through a transom, and being noticed by a member of the posse, received a bullet from a Sharps rifle and was instantly killed.

This episode spoiled the arrangement for a bloodless affair as had been promised, but the rest of the program went through without a hitch. The killing of Little was called murder by the proslavery folks, but the other side called it self-defense, which is nearer the truth, for armed men seldom fail to return a shot when fired upon. Some paragraphers have stated that Little used duck shot, as he had been out duck hunting the day before. This is a mistake; he had been up on the Osage hunting men with a posse, and had been in a skirmish at Fort Bain, where they were repulsed, and he had returned, probably in a bad humor.

I helped to remove some of the shot from the wounded men, and I know what they were. I have been told that the intended raid had leaked out through someone, and that the Fort Scott men expected it and had agreed that each man should fire from his house and do what they could in that way, thinking to drive the posse off, but they had made a bad guess and failed.

The two prisoners were soon released. Their chains were cut by a member of the party, a blacksmith named Dorey, the father of Charlie Dorey, now in Fort Scott. They were armed and were soon in the ranks, standing guard over the men who had been guarding them. There were also many others under guard—Judge Williams of the federal court, old Judge Ransom, and, in short, about all the marshals and deputies and court lackeys in Fort Scott, with many of the citizens. They were hustled out into the square and a Sharps rifle pen was formed around them, and as it was frosty (December 16) a fire was built for the comfort of the prisoners. The furniture of Judge Williams' office and all his books were used for fuel. Judge Ransom and Marshal Campbell complained bitterly, and protested that it would go hard with us for handling United States officers in such a manner, but the boys ridiculed them, and one little insignificant fellow, Avia Flint, ordered them to keep still, and pushed them around with his little old squirrel rifle. He was a very small cadaverous-looking fellow, weighing not over one hundred pounds, and ex-Governor Ransom was far above six feet, and portly, and he made a ludicrous spectacle, marching at the command of such a very inferior guard. Judge Williams was jolly and good-natured, and asked the boys to spare his fiddle and wardrobe, which they did; but his court and all the belongings were literally destroyed, and he was compelled to witness it. He ran away down through Missouri, and I don't know when he came back, but I think he was there a year later.

The accounts written in regard to the looting of Little's store are quite absurd. Some say $7,000 worth of goods were destroyed, but I think $700 would have covered all there was in that little shack. It contained whiskey, tobacco, and a few groceries. As soon as possible Montgomery ordered the store nailed up, and the looting ceased. Some of the fellows were helping themselves to whiskey and tobacco, and perhaps other things. No doubt there were men there that would steal; but for the most part that crowd was composed of the best men in Kansas, and nearly all of them afterwards joined the Union army, and many held offices all the way from lieutenant to brigadier general. And later the state of Kansas as well as Linn and Bourbon counties, elected them to the best offices in the gift of the people. One member of the company became treasurer of Bourbon County, and another was United States Senator for a long time, and if I am not mistaken, one was sent to Congress from this district. I was only twenty-two at the time and the leaders of that force were nearly all men of mature years, but I had a speaking acquaintance with a good many of them, including the Bains, two of them, the Thomas brothers, Maynes, Stevensons, Stewarts, Steel brothers, Barnes, Dentons, Haslets, Seamans and many others. Only three or four of that party ever went wrong that I know of. In fact, they were just the rank and file of a good citizenship, and led by a man that historians have failed to do justice to.

Some may wonder why an account of this has not been written before by those who took part. I will own that it was not a very popular move; more than half of the free-state men disapproved, and many denounced it outright. It was a very serious crime against Uncle Sam, and today would probably be punished relentlessly. It was conceived in secret, and secrecy was enjoined at the time, and I am not sure that I ever heard anyone brag about it unless in the company of some of the participants. Today there are living, of those whom I knew, only four or five, and of course, they were very young at that time. The leaders have long since passed over. But I think they did just right, and that they lived and died with a clear conscience. We kept still a long time. We had to; the administration was against us. Jefferson Davis was in the cabinet and the South had control of everything, and the only reason we were not punished was because the army would not help, and they had no other way to bring us into court. Two years later Lincoln was elected, the war came on, and we were in the hands of our friends; and I don't believe any one of that company was ever tried for the offense."

During this time Plumb was head of a local Emporia militia tasked with protecting the town should it ever come under attack from proslavery enemies. In 1857, he was appointed to protect the ballot box as votes were cast to determine the territory's constitution to be admitted into the Union. James Lane had appointed Plumb to serve as Superintendent of Enrollment of the 4th Brigade, 2nd Division. His job was to recruit other men to the militia for the purpose of protecting the ballot box. Voting at that time was often a dangerous affair which necessitated the need for ballot and poll protection. Routinely, proslavery citizens of Missouri would cross into Kansas and vote in an attempt to sway the elections, or intimidate legal voters away from the polls. Confrontations between these people and the citizens of Kansas often resulted in violence.

On December 17, 1857, Lane appointed Plumb as his Aide de Camp for the Free-State territorial militia. In 1858, Plumb was a delegate to the constitutional convention held at Wyandotte. Voting records from within the convention still survive and show that Plumb was in favor of women's suffrage as well as African American suffrage. Unfortunately, he was in the minority regarding women's suffrage and it did not make it into the final constitution that was put to the vote of the people. The constitution was approved by the citizens of the territory, but failed to pass the United States Senate to admit Kansas into the Union.

As an example of Plumb's growing influence within the Free-State party, he successfully introduced election reform in the nominations of candidates. Early Emporia resident, George Walker told Connelley:

> Plumb was always an independent man and thought for himself. The old Free-State party at first made nominations of candidates for office by the caucus method—a few leaders would get together in caucus and name the candidates, and this had become the accepted manner of naming party candidates. Plumb believed the people should name their candidates. In 1861 Plumb drew up a petition or declaration for a county

Original certificate issued to Preston B. Plumb and signed by renowned Kansas Senator James Lane for the Protection of the Ballot Box in 1857. Image courtesy Plumb Family.

Wanted!

A GOVERNOR for Kanzas! Men of principle and conscience need not apply.
aug19   PLUMB & McCLUNG.

Wanted!

A Purchaser for two good Yoke of work Cattle. Cheap sale.   PLUMB & McCLUNG.
aug19

Notice.

THE undersigned having filed upon the Southwest Quarter Section of Section No. 14, in Township No. 19, Range No. 11 East, and intending to pre-empt it, hereby warns all persons from settling on the same.
aug15–tf   R. J. HINTON.

Valuable Claim for Sale!

CONTAINING 40 acres timber, plenty of stock water, ten acres improved, a good well of water and a dwelling house, and is but two miles from town. Will be sold cheap. Apply to
sep12   PLUMB & McCLUNG.

The classified excerpt above from Plumb's December 12, 1857 Kanzas News shows his sense of sarcasm rather well. He was referring to the revolving door of governors in the Kansas Territory. At the time of this newspaper, Kansas had already had five governors in 1857 (and would claim yet another that December). Also in this ad is a listing for land being sold by Plumb and his friend and co-worker at the news, Leigh McClung. Plumb sold real estate, insurance, and provided notary services during this time. Image courtesy Newspapers.com: Kanzas News, December 12, 1857.

convention. His name made the movement popular at once, and the convention was held at Fremont. A ticket was nominated and elected. From that time the convention method prevailed. It was a great reform when introduced by Plumb.

Between 1857 and 1859, Plumb worked tirelessly on his *Kanzas News* newspaper. Without telegraph lines in Emporia, gathering news meant physically going somewhere, interviewing people, and then returning to the paper to report it. For Plumb, this meant traveling to Lawrence frequently to gather up items of interest for his paper. When the family horse was in use on the family farm, he was forced to walk the roughly seventy miles each way. When he rode, he proved a hard rider and was difficult to keep up with. Occasionally, he would travel with a companion on these long treks to Lawrence. On one such occasion, he traveled with Addison Gilbert Proctor (proprietor of a local Emporia store) to Kansas City who related the following incident:

> We decided not to follow the Santa Fe Trail to Burlingame, but to cut across the country into the Neosho Valley, via the Osage Agency and the valley towns. We left Westport early on an October morning, intending to reach the Agency that evening. We knew it was a long ride, and we let the horses jog along in their own way. We hardly met a man or saw a house all that day, but kept going on a grassy trail toward the southwest. Night closed down on us with nothing in sight but the stars and the dim trail through the grass. We knew we must be somewhere in the region of the Agency, but had no means of knowing how near. Along in the evening, we came to a river. We found our way down the path, crossed by the starlight, but when we reached the other side the overhanging trees completely blotted out our path, and search, as we did, leading our tired horses up and down that narrow shelf between the water and the steep bank, it was nearly midnight before we discovered a narrow footpath leading up the bank. We struggled up this steep way, fairly dragging the horses after us, and we mounted in the opening on the level river bank above. It was just light enough by the stars to push our way along through the open wooded section. As we were slowly feeling our way along, all of a sudden we found ponies all about us feeding, and in a few moments the

flickering light of smoldering camp-fires appeared in every direction; and all about us, seeming to cover the ground, moved the form of waking Indians, tossing and twisting about. We were right in the midst of an Indian camp. Before we could hardly think, all about us the Indians were jumping to their feet and in the confusion uttering all sorts of guttural, both loud and deep. We instantly realized our danger. "Put spurs to the horses and rush out," says Plumb. Instantly the two horses responded with a jump and a dash, my horse ahead. The Indians gave a most unearthly yell and whoop that fairly lifted the horses from their feet as they plunged headlong through the trees, we clinging close, with heads low to escape the branches. Dashing through an opening in the woods with the crowd of wild yelling Indians close on our path, we came to a ravine, down which we went, the Indians running close to us and yelling every jump. As we struck the other side of the ravine an Indian running ahead of his gang caught Plumb by the ankle and attempted to throw him from his horse. Plumb carried a short riding whip with a heavy handle. He instantly turned and struck the Indian a solid blow square in the face with that heavy handle. The Indian fell to the ground with a yell, losing his hold on the stirrup strap.

It was now getting desperate. A halt would mean instant death, for the Indians close behind us were wild with excitement, evidently taking us for a pair of horse thieves. As we rushed ahead with horses quivering from excitement, all of a sudden we came to a road, just the road we had been hunting for since coming to the river. Down this road the horses swept with new life, seeming to realize their good fortune. Suddenly just before us, a big cluster of buildings loomed up in the starlight. We rode at full speed directly to the main building, which stood some hundred feet from the road. A high fence was before us with no open gate. Up we road, threw our bridles over the projecting rails, leaped over the fence, and ran to the house. A partly open door showed a dull fire. We made a rush, pushed open the door, and shouted. Startled men, sleeping on cots and on the floor, instantly sprang to their feet, with the clicking of revolvers. Plumb knew the agent and shouted his name, and we were able to make the situation understood, though for some moments it looked desperate. The Agent said it was a close call; that the Indians were a bad lot, just in from a buffalo hunt, and many of them had been drinking and were very dangerous.

On another one of his many trips to report the news, Plumb came down with the dreaded smallpox disease. There are several versions of the story of how he got smallpox, and unfortunately, there are no surviving accounts from him personally. The following story from Mrs. Storrs, seems to be the most accurate:

A man by the name of Wright went to Mrs. [G.W.] Brown's house [in Lawrence] and asked for Mr. Plumb. She told him that Plumb would be in after a while so he waited, thinking he would get his dinner. In a couple of weeks, Wright, Plumb, and some others started to Emporia. Wright was a carpenter and Plumb had told him he thought he could get him a job. They stopped at Burlingame for dinner and the man fainted and fell off the stool he was sitting on. They thought he was overcome by the heat as he was not used to this climate. But they found he had a high fever and decided he better stay there till he felt better and come down later; they could not wait for him. The man at whose house he was, sent for Doctor Titus who said he had smallpox, and the man had him taken away to a little shanty. Plumb heard of this and sent a man to take care of him and afterward got a woman, a Mrs. Collier from Xenia, Ohio. When the man was 'bout well Mr. Plumb was coming down from Lawrence and stopped and shook hands with the man, and from that he took it. We were living in a little house close to the hotel and one of the boys came over and said, "Mrs. Storrs I wish you would go over and see Plumb; he has a high fever. The doctor has ordered him to have some gruel and Mrs. Hammond says she don't know how to make it." I said I could make the gruel. I took my little girl with me as I had no one to leave her with. Plumb was tossing about on his bed, and when I went in, he said, "You are an angel of mercy." Morris the Methodist minister was trying to make him some gruel. I took charge of that but soon found Mrs. Hammond did not like to have me do it. Later,

[Leigh] McClung came over and said Plumb had broken out with the smallpox. We had Doctor Swisher who lived on Allen Creek come in and vaccinate us and none of us took it. They moved Plumb out to a little shanty on Mrs. G.W. Brown's claim and sent for the Mrs. Collier who nursed Wright to take care of him. Every bit of his hair came out and he was badly marked. Soon after he was well they had a convention here and Plumb had to make a speech. He began to speak with his hat on and somebody kept calling to him to take off his hat. Finally, he raised his hat and showed his bald head.

Plumb retained the smallpox scars for the rest of his life, and was occasionally mocked for them by unsavory reporters and politicians.

In 1859, Plumb decided to pursue becoming a lawyer hoping it would be advantageous to him as a political leader and as a profession. He decided to sell his interest in the *Kansas News* (renamed from the *Kanzas News* in July 1858) to Jacob Stotler who had been a part owner up until that time. Plumb's last issue was January 15, 1859. He left Emporia in October 1859 for Cleveland, Ohio to study and returned in February of 1861. It is unclear which school he went to in Cleveland and what the curriculum may have been. The *Kansas News* wrote upon his return, "He is accompanied by Mr. H.G. Plantz who intends making Emporia his permanent home. Plumb and Plantz have hung out their 'shingle' and intend to practice law in the Courts of this Judicial District, all business entrusted to their care will receive prompt attention. Their office is under Masonic Hall on Commercial Street."

During this time, Plumb worked and resided in a particularly modest fashion. He and his later partner Bailey had a law office at Masonic Hall, a building located at the southwest corner of 7th and Commercial streets in Emporia. Describing the layout, L.T. Heritage said, "Their office was in the front room, first floor and in it was a double bunk in which they slept; (Two berths one above the other like a Pullman). They had a pine box for a table. Someone asked Plumb if he could not afford a better table. He said the table was as good as the lawyer."

While working as a lawyer, Plumb took on clients throughout Kansas and even into neighboring states. One such client was an Ohio widow who needed his help disposing of some property in Kansas. While in Ashtabula, Ohio, he made the acquaintance of her niece, a young woman named Caroline (Carrie) A. Southwick. She was the daughter of Abijah Southwick who ran an integral stop on the Underground Railroad in Ashtabula. The two made an impression on each other, and the teenaged Carrie was smitten with the handsome lawyer from Kansas. Although Plumb returned to Emporia, the two corresponded through letters.

Chapter 4
War Breaks Out

On April 12, 1861 the first official shots of the Civil War rang out at Fort Sumter in Charleston, South Carolina. But many Kansans had been fighting pro-slavery bushwhackers for years, and they rushed at the chance to enlist and serve their country.

At this time, Plumb served as a Supreme Court Reporter and in the State Legislature. Plumb was also eager to join the fight but was convinced by local Emporians to remain in the legislature until the matter of a county seat for Lyon County was decided. Plumb's brother, George, did not wait and enlisted in the 8th Kansas Cavalry right away.

During this time, Plumb became better acquainted with Thomas Ewing, Jr., who was serving as a judge. Plumb also got a bit of notoriety for serving on a military court-martial with Colonel James Gilpatrick Blunt.

Plumb was effective in the State Legislature and was Chairman of the Judiciary Committee in the House. Kansas was a very new state, having been admitted to the Union in January 1861, and consequently, there were a great many new laws being created. Plumb took an active role in proceedings and often spoke on issues he was passionate about.

Plumb was a key player in founding the Emporia Normal School while he was serving in the State Legislature. When the matter was being discussed in the legislature, it was necessary to have a deed to the site there by a specific time. In order to accomplish that, Plumb rode from Topeka to Emporia through a terrible blizzard and returned immediately with the deed to 40 acres of land so that the bill for the school could be adopted.

Paul Havens was a member of the Kansas State Legislature in 1861 with Plumb and knew him well at that time.

> He remembers that Plumb was very active in the Legislature, but was not over-talkative and never talked himself out as many members did. He usually had something to say on every measure before the Legislature but it was pointed and briefly said, and very effective. Havens remembers that he was particularly valuable in the House for his knowledge of business affairs. He seemed to know everything about business and how it should be transacted. A great deal of the business of the State was left to him and committees he was on.

After a question had been debated sometimes for half a day and the House was muddled and befogged about what ought to be the outcome, Plumb would get up and talk five minutes in a practical way about what ought to be done with the measure or about the matter under discussion, and men would then for the first time see what the real question had been all the time of the discussion. Plumb's suggestions were usually adopted.

In January 1862, a committee of five was appointed to investigate embezzlement in the offices of the secretary and auditor of the state. The committee reported a resolution impeaching Governor Charles Robinson, Secretary of State John W. Robinson, and State Auditor George S. Hillyer for misdemeanors in office. Plumb was appointed chairman of the house committee to conduct the trial before the senate. Plumb was successful in his trial and those who knew him recalled later that he was fair and just in his prosecution, and did not hold any ill will against Charles Robinson, whom he had supported previously for governor.

By August 4, 1862, another regiment of troops was being raised with Thomas Ewing, Jr. in command. Ewing had been appointed by General Jim Lane to raise the regiment. Plumb set about recruiting a company of men from Emporia and the surrounding area. On August 16, 1862 Plumb ran an ad in the paper to recruit 100 men from Lyon, Morris, Chase, Butler, Greenwood, and Coffee counties. Among the men who enlisted under him, were his brother William, Jacob Stotler's younger brother, Charlie; and numerous friends of his, including Lemuel T. Heritage and George M. Walker. Many of these men knew and respected Plumb and were convinced to enlist without any grandiose promises or assurances that the war would be over quickly. In an issue for August 30, 1862 was a notice, "More Bounty" – "A fund is being raised in Emporia for the purpose of paying to the needy families of those who enlist in the Lyon County Company, a bounty of Twenty Dollars each per annum, until the war is closed." Plumb was the first to contribute to this fund with the sum of $100 per year. Ewing delivered a speech in Emporia on August 26, 1862, which was published in full in the *Emporia News* on September 6th, along with this local item, "Our town is about dried up, since the boys left it is a rarity to see a man, the other day we went down Commercial Street, in business hours, but there was no business. What a change, the once busy town is as lonesome as a deserted village. It is war times and we are realizing it."

This image depicts a court-martial with Colonel James G. Blunt (seated at table) and Plumb (standing and pointing). The illustration was made several years after the original date of the trial, October 18, 1861. Plumb accompanied Blunt as a civilian militia member on a retaliatory strike against John Mathews for sacking the town of Humboldt, and led the prosecution against those arrested for aiding the Confederacy. The trial ended in a stalemate and the arrested were acquitted. Image courtesy Kansas State Historical Society.

Thus, Company C of the 11th Kansas Infantry was raised by Lieutenant Preston B. Plumb. L.T. Heritage furnished this account:

> The soldiers which had enlisted under Lieut. Plumb took their departure on Tuesday morning. Before they left they were presented by the Citizens of Emporia with a splendid flag, made by the ladies. The presentation speech was made by old "Father Fairchild", and the flag was received by Mr. Plumb in one of his happiest efforts. The scene at parting was very affecting, parents, sisters, daughters, wives, children and friends were present to bid the soldiers farewell, many of them feeling that it was the last parting on earth. Few eyes that did not shed tears, but all felt that the sacrifice must be made, stout hearts trembled. Twenty teams had been furnished by the generous citizens to convey the boys to Fort Leavenworth; they were accompanied by the Elmendaro Band.
>
> About 300 people had congregated to see them off. As they passed over the hill, cheers on cheers went up from the long line of wagons, which were responded to from the citizens left behind.

There were 140 total enlisted, of this number 134 were accepted, 101 being mustered as Company C and 33 mustered into Company E (those under Captain Edmund G. Ross), being mostly from Americus and vicinity. Those who were not accepted were later allowed to join the regimental band. Plumb was promoted to Captain of Company C and took charge of the very men he had recruited, a fact that would weigh heavy on his mind throughout the war. Plumb was sickly and very thin when he went into the army. His brother, George, later said that he'd suffered two hemorrhages and had been coughing up blood. Despite the illness that may have been consumption, he was full of energy and enthusiasm for the service.

Chapter 5

Off to War

Serving in the military became one of Plumb's proudest accomplishments. In late 1862, he was a prominent Emporian and Kansan. He had advocated tirelessly for the Free-State cause in his Ohio and Emporia newspapers, risked his life for the same cause by smuggling weapons into Kansas to arm the Free-State settlers, and aided John Brown in whisking escaped slaves to freedom. He had helped build the state government of Kansas under those same principles while serving in the state legislature, participating in a state constitutional convention, and practicing law. The men of the regiment elected their officers and selected Plumb to serve as Major. At 24 years old, Plumb was now a Major of the 11th Kansas Infantry, a rank that made his father very proud, as his father (Plumb's grandfather) had also served as a Major in the United States Army during the War of 1812.

The early movements of the 11th Kansas are filled with near-constant marching and very little engagement with the enemy. Like his letters nearly a decade earlier to the *Xenia News*, Plumb chronicled nearly every step within the regiment's *Buck & Ball* newspaper:

> We have been furnished by Lieut. Gregg, Sergeant Taber, and Private Rivers, of the Eleventh, notes from their diaries of the march of that regiment from Fort Leavenworth, from which we are enabled to make up the following history of that long and tedious expedition. We propose, in the future numbers, to continue the history, so that at the end of the war the members of the Eleventh, and their friends, may be supplied with a complete record of all its marches, and battles–a record which cannot but possess rare interest to all concerned.
>
> The Regiment was regularly mustered into the service for three years, or during the war, on the 14th of September, with Thomas Ewing, Jr., as Colonel. Thomas Moonlight was subsequently mustered as Lieut. Colonel, and P.B. Plumb, as Major. After a course of instructions by Capt. Walkinshaw, the regiment was ordered to reinforce the division of Gen. Blunt, then operating in Missouri. Accordingly, it took up the line of march from

Portrait of Preston B. Plumb taken in Leavenworth, Kansas in August or September 1862 at the time of enlistment. Notice the infantry kepi in his hand, but lack of uniform. Image courtesy Robert and Lesa Reves.

camp Lyon, near Fort Leavenworth, on Saturday, the 4th of October. Made camp after a march of 12 miles, on a prairie south of Leavenworth, and in honor of the colonel, it was christened camp Ewing.

The next day's march was 15 miles, crossing the Kaw river to Camp Moonlight, immediately south of the town of De Soto. The next was 30 miles, to camp Plumb, on Bull Creek, 2 ½ miles south of the town of Marysville.

Nothing special occurred on these marches. The men, being mostly unused to traveling on foot, were of course very much jaded by starting off thus briskly on a long journey, but were content, and bore the fatigues of the march with unexampled cheerfulness and good humor. Many were the jokes passed at the meagre and ragged appearance of the respective companies as they came filing up the banks of Bull Creek into camp, caused by so many falling out by the way from over-fatigue.
The road thus far had been extremely dry, and there being much wind, the men suffered from thirst and dust.

On the 7th the regiment marched to Twin Springs, a distance of 23 miles, crossing the Marais des Cygnes. At Paola the 12th Regiment, Col. C.W. Adams was drawn up in line and saluted the 11th military style as it passed.

At Twin Spring a heavy rain and wind storm occurred during the night, blowing down several tents, drenching the earth, and creating much confusion throughout the camp, delaying the command until afternoon, when it again took the road, and marched to Sugar Creek, near the town of Paris.

The 9th was as disagreeable a day as it is often the lot of a soldier to travel. The rain was cold and incessant and coming much of the time in the faces of the men, was, with the constant mud, very trying. Passed through Paris, Moncka, and Mound City to Fort Lincoln, a distance of 12 miles. That march will long be remembered by those who were required to make it, as one of great discomfort and suffering. It was somewhat relieved, however, by a train of wagons sent from Fort Scott by Gen. Lane to carry the arms of the regiment from Mound City to that point. That part of the march, 12 miles, was made in extremely quick time, although in the face of a driving storm.

The march from Ft. Lincoln to Ft. Scott, on the 10th, a distance of 12 miles, was comparatively comfortable. At Ft. Scott the regiment lay until the afternoon of the 12th awaiting the ammunition and provision train of 60 wagons which it was to convoy to Gen. Blunt, then in South-western Missouri, and operating against the enemy.

Left Camp Blunt, near Fort Scott, on the afternoon of the 12th, accompanied by Lieut. E.A. Smith, with a section of Blair's battery, and camped 12 miles south, near the scene of the battle of Dry Wood, in which (then) Capt. Moonlight, with his "battery," (the little howitzer,) checked the advance of the rebels upon Kansas, protecting the State from invasion.

On the 13th, marched 10 miles to Camp Stanton, on big prairie, in Missouri. Target shooting was practiced here by companies for the first time, and the muskets, owing to their large caliber and forcible shooting, were dubbed by the Col. "light artillery," causing much amusement.

On the 14th marched to Camp Henning, 23 miles beyond, camped near the little town of Preston, once quite a pleasant and thriving village, but now entirely deserted and the streets grown to grass—a sad relic of war's devastation and ruin. The inhabitants were said to be mostly loyal to their government, and for this were driven out by the secession marauders, and many of them murdered.

On the 18th passed over the scene of Gen. Sigel's celebrated retreat, near Carthage, the men picking up many relics of that hotly contested fight. Forded Spring river, and it being the first instance of having to walk through rivers, many were the grotesque and laughable incidents that occurred.

Passed through the once prosperous town of Carthage, now fearfully wrecked by Sigel's guns and soldiers, camped five miles beyond, at Camp Sigel, after a march of 17 miles; met at Carthage, a long train of U.S. and emigrant wagons, bound for Kansas, with the wounded from the battle of Newtonia, of a few days before –the emigrants on their way to permanent residence in Kansas, having been driven out by their rebel neighbors. Were joined here by two companies of the Wisconsin 3d.

On the 16th marched 20 miles to Camp Schofield; pleasantly situated in a small valley between high hills, but a rather dangerous locality under the circumstances. The camp was somewhat disturbed by rumors of the near proximity of large guerrilla forces, but no serious alarm occurred.

On the 17th marched 18 miles, through Newtonia, the scene of a recent hard fought battle, to the little town of Stony Comfort, a very comfortless place, though well named, as far as the stony part was concerned. Roads very hilly and rocky, and pure running water abundant, affording simple opportunity for the men to practice on "wading in"–a lesson they did not forget on the great march of the 27th and 28th ult.

October 18th, marched 20 miles to camp Totten, three miles south of Keatsville, on Springfield and Fayetteville road. Passed through Keatsville, which looked desolate enough–the inhabitants nearly all left, and all kinds of business stopped. This in fact was the case along the entire march through Missouri and Arkansas.

Sunday, October 19, overtook the main command at Elk Horn Tavern, the scene of Gen. Curtis' great battle with the rebels last summer. The regiment was here reviewed and addressed in very complimentary terms by Brig. Gen. Schofield, commanding Division, and hospitably dined by Col. Weir's brigade, for which kindness the Eleventh takes this occasion to again express its sense of obligation. Made camp Cloud immediately to the right of Pea Ridge, after a march of 16 miles and was introduced to its present brigade commander—the gallant and accomplished soldier and gentleman—Colonel Cloud.

Oct. 20, again resumed the line of march in pursuit of the enemy, at 6 p.m., for Bentonville, 15 miles distant, which was reached without unusual incident at daybreak next morning. This was once a beautiful place but is now in utter ruin.

The 21st was another night's march of 18 miles to near Maysville, supposing the enemy to be there. They having fallen back, the pursuit was continued next morning, the 22d, to Fort Wayne, 8 miles further, most of the distance on a "double quick," but arrived on the field only in time to see the enemy "double quicking" the other way, leaving their 4 pieces of artillery in the hands of four companies of the Kansas Second, who had just taken them by a most intrepid and daring charge, and with a loss of 3 killed and 6 wounded. Made camp on the site of old Fort Wayne, where the command rested until the 31st of October. An alarm was raised in camp the next day, by the appearance of a body of rebels, supposed to be seeking the rebel command of Cooper, which had been driven out the day before. The men were in perfect line of battle in three minutes from the beat of the drum, and on the field in the direction of the enemy, one mile distant, in ten minutes afterwards. No enemy however, made his appearance, and the regiment marched quietly back to camp.

On the 30th a grand division review was made by Brig. Gen. Blunt, making a line of battle, of infantry, cavalry and artillery nearly two miles in length. The forces present were the 2d, 6th, 10th, 11th and 13th Kansas, 1st and 3d Indian, and Rabb's, Allen's and Hopkins' batteries, about 6,000 men and 18 pieces of artillery.

Oct. 31st marched 18 miles to Camp Ewing, on the Spavinaw, a beautiful level prairie surrounded by high hills and timber. On the 1st Nov. the brigade was mustered and inspected by Colonel Cloud, brigade commander, and on the 3d marched to camp Bowen, 4 miles south of Bentonville, distance 15 miles. A pleasant locality, and good position to meet the enemy. Here the regiment remained until the 13th while companies E and D under command of Maj. Plumb, were detailed on a milling expedition to Brown's mill, in Washington county, ten miles to the southwest, for the purpose of supplying the command with flour. They succeeded in getting some five or six thousand pounds, which was quite a relief, in the then condition of the commissary department. In commemoration of the change, they christened their stopping place camp Plenty. While here, they, in conjunction with a force from the 2nd Kansas made an expedition to Robinson's tannery, 8 miles west, and destroyed about $15,000 worth of hides which were being prepared there for shoes for the rebel army. Enough leather was destroyed to have shod ten thousand men, and many will be the cold toes among them the coming winter, in consequence of the loss. On the 14th the command moved forward 22 miles to camp Babcock, where it was joined by the milling party, and a portion of Co. F, under Capt. Reese, sent out to another mill to the west of camp.

The command laid here until the 27th, when intelligence having been received that the enemy had made a stand in force at Cane Hill, it was ordered to march upon and attack him. Each man was required to carry his blankets and provisions, leaving the wagons in the rear. The distance was 30 miles of very rough road, and was accomplished between 9 o'clock of the morning of the 27th and 11 of the morning of the 28th. Here commenced the battle of Cane Hill, a succinct account of which will be found elsewhere, and here ends for this number, our history of the Eleventh Kansas.

It may not be inappropriate, in this connection and as a part of the history of the Eleventh Regiment, to add some remarks in regard to the policy pursued by its commander during the march, with reference to the great issues of the war. Thoroughly comprehending those issues and imbued with the spirit which animates the entire North in this contest, he has universally acted upon the trite admonition of the pugnacious Hibernian—"whenever you see a (rebel) head, hit it." Along the entire march through Missouri and into Arkansas, he has by a most judicious discrimination, afforded protection from despoilment, to these whom he had good reason to believe were at heart loyal to the government, while the heavy hand of war has not been withheld from those whom he had equally good reason to believe had plotted and assisted in the efforts for its overthrow. Believing with the people at large, that secessionists were aliens and not entitled to the protection of the army, no such protection has been afforded by him.

In this way, he has succeeded in satisfying in part, so far as the men under his command are concerned that spirit of vengeance which this monstrous and causeless rebellion has awakened, and also acted according to one of the most essential and universal rules of warfare, that the enemy shall be required as far as possible, to support the army, as the most effectual method of teaching him the legitimate lessons of rebellion against a good and powerful government. In this way, too, the soldiers of that regiment, entering this country as they did, with an unalterable conviction that secession was to be rebuked by every effectual and legitimate means, have been saved, on the one hand, the shameful farce of protecting rebel property, and on the other, the stigma of pillaging the homes of families, and restrained, to a very great extent, from a private and unauthorized exercise of the power of confiscation. In no other way could this result have been so effectually attained, while the proverbial good conduct of that regiment, and the cheerfulness with which the men obey his every command in this as in every other respect, attest their approbation of his course, and their appreciation of him as a commander.

During this time, the regiment had been issued antiquated large-caliber Prussian muskets dating to the 1830s. These guns fired a shot of a single musket ball and buckshot together, giving rise to the name "buck & ball" shot. Ewing once jokingly remarked that the regiment should be reclassified from infantry to light artillery given the nature of the shot.

As previously mentioned, the regiment's first fight came at the Battle of Cane Hill in northwestern Arkansas on November 28, 1862. Brigadier General Blunt's Union forces moved into Arkansas and were intercepted by Brigadier General John Marmaduke's Confederate army. The ensuing fight set the stage for the Battle of Prairie Grove with Blunt's command breaking through Marmaduke's line and pursuing them until nightfall. The *Buck & Ball* printed a more detailed account of the battle and their involvement in it:

> Owing to the space required for the details of the great battle of the 7th inst., and to one half of this sheet having been previously printed we are compelled to reduce the account of the above engagement to a mere mention of the main incidents of the conflict, and of course to omit many circumstances and facts of interest.
>
> The battle commenced by Rabb's and Hopkin's batteries, at 11 o'clock on the 28th of Nov. the infantry then being about two miles in the rear. Immediately upon hearing the cannonading, the 11th Kansas and the 1st and 3d Indian Home Guards, being in the advance were hurried forward at a double quick, and shortly brought into the battle, the 11th in support of the batteries.
>
> On arriving in presence of the enemy, the 11th was divided, the left wing following one section of the battery, and taking position at the foot of a high hill immediately in the rear of the village of Cane Hill, and the right taking position about a mile distant, upon a high bluff to the North-west. The fight was kept up in this position mainly with artillery, for about one hour, when the enemy's lines were seen to break and fall back, in retreat.

At this stage a running fight commenced, through woods and over almost inaccessible bluffs, for about five miles; the artillery keeping the road and pouring volleys of shells upon the enemy from every eligible point. At this time the enemy attempted to make a stand across the road leading to Van Buren, when they were charged upon by the Second and Sixth Kansas cavalry, in the road, and the 11th infantry and Indians in the woods. A severe but short engagement ensued, the 11th having a regular bushwhacking fight and fairly beating the enemy at their own game. Three miles further on another stand was made, when the Sixth again charged upon them, but were compelled to fall back. The artillery then came up and attacked, driving them into the mountains. It being now quite dark, the pursuit was discontinued, and the enemy continued his retreat for several miles, getting entirely beyond pursuit in the fastnesses of the Boston Mountains.

The casualties on the side of the Union forces were slight, with the exception of those of the Sixth, that regiment losing some 20 or 30 killed, wounded and prisoners, among them Lt. Col. Jewell, since died, and Lieut. Johnson, now recovering. The 2nd also lost one killed and two or three wounded. The 11th lost several wounded, but none killed. On the side of the rebels, the loss was much heavier, both in killed, wounded and prisoners, although the exact number is not known. Among the killed was Col. Munroe, commanding a regiment of their forces. Some 30 or 40 others are known to have been killed.

The distance marched by the 11th that day was not less than 38 miles, much of it on a double quick, and through the woods, being one of the severest and most fatiguing marches on record. At the end of the day the men were so thoroughly exhausted that they were content to drop down upon the ground without supper, blankets, or tents, and seek that repose, of which they had been deprived by the hard marches of the two previous days and nights.

Veterinary Surgeon Thomas Barber of Emporia described seeing Plumb on the field during the Battle of Cane Hill:

> At Cane Hill the Eleventh was charging on the retreating rebels – had driven them back by the charge. A part of the Sixth Kansas came into the charge from an oblique direction and took place just by the side of the Eleventh and overlapped it a little. Barber remembers that Plumb's horse was shot and disabled. Plumb had no time to get another one, but kept his place in the charge on foot, running abreast of the charging column. He was present when Colonel Jewell was killed. He rejoiced when the rebels were driven away but there were tears in his eyes when the dead and wounded were being gathered up.

Sergeant Sherman Bodwell's diary of Company H also offers a glimpse into Cane Hill through his experiences:

> Saturday [December] 6th
> Broke camp as usual. Marched to our line of battle, south of Newburgh, lay there till about noon. "A", "F", "D" and "H" ordered to the front to foot of hill where we went into action on the 28th. "H" ordered up the hill, and deployed right and left under the rest lying down. Waited an hour or more, a few scouts keeping up a scattering fire with enemy in front and trying to draw them within our reach. Fell back to foot of hill and commenced getting supper. Firing in front. "H" went up deployed, and drove enemy through timber some ¼ mile. Ordered back by Maj. Crawford, the enemy following until we regained our first position, where we checked them.
> Enemy fell back, formed, and charged on us in force, showing colors. Met them with a heavy fire, as they rode upon us in column. Ordered back down hill, under a heavy fire. Myself, Corp'l. Ward and Private Evans wounded. Evans seriously. "H" formed on hill side, and marched back ½ mile, it being nearly dark. Walked into Hospital, had my wound bandaged (Dr. said, better call it square for this time and stay, leg would be stiff in morning) and returned to company, passing the Regt which had marched to front. Bivouac at night our position as picket.

The *Buck & Ball* regimental newspaper serves as a great record of the 11th Kansas' history through Cane Hill and immediately following the Battle of Prairie Grove. Later in life, Plumb recalled how the paper came to be and his involvement in it to a newspaper reporter of the *Globe Democrat*:

> The 11th received its baptism of fire at Cane Hill where there was a running fight of five miles. Then came a rest of several days. Hidden away in a log cabin on the outskirts of the town was found the outfit of a country printing office. It had been in service at Tahlequah, the capitol of the Cherokee Nation. There were Cherokee characters as well as English type, so that the paper could be gotten out in both languages. The owner, fearful of the capture of Tahlequah and of the destruction of his printing office, had moved his type and press across the country and had hidden the property at Cane Hill, never dreaming that that out-of-the-way hamlet would be reached by the invading army.
>
> But, the battle over, the soldiers found the Cherokee editor's plant, and when 11th Kansas came along the type was scattered over the floor and some of it in the street. The press was in fragments and some portions of it missing. Then it was the instinct of the "art preservative" asserted itself. The 11th Kansas took possession. Maj. Plumb became once more an editor. Ross, who afterward was United States Senator and is now Governor of New Mexico, was of the first to arrange an apology for cases and to commence sorting the "pi," S.J. Crawford, who became Governor of Kansas, and who is now the State's legal representative at Washington, was another of the force. There was no lack of recruits. The 11th had printers enough to man a dozen composing rooms.
>
> "One of the first difficulties we had to contend with," says Senator Plumb, in telling the story "was to get big letters enough to set up the title. The boys who had been there ahead of us had picked out the job type for initial letters, and had carried them

off. We finally chose a name for the paper to conform to our scanty stock of big type. The exigency of the font rather than the appropriateness of the name was what we had in mind when we fixed upon 'Buck & Ball'. Even then we found we were short a letter; and I remember that Crawford or Ross, or somebody else, had to whittle out one from a stick. You will notice that we didn't always capitalize proper names, and that we occasionally employed italics in the middle of a word. That wasn't because we didn't know better, but because our assortment ran out on certain letters. We finally got together enough material and set up the six columns. By the time the form was ready the old press had been tinkered so that we were able to work off one side. The next problem was the white paper. The best we could do was to use the foolscap supplied the army and we had to skirmish for that. Then some of the boys got several rolls of wall paper and we worked that off. We offered to exchange one printed sheet for so many blank sheets and that yielded us considerable foolscap which the boys found somewhere. One way or another we managed to get together enough paper to print 1500 copies on one side. Just as we were striking off the last the word came that Hindman's army was approaching. Our pickets had been driven in. I was ordered to take my men and go a certain point on the picket line and hold it. We dropped the printing business right there and hurried forward.

The Federal troops moved out of Cane Hill to take up a different positon, leaving Maj. Plumb and his detachment of intelligent compositors out in the woods holding a picket line. There a staff officer of Gen. Blunt found them next day, and asked in surprise if Maj. Plumb didn't know the troops had evacuated Cane Hill.

"Yes," said the fighting editor.

"Then, what in thunder are you staying here for?" asked the staff officer.

"I haven't had any orders to fall back," replied the editor.

"Well," said the staff officer, "I'll take the responsibility of ordering you back."

By that time the main body of the army was several miles from Cane Hill. As Maj. Plumb and his men went back through the village, the editor true to his professional instinct, couldn't resist the temptation to have one more look at the temporary printing office. He went in. There, on the floor, lay the half-printed edition of the Buck & Ball.

"I rolled the papers up in a bundle," says Senator Plumb, "tied a cord around them and carried them to the door. An ambulance, the last, which had remained behind, for something was just being driven off toward the army. I threw the bundle of papers into the rear end of the wagon, joined my men and marched in another direction. The next day we fought the battle of Prairie Grove, and the day after that we had enough to do to take care of the wounded and get things into shape. About the third day I went in search of my papers and found them all safe in the ambulance. After that we reoccupied Cane Hill, took possession of our type and set up the other side and printed the paper complete. You see the outside is dated the 6th of December, while inside appears a full account of the battle of Prairie Grove, which wasn't fought until the 7th. That slight discrepancy in date is explained by what I have told you. We got out and distributed the 1500 copies. Gen. Blunt thought it was a fine idea. He proposed to have the 'Buck & Ball' continued. He furnished some wagons, told me to take possession of the type and material where I could find them and go on getting out the paper. But about the time I got an outfit together and was prepared to resume publication Gen. Schofield came down to take command of the army. He wasn't so well impressed as Blunt had been with our journalistic enterprise and we didn't get out any more issues. So 'Buck & Ball' began and ended with Vol. 1, No. 1."

Almost half of the little paper is given up to excellent accounts of the battle of Cane Hill and Prairie Grove. One of the most interesting features is the address issued by Maj. Gen. Hindman to his troops. This address is dated December 4. The battle was fought December 7, and a couple of days later the "Buck & Ball", published by the victorious Federals, prints the Confederate General's appeal to his soldiers. The address closes as follows:

"Remember that the enemy you engage have no feelings of mercy of kindness for you. His ranks are composed of Pin Indians, Free Negroes, Southern Tories, Kansas Jayhawkers and hired Dutch cut-throats. Those bloody ruffians have invaded your country, stolen and destroyed your property, murdered your neighbors, outraged your women, driven your children from their homes and defiled the graves of your kindred. If each man of you will do what I have urged upon you, we will utterly destroy them. We can do this. We must do it. Our country will be ruined if we fail. A just God will strengthen our arms and give us a glorious victory."

The motto of "Buck & Ball" was the exclamation of John Kitts during the battle of Cane Hill. Kitts was one of the printers who helped set up the paper. Rivers, who afterwards edited a Kansas newspaper, was another. The Buck & Ball contained a great deal of news and very little editorial, and thereby, Maj. Plumb shows that he would have made his mark as a newspaper man if he hadn't turned statesman. The "leader" is a ringing appeal to the people of the conquered counties.

"Eighteen months ago Western Arkansas was prosperous with peace and plenty, "it begins, and this is the conclusion:

"Men of Western Arkansas! Most of you went into this rebellion against your convictions. Will you continue in it to your own utter ruin and that of your country? You have it in your power to bring peace back to your borders. Unite with the Union army in driving out those who are in arms against the Government, and you can then return in peace to your homes. If you do not, the Government must continue to treat you as its enemies. Your choice is between peace and war – peace in the Union, and war against it. Chose ye!"

In another place the fighting editor has this explanation of the choice of the name of the paper: "Buck and ball, when applied to musketry, means death to rebels; when applied to newspapers, the enlightenment of the rebel mind to the reception of the truths of freedom. Take it either way, and it's death to treason - the herald of freedom and good government. The rebels appealed from ballots to bullets; so we will give them first 'buck and ball' from the muskets and then from the press."

Chapter 6

Battle of Prairie Grove and Aftermath

In the fall of 1862, the Union army was attempting to retain control of northwest Arkansas. Confederate General Thomas Hindman held the high ground known as Prairie Grove, while Union General James Blunt's Federal forces attacked it. Each attack from Blunt's forces was repulsed and answered by counterattacks from Hindman's army. The deciding factor came when Blunt's reinforcements, including the 11th Kansas, arrived and Hindman disengaged and withdrew, abandoning the ground to the Union Army.

Thomas Barber was with Plumb during the fighting at Prairie Grove and remarked:

> At Prairie Grove Plumb was in command of the right wing of the Eleventh Kansas. Acted the part of a soldier–cool, brave, level-headed. Captain Heritage was shot just as orders were given to fall back to draw the enemy from the woods. The boys picked him up and carried him and put him over a fence and Plumb was one of the first to come to him and take him by the hand and he directed where he was to be taken to in the rear. Plumb was always at the front–that is, in his place with the regiment in battle.

Sergeant Sherman Bodwell's diary entry for December 7th as well as the few days immediately following, offer a glimpse into what the conditions were like for the 11th Kansas troops:

> Sunday Dec. 7th
> (Firing recommenced on hill. Form to go up but suddenly ordered north. Blunt flanked.) Marched at 9 A.M., north overtaking Regt some 3 miles N of Boonesboro. Train taking the road to Rhea's Mill. Cannonading east of us at time of starting. In sight of Rhea's Mill about 1. Rested a few minutes, and marched E toward Herrons position, hearing his artillery and seeing the smoke. About 5 miles out having double quicked much of the way, came upon the battlefield of "Prairie Grove", division marching in upon open fields passing to opposite

Prairie Grove. Rabb taking position opened fire upon the enemy engaged with Herron on the right of their line. Our [?] of Regt (left) lying down on the left of Battery, Rose up faced to the right, filed right, and lay down under a light fire, fronting the Grove, and on the right and rear of Rabb, Right wing com by Col. the Grove, with 10th, 13th, 2nd Indian hotly engaged with enemy, his line stretching a mile or more, 20 pieces of our artillery, and some of Herrons firing upon the whole line. About sunset, our men in timber driven back to edge of timber. Enemy heavily massing in front, to charge upon Rabb. Left wing up, to the front fire and lay down under a smart fire burn timber some 20 rods in front. Rabb passing to the rear. Lay some 15 m, rose, paced about, marched back to old position, and lay down a half hour rose and marched back some 20 rods and halted, till Col. brought down Rt. Wing and firing ceased. Waited sometime in the darkness, men bringing in the wounded. Marched back ¼ mile, and lay down till morning. The enemy kindling his fires opposite the length of grove. Very cold and no blankets.

Monday Dec 8th
Truce of eight hours to bury dead. About noon were informed that Hindman declined fighting having been withdrawing his force during the night. Marched out of timber and lay down in edge of prairie for night.

Tuesday Dec. 9th
Visited battlefield in forenoon. Saw where the heaviest fighting was done by Herron. Counted 97 of our dead, parties bringing them in, and digging trenches to bury. Dead bodies of rebels, probably 150 lying in rail pens, to keep hogs from them. More than 40 in one pen. Where the rebel battery stood, 5 dead horses in one pile, 4 in another. Back to Ray's Mill [Rhea's Mill], getting tents and blankets for first time since Friday last.

Wednesday 10th
Still in camp. My wound quite painful. Hardly able to get about. Took off bandage and dressed it for first time. Raney Led pm [prayer meeting] in evg.

Thursday Dec. 11th
Marched back to our old camp. My leg feeling better, but rode most of way. Met rebel ambulances going to field to get their wounded. Found them filling buildings in Boonesboro with them. Hear that their loss of Sat. night according to their account, was not less than 25. Col. Shelby's Regt attacked us. Wrote Father."

Corporal Stephen H. Fairfield recalled the Battle of Prairie Grove to Connelley:

In the battle of Prairie Grove the Eleventh Kansas got on the field after Rabb's Battery had been in action for some time. The battery had been repeatedly charged, and as the Eleventh passed it the men saw the horses lying dead about it. Plumb had one wing of the regiment and General Ewing the other. Plumb charged into the timber in front of the battery and drove out some rebels, then supported the battery. General Ewing became engaged with the rebels in the woods to the right of the battery and was engaged there until after dark. After having cleared the field in his front he led his men back to the line to camp. As he emerged from the woods the men of the battery supposed it was the rebel force breaking out there to charge the Union lines. The artillery men were preparing to fire but were restrained by Plumb, who know that Ewing was in that quarter. Just as the gunners were about to fire, Plumb became convinced that it was Ewing's men advancing there in the gloom and as the lanyards were lifted he cried "Hold! Hold! Those are our men. For God's sake do not fire!" In a moment General Ewing appeared at the head of his men. If the artillery had been fired a frightful slaughter would have resulted. "Major Plumb was always on the alert," said Fairfield, in relating this incident. "He was always looking out for everything which might happen."

After the battle, Plumb came across Edmund Mercer of Company I who had been wounded near his spine at the back of his neck. The wound had knocked him unconscious for several hours while continued to bleed. He eventually came to and stumbled back to his company, where he had been assumed dead. Plumb cleaned and dressed Mercer's wound and he was able to rejoin the regiment and continue fighting in the war.

Exhausted from the battle, the 11th Kansas continued to pursue the enemy through terrible weather conditions and bitter cold.

> [Corporal] Fairfield was in the march down Cove Creek in December 1862. This was an awful march. The water at first was not deep, but the stream grew in volume as they descended it, and it ran zigzag through a narrow gorge. The road led down this gorge and the men waded the creek thirty-two times. Often the water was waist deep, and it was icy cold. After this march, the men camped in the timber a few hours in their freezing clothes. Plumb was all along the line during the march cheering the men and sympathizing with them, but not for an instant entertaining any grumbling or any talk blaming anyone. He appealed to the men to do their duty and discharge fully every requirement, no matter what the hardship – otherwise their action was not patriotic. "And the men always relied on him for aid in every matter which came up."

> At Kansas City, Mo., the Headquarters were in the Pacific Hotel, which stood on the street leading west from the south end of the square where the City Hall is now. Fairfield thinks it is still standing and is still the Pacific Hotel. General Ewing had his offices there, and Plumb was chief of staff.

> General Ewing stationed troops along the line between Kansas and Missouri as far south as Fort Scott. The stations were about twelve miles apart. Shawnee Mission was one station below that was Oxford or Little Santa Fe; then came Aubry; then Coldwater Grove, Trading Post, Barnesville, and perhaps one or two others. Sentinels were to pass constantly from post to post, and couriers were to be sent with any intelligence of importance from post to post until it reached Kansas City headquarters. At first some of these posts were guarded by troops of the Eleventh Kansas, but on one emergency or another most of these had been sent on other duties and their places filled by men of the Ninth Kansas.

Thomas Barber recalled:

> On the 8th (Barber thinks) Plumb led his men down Cove Creek, when it was forded 32 times. Crossed it last about dark. Then continued to Dripping Springs, where they captured some of Hindman's rear-guard. Hindman had come to General Blunt and bluffed him and got his army away from Prairie Grove. After the fight at Dripping Springs, they followed the rebels into and through Van Buren, capturing more men in the town before they got on the ferry boat. On all this march Plumb was right with the men–always talking to the men, cheering them up and sympathizing with them.

The following story related by Barber, either happened while the regiment was on its way to Prairie Grove, Arkansas, or after the Battle of Prairie Grove. Unfortunately, Barber was not clear on the timeline involved. Confederate General Sterling Price had fought in the Battle of Pea Ridge against Federal General Franz Sigel and had left behind a large cable chain affixed to trees to block Sigel's pursuit of his forces following the battle in March of 1862. In December of that year, the 10th Kansas Infantry along with the 11th Kansas Infantry encountered the same cable chain while trying to cross the White River near Eureka Springs, Arkansas.

> Colonel Weir, Tenth Kansas was trying to cross the White River, which was swollen with recent rains, in wagon beds with tarpaulins wrapped around them, but this was a failure. Plumb saw something else would have to be provided. He sent wagons and teams back to Cross Hollows to bring up Price's cable chain. He put men to chopping down trees and hewing gunwales for a boat–four long pines. Other teams, he sent to a mill to bring up lumber and some men he sent to get tow [a natural fiber] to caulk the seams of the boat. While the boat was being built some men were stringing the cable across the river–to do which someone had plunged in and swam to the other shore with a rope which was attached to the cable. Some were making pulleys. Soon there was made one of the most perfect ferries,

Barber ever saw and the whole army crossed over the stream safely.

At Cane Creek, the regiment was short of rations and Plumb took charge of a water mill and ground corn for bread. Was always looking out for the men – no one else seemed to do so.

Prairie Grove was a defining moment for Plumb and his men. This was Plumb's first experience in command of a large number of soldiers in combat and he had made a definite impression on them. Lt. George Walker later told the following story to Carrie Plumb:

> We had marched all night much of time in timber, had passed Maysville Ind. Ter. [Indian Territory] and were out in the open high prairie, two batteries of artillery and some cavalry had passed us since daylight. We heard firing in front of us and the order "double quick" was given and we started forward on the run with Capt. Heritage in lead of our company. I said "on the run" we were as near a run as weary men who had marched all night carrying heavy muskets and forty rounds of 69 calabre [caliber] ammunition could run. While thus making best of speed we could. Adjutant Williams met us with "Hurry up boys or all will be lost." We needed encouragement this was not very encouraging. Then Lt. Col. Moonlight met us with "Hurry up boys or you will miss all the fun." We were not in for fun. Then Maj. Plumb met us with "Hurry up boys you are needed." We had gone in from a sense of duty and here was the message we needed and every man who heard it was goaded to do his best. In these three sentences or orders I read the character of the men who gave them.

Sending letters home was the only real connection the men had with their families. That connection with home was just as important to the soldiers in the field as it was to their loved ones left behind. Parents, wives, sweethearts, and friends were desperate for any news of how their loved ones were faring, what battles they had been involved in, and unfortunately, whether or not they still lived. Corporal Fairfield recalled the following story of Plumb's dedication to his men:

Portrait of Major Preston B. Plumb taken at Fort Smith in 1863. Image courtesy Mollus-Mass Collection, United States Army Heritage and Education Center, Carlisle, PA.

Fairfield was Regimental postmaster, then postmaster Army of the Border, then postmaster for the entire District under General Ewing at Kansas City. And in connection with his duties as Military postmaster, he tells of one of the acts of Major Plumb, which is to his credit and which is characteristic. There was no provision to furnish the soldiers with stamps for their letters, and they were constantly writing to their wives and children at home. A letter could pass through the mail if it contained the frank of a commissioned officer. Hundreds of these letters were brought to Plumb for his frank. Fairfield has known him to remain up until three o'clock in the morning writing his frank on these letters. Every day he would have as many as a hundred–often several hundred if any movement of the troops had been ordered. He had to write his name and rank on each letter. He could never be prevailed on to leave a portion of his work for the next day, always saying that some anxious wife or mother or father would be painfully disappointed to receive no letter when the neighbors received theirs.

Drawn to military service through a strong sense of patriotism and abolitionist views—the battle of Prairie Grove served as a grim reminder of the human cost of the war. Plumb sent the poem below and a short letter to his family sometime in January of 1863, about one month after the fight.

"Shot through the lungs" how he lay, how he lay
At Antietam, all the fearful day,
Slowly bleeding his life away!

And there comes to us now from the scenes of strife,
Soiled with the camp-dust with memories rife,
All we have left of the soldier's life.

Only a book with "This for my friend
When I am done with it" thoughtfully penned,
Long ere the battle. Is this the end?

Is this the end for the voice of song
For the hand so skillful and yet so strong
For the earnest will that bore him along?

I mind me now of his school boys ways;
"Brave and gentle" the fitting phrase,
And the patient toil of the after days.

Courteous as knight of the times of old,
With a heart as pure and withal as bold,
And his manhood's story all untold.

Yet why our life but to spend it free
As the snow that falls on the angry lea,
For the Right, for the Truth, for Liberty?

And the brave heart knows, with a quiet content,
When treason and murder their shafts have sent,
That the time is at hand for which it was lent;

But oh! Fatherland that we love so well,
Shall the future's annals shuddering tell
It was all in vain that our heroes fell?

We give them up at thy bitter cry,
We say no word when they go to die
Is it Freedom's dawn that reddens the sky?

Ah, Comrade, sleep well in thy soldier's bed
At Antietam in the field of our dead,
Who knows who watcheth overhead.

The above I call good. I clipped it from the Missouri Democrat. Charles Stotler died one week ago today. Mr. Anderson is getting better. Alex. Drake of Americus died about the same time. Emmet Crane of Greenwood County also died a few days since. This makes four of those recruited by me who have lost their lives in the service. Some more are dangerously sick. I feel glad that Frank has lost his military appetite & gained one for beef. It is better. I got a little shotgun from a rebel at Van Buren which I shall send by Will if possible.

Plumb's younger brother, William ("Will" in the letter) served in the 11th Kansas alongside him, and was discharged for disease on January 8, 1863. He had enlisted only a couple of months after turning sixteen years old. Charles Stotler was the younger brother of Jacob Stotler who had come to Emporia from Ohio with Plumb and worked for him at the *Kanzas News*.

Plumb along with the other officers of the regiment had been campaigning for some time to have the 11th converted to a cavalry regiment. Their wishes finally came true in April 1863. Corporal Fairfield recalled:

> Ewing had practically no cavalry. He appealed constantly to General Schofield for cavalry, and said he was virtually a prisoner in Kansas City. The guerrillas came into the city sometimes and the owner of the Pacific Hotel was assassinated two miles out. He had been threatened for allowing the hotel to be used for Headquarters–a matter he had no control over. Couriers and mail carriers were often killed in sight of Kansas City by guerrillas. Disloyal men complained to the Government constantly of every commander stationed at any post, and such men as Pennick removed to other places. These complainants always falsely paraded themselves as loyal citizens. Immense harm to the Union cause was thus done. This was the situation in the summer of 1863 at Kansas City.

It took some time for the orders to mount the regiment to materialize into actual horses for the men. Sergeant Bodwell wrote in his diary on July 13th that he had just received information that the regiment was to be mounted; "An order from Gen'l Schofield said to be in print, mounting the 11th." He mentioned in his entry for July 30th, that Company F finally received their horses.

Chapter 7
Quantrill's Raid

In addition to fighting the Confederate Army, the 11th Kansas also found themselves fighting "bushwhackers"–pro-Confederacy civilians with peripheral ties to the Confederate Army. One of the most infamous bushwhacker leaders was William Quantrill. Originally a member of Sterling Price's Confederate Army, Quantrill deserted and formed a band of outlaws. Quantrill's Raiders, as they were known, counted Frank and Jesse James as members. William "Bloody Bill" Anderson and Cole Younger also joined Quantrill's forces. Between March and November of 1862, Quantrill's band attacked and burned several Kansas towns and settlements. During that time he was also welcomed back into the Confederate Army with the formal rank of Captain.

The topic of this biography does not warrant a full examination of Quantrill's motives, but it is important to point out that the guerrilla warfare along the border of Kansas and Missouri can be traced back for years. Although not official U.S. Government policy, several federal regiments burned the homes of pro-secessionist civilians in Missouri. This only served to foment more violence and the need for revenge. The situation became desperate as the U.S. Army was operating in a mixture of friendly and unfriendly territory. Secessionist civilians were running out Unionist civilians, and vice versa leaving both sides wondering who they could trust.

There were a number of spies acting on behalf of the Confederacy and the gangs of bushwhackers. Molly Anderson, the sister of William "Bloody Bill" Anderson was just such a spy. She was captured by both Preston Plumb and his brother George after trying to scout information on the federal army and smuggling weapons and supplies. George Plumb described how Molly Anderson was captured to William Connelley:

> It was sometime in the fore part of August 1863. There were two girls who came to the District Provost Marshall's office just about the time the office force left the office. Major Plumb was finishing up signing some papers. They asked for a pass to the Guard House, which at that time contained about 80 prisoners. At first, he refused but later called them back and gave them a pass. He turned to me and told me to follow them and watch

them closely to see what happened when they were in the Guard House. I followed them but the Sergeant of the Guards and officer of the day who was there refused to let me go in as he did not know me and I did not have a pass. I said to the Sergeant, "Then you better follow those people and see what they want." He came back a little later and said they looked the prisoners over carefully but did nothing more. I started to go back to headquarters and met Major Plumb coming at a rapid pace. He asked me where the girls were. I told him what had happened. He said, "Get your horse, and don't you stop till you get them." I went up to headquarters where my horse was tied. John Scott, one of General Ewing's orderlies, was coming out of headquarters, and I asked him to get on his horse and go with me and he did so.

At that time there were just two roads to the south and east leading out of Kansas City that anyone coming in from a distance would be likely to take. One was the pike or macadam road leading to Westport; the other led in the direction of Independence. I took the road to Westport, and just as I arrived at Westport I overtook the girls. They had a lumber wagon and a span of mules. A soldier that belonged to a little detachment of the 5th Kansas, that was camped near Westport, was driving for them. I stopped them and told them they would have to go back to Kansas City. They protested very strongly against it, and the soldier said that he would vouch for the girls being all right, etc. I ordered the soldier to get out of the wagon and go to his camp and told the girls to turn the team around. They parleyed and finally, I took hold of the bridles and turned the mules around. I told them it would not take long to drive back to Kansas City, and if they were all right they would soon be at liberty to go again. It was between sundown and dark, just beginning to get dusk. John Scott spoke up and said he did not enlist for any such business as this; he was going to go over to where the 9th Kansas was camped, a short distance away, on the edge of Westport. I urged the girls to drive as rapidly as possible. As we came into McGee's addition which was the extreme south portion of Kansas City, at that time, we overtook an ambulance containing the Colonel and other Regimental officers of the 11th Missouri, that was camped at that time, somewhere below Westport, at what was known as Ray's [Rhea's] Mills. The girls appealed to the officers for help. The Colonel turned to me and said he would vouch for the girls, - knew they were all right, etc. The other officers in the carriage said the same. I had no intention of giving them up but just at that time, General Ewing, Major Plumb, and a few other officers came hurrying along the road. General Ewing ordered the Colonel to go along and tend to his own business, and if he ever interfered with a man on duty again he would have him court-martialed. Major Plumb then told me to take the girls to Gillis House where I would find a certain officer who would see that they were taken care of, and to take the team to Ham's Livery Stable which I did. When I had unhitched the team I began to take the things out of the wagon and found they had a large quantity of powder and shot, principally buckshot, and a number of other articles as were used around camp. The girls proved to be Molly Anderson and Jane Chamberlain, who had been acting as spies for Quantrill. Afterwards, there were a great many more taken. Evidence was found against some of them and others were released because they could get nothing against them. Quite a number including Molly Anderson and the Chamberlain girls were kept prisoners till the close of the war.

The prison housing the women collapsed on August 13, 1863, resulting in the deaths of four of them. One of the women killed was Josephine Anderson, a sister of "Bloody Bill" Anderson. Rumors immediately swirled that the prison had been sabotaged to cause its collapse, but those have since been disproved. Nevertheless, the rumors served to fuel more violence, for which the citizens of Lawrence, Kansas would pay the price.

Lawrence Raid

Lawrence, Kansas was a frequent hotbed of violence prior to the Civil War between Free-State and proslavery men. It became the scene of another vicious attack on August 21, 1863. Quantrill's band of about 450 guerrillas stormed the town around 5:00 am looting and burning stores and banks. They murdered roughly 150 men and boys, mostly civilians, aside from eighteen unmustered army recruits. The brutal attack was in retaliation for the collapse of the women's prison and because Lawrence was a well-known Free-State town and was associated with the Jayhawkers, a violent abolitionist group.

Plumb was stationed in Kansas City, Missouri, roughly forty miles from Lawrence when the attack occurred. General Ewing was away visiting his wife, and Plumb's immediate duty was to start a pursuit and notify Ewing in the hopes of receiving reinforcements. He did this to the best of his ability, but was hampered by a long pursuit with exhausted horses and men who were collapsing along the chase. He also was at the mercy of intelligence that was not always accurate in order to determine which direction Quantrill's band may have gone.

> [Corporal]Fairfield says General Ewing sent Major Ross with a Company of men to guard Lawrence some time before the raid. Lawrence was then full of saloons, and these saloons sold liquor to Ross' soldiers after being ordered not to do so. When Ross saw that the saloon keepers would not obey his order he took a body of his men and knocked in the heads of the liquor barrels in such saloons as had disobeyed his orders. The saloon men made a great outcry and appealed to Ewing and Schofield to have Ross and his company removed from Lawrence. They asked for guns to arm the citizens, saying that if these were furnished Lawrence would guard herself. The guns were furnished and Major Ross and his men sent back to Kansas City. "That is the true story of the removal of Major Ross from Lawrence," said Fairfield, "but it would not do to print it. The people of Lawrence would resent it, the truth though it is."

> Fairfield was at headquarters the night before the Lawrence raid. General Ewing had gone up to Leavenworth in the afternoon on a boat to see his wife. He had not been away from Headquarters [located in Kansas City, Missouri] for weeks. Plumb was left in charge, but if he had any specific orders for any emergency Fairfield did not know it–never heard of it. About nine o'clock at night a courier arrived at Headquarters with a dispatch stating that guerrillas and rebel troops to the

number of one thousand men were assembling or had assembled in Missouri just east of Aubry, Kansas. What orders Plumb sent out when he received this dispatch Fairfield does not know, but thinks he sent some orders.

About eleven o'clock other couriers—a number of them—arrived at Headquarters with dispatches saying that the rebel forces had crossed the state line into Kansas. Plumb realized that quick action was necessary. He moved rapidly in his preparations to take the field—energetically, as he always moved. He summoned every cavalryman in the city with a sound horse. He did not get more than twenty, perhaps not so many. With these he set out for Kansas—Fairfield thinks he went by the Shawnee Mission and may have secured a few men there. He then rode for Olathe and in the pursuit of Quantrill, but Fairfield was not one of the men and can not say from personal knowledge anything about the pursuit, but he afterwards talked to Major Plumb about it and Plumb told him that he came up with Captains Coleman and Pike and then turned South to intercept the guerrillas. In the pursuit, his horses were exhausted and several died, and they could not overtake the guerrillas. They found a rear-guard across their path always to impede their pursuit of the guerrillas.

Pursuit of Quantrill

Plumb's brother George provided a fairly detailed account of Plumb's pursuit of Quantrill immediately following the raid:

> I left Emporia the day before the Raid and passed through Lawrence in the evening, arriving at Kansas City sometime between 12 and 1 o'clock in the morning. I went up to headquarters where General Ewing's orderlies and some scouts had a tent in front of Milt McGhee's residence, unsaddled my horse, tied him to the picket line, and laid down for a few minutes. A boy came running through the tent and stumbled over me, got up and shook me, and wanted to know who I was. He said, "Come over to headquarters Quantrill has gone into Kansas." This boy that stumbled over me was one of General Ewing's orderlies, Eugene Cloud, a nephew of Colonel Cloud.

The cry of Quantrill gone into Kansas was nothing new as it had been of almost daily occurrence for a month. I told him it did not make any difference to me where Quantrill went, I was too tired to go anywhere. He went away, was gone a few minutes, and came back, saying Major Plumb had sent for me to come over. I got a fresh horse from the picket line saddled him and went over to headquarters. I found my brother with 17 soldiers belonging to the 2nd Colorado. They informed me that Quantrill had gone into Kansas and we were going to start in pursuit. We rode to Olathe arriving there about daylight. We stopped a few minutes and got a few extra soldiers, stragglers, - Cy Leland was one of them and several officers. From there we went right up the Santa Fe trail until we got up as far as Gardner; then we took across the country toward Lawrence. By that time we could see the smoke from Lawrence. We stopped a few minutes to decide what was best to do. We could not get to Lawrence till Quantrill would have left and we wanted to intercept him. We decided Quantrill would do either one of two things,–would divide up into small bands and go back into Missouri along the Kaw River, or he would go west on the Santa Fe Trail to some point near Burlingame then South to the Indian Territory thereby avoiding all pursuit of the soldiers on the border. My brother could not get it out of his mind that there was but one thing to do,–keep on the Santa Fe Trail till we got beyond Quantrill so as to stop him if he went further west. We went towards Lawrence till we crossed the Wakarusa. After we came up and had gotten out of the timber along the river we discovered that Quantrill had gone south from Lawrence, by the smoke of the burning buildings. We turned straight south, recrossed the Wakarusa went thru the black jack timber along the stream, across a big prairie to the Santa Fe Trail about halfway between Brooklyn and Baldwin City. Then we were undecided which way to go fearing that Quantrill might slip down and burn Baldwin City, and still feeling that we were losing time as he might take the other course and go west. Major Plumb sent two men up on the high ground west of where we were to see which way he went and report as quickly as possible. We waited some little time and Major Plumb became impatient at the delay and told me to go up and find out what was the matter and report. I met the men coming down waving their hats to indicate that Quantrill had gone south. Major Plumb then started his forces on the gallop and overtook us near a cornfield. I with a number of others was ordered to get off my horse and let down the fence to let part of the command into the field. Major Plumb went round the field, to the South.

Lane was pursuing Quantrill with a squad of men and overtook him right by this cornfield. When we came round the field we did not see Quantrill till we got nearly down to him and he did not see us. When he did see us he and his men turned west like a flock of birds. Then Quantrill found that he was going to get into the brushy ground and so swung round and got turned back east and crossed Ottawa Creek onto the high ground. Just as we came Coleman and Lane had gone thru the cornfield and all the forces came together. Lane came up to my brother riding an old brown nag bareback. He had on an undershirt and a pair of drawers. My brother said, "Jim haven't you any firearms?" and he said "None." Preston said he had two pistols and would give him one and took off his belt and gave it to him saying he could keep his pistol in his holster. Then Lane wanted to take command of the whole of the forces, but my brother said no he could not do that. He said to Lane, "You organize the militia and I will keep my forces up and we can cooperate." The citizens were coming from everywhere and Lane organized 10 companies. A few men were rushing up and drawing fire from Quantrill's rear guard. The amusing thing was that those 10 companies of militia would fire whenever they saw Quantrill's men even if they were five miles away. I looked for people to get hurt; everything was excitement. I never saw such a stampede in my life. If Quantrill had turned back on that mob of men in the condition they were with so few soldiers, he could have killed more people than he did in Lawrence with less trouble, but he knew what was on the border; he was saving his strength for what was ahead of him. If Clark had done his duty instead of staying in Paola, he would have met us further up; but it was open country and it was pretty hard; Quantrill kept the high divide so he could not be surprised; only at Paola, he went into the timber. Every hour we were expecting to hear from Clark. Every little bit Lane would speak to Plumb and he would say "Keep your men together Clark will surely be heard from soon."

The instructions to all the posts along the border reaching from Westport to Fort Scott, were, whenever there was any body of men crossed the State line into Kansas, to at once report to the nearest station on each side and to send word to Kansas City; then to pursue with all the available force immediately. I had carried instructions many times. Very likely Major Plumb had sent a messenger to Clark,–I don't remember.

Major Plumb thought the people along the Kaw River ought to be notified and I went on a side trip of several miles and got a dozen or fifteen men on their horses spreading the news along the river. After we left Gardner until we got up to Wakarusa I was not with them as it took me quite a little time to make the circuit and get back.

I don't recall where Captain Coleman came up to us; it was probably near Blue Mound just before we turned to go south from the Wakarusa.

Major Plumb's men were mounted on very soft horses. They rode fast and winded their horses in the start so they were worn out before we really got in pursuit of Quantrill. It was as hot as it ever gets. I have often wondered how the horses stood as much as they did. After we left the Santa Fe trail south of Baldwin City my brother's horse gave out. I saw some men hauling hay across the prairie. I went over to where they were and said I wanted one of their horses and asked which one was the best rider. They were what we called refugees from Missouri and wanted to know what difference it made to me which horse was the best riding animal; I could not have one of their horses. I said I had got to have a horse and began to unhitch one with them threatening me all the time but they had nothing but pitchforks. I lead away one of their horses, a mare with a colt, and told them there would be a little brown horse left on the trail and for them to come up and get it. We saddled the mare and got my brother on to her. The farmers got the mare back at Kansas City and pay for the colt which was lost but they did not return my brother's horse. Sometime later the 11th Kansas recognized my brother's horse in the possession of some soldiers and brought him in. He had a "U.S." branded on him.

When we got to Paola that night Captain Coleman and Major Plumb were both so exhausted they could not dismount from their horses without assistance; indeed none of us were in much better condition as we had all been in the saddle for twenty-four hours with nothing to eat or drink.

For years after the Lawrence Raid, Plumb was wrongly blamed for not catching Quantrill. Numerous firsthand accounts indicate that Plumb made every effort possible attempting to anticipate which direction Quantrill would go and sent what limited men he had available in those directions. It is also worth pointing out, that had the entirety of Plumb's forces managed to catch up to Quantrill, they would have been hopelessly exhausted and outnumbered, likely resulting in more casualties for the Union.

Thomas Barber's interview with Connelley is especially interesting as he talks about several dispatches Plumb sent during the pursuit to Ewing in an effort to update him on their position and requesting reinforcements. Unfortunately, these dispatches were not heeded and Ewing did not come to Plumb's aid.

> Plumb kept sending dispatches back to Kansas City explaining how things were and all his actions in the pursuit of Quantrill and asking Ewing to get every available man and assemble on the state line, and they would there get Quantrill. Ewing being away, these dispatches went to regimental headquarters and were sent to Fort Leavenworth to Ewing by Major [Martin] Anderson. But Ewing did not get them having started down to the field of action by De Soto. Plumb was expecting that Quantrill would find Ewing and several companies across his path at the state line, but he could never hear a word from any dispatch he sent. Major M. Anderson took what men he could and followed Plumb, on the 21st, and Barber went with him. At

Olathe, they met a courier coming on the run, his horse in a foam. He saluted Major Anderson and said he had a dispatch from Plumb. Major Anderson took it and looked at it. It was to General Ewing and Major Anderson sent him on to Kansas City with it. Major Anderson met two other couriers with dispatches from Plumb to Ewing, and sent them on to Kansas City. Barber knows this for he saw them. But Ewing was then on the road south from Leavenworth to De Soto and did not see them. And Plumb was relying on him to be at the State Line. Major Anderson got to Olathe and from the vicinity of Olathe went to Aubry and then into Missouri in pursuit of Quantrill. Major Anderson, Dr. R.M. Ainsworth, James S. Snow, Barber, and a man who was convalescent, from the hospital, made up the party that started to see Plumb and help him. The convalescent man and Snow were in the ambulance. The others on horseback. About Aubry, they found two or three of Captain Coleman's men and took them along. These men had been on some detached service. They found in Missouri–the next day–five straggling guerrillas and killed them. The convalescent man was obtained at the hospital on Grand Avenue at 20th Street.

At the end of his interview with Thomas Barber, Connelley left the following note:

> I am now seeing that in order to aid General Ewing in his candidacy for the U.S. Senate Major Plumb assumed much of the blame which ought to have fallen on Ewing, and Ewing was not man enough to publish Plumb's dispatches.–W.E.C.

Connelley was well versed in Kansas history and this was new information to him. Among his other interviews with 11th Kansas soldiers, there was also a sentiment of ill will toward Ewing. The reasons for that were not elaborated on, but those feelings may have been related to this incident, or to the fact that Plumb was unfairly "blamed" for the results of the pursuit.

Order #11

The result of Quantrill's raid on Lawrence was the now infamous General Order No. 11 issued by General Thomas Ewing, Jr. on August 25, 1863. The order read as follows:

General Order № 11.
Headquarters District of the Border,
Kansas City, August 25, 1863.

1. All persons living in Jackson, Cass, and Bates counties, Missouri, and in that part of Vernon included in this district, except those living within one mile of the limits of Independence, Hickman's Mills, Pleasant Hill, and Harrisonville, and except those in that part of Kaw Township, Jackson County, north of Brush Creek and west of Big Blue, are hereby ordered to remove from their present places of residence within fifteen days from the date hereof.

Those who within that time establish their loyalty to the satisfaction of the commanding officer of the military station near their present place of residence will receive from him a certificate stating the fact of their loyalty, and the names of the witnesses by whom it can be shown. All who receive such certificates will be permitted to remove to any military station in this district, or to any part of the State of Kansas, except the counties of the eastern border of the State. All others shall remove out of the district. Officers commanding companies and detachments serving in the counties named will see that this paragraph is promptly obeyed.

2. All grain and hay in the field or under shelter, in the district from which inhabitants are required to remove, within reach of military stations after the 9th day of September next, will be taken to such stations and turned over to the proper officers there and report of the amount so turned over made to district headquarters, specifying the names of all loyal owners and amount of such product taken from them. All grain and hay found in such district after the 9th day of September next, not convenient to such stations, will be destroyed.

3. The provisions of General Order No. 10 from these headquarters will be at once vigorously executed by officers commanding in the parts of the district and at the station not subject to the operations of paragraph 1 of this order, and

especially the towns of Independence, Westport and Kansas City.

4. Paragraph 3, General Order No. 10 is revoked as to all who have borne arms against the Government in the district since the 20th day of August, 1863.

By order of Brigadier General Ewing.
H. Hannahs, Adjt.-Gen'l.

The contents and intent behind General Order No. 11 are still hotly fought over today. Plumb's main connection to the order was that he is said to have been present when it was discussed or written, and that as an officer of the 11th Kansas Cavalry, he was tasked with carrying out said order.

Many years after the war, Brigadier General John Schofield sent a letter to Ewing describing his reasoning behind the order. While issued by Ewing, the order itself was discussed with many other high-ranking Union officers. Ewing bore the brunt of the repercussions for the order at the time and for the rest of his life. Schofield's letter is as follows:

West Point, N.Y., Jan. 25, 1877
General Thomas Ewing, Lancaster, O.:

My Dear General: I avail myself of the first opportunity that has presented itself to reply in detail to your letter of the 30th of December last.

It was in May, 1863, that the command of the Department of Missouri devolved upon me, and you were soon after assigned to command the District which embraced the border of Missouri and Kansas. The condition of that border at once became the subject of earnest consideration. The guerrilla warfare which had been waged in that district, with only temporary intermissions, for two years, had finally degenerated, as all such contests are liable to do, into revolting barbarism. Civilization and humanity demanded its prompt suppression, whatever might be the means necessary to that end.

A large majority of the people had already been driven from their homes or had voluntarily left them. None remained, beyond the immediate protection of the military posts, except such as were, whether voluntarily or not, useful to the guerrillas. Those who remained were simply purveyors for these border warriors, furnishing them the provisions, forage and temporary shelter necessary for their operations.

There were two, and only two, possible ways by which this border war could be stopped. The one was to permanently station in that region troops enough to protect all the people, drive out the guerrillas and prevent their return. The other was to remove the source from which the guerrillas obtained their supplies. The latter was proposed by you and at once admitted by me as a measure absolutely necessary to be adopted if the former was impracticable, but I preferred the former and hence hesitated to adopt the latter. But I had the states of Missouri, Arkansas and Nebraska and Colorado and the Indian Territories—over four hundred thousand square miles of disturbed territory—to take care of, and operations against the Confederate army in Arkansas to be prosecuted. It was difficult to spare even a small force to guard the border of Kansas and Missouri. There had already come a demand upon me from Washington to send all possible reinforcements to Gen. Grant, who was besieging Vicksburg. To this all minor considerations had to yield. The preservation of a few farms with their crops in Western Missouri or anywhere else, could not be considered for a moment in comparison with the success of Grant's army in opening the Mississippi, to the Gulf. Of course I had sent to Gen. Grant all the troops I had in reserve and had at that time none left to reinforce you on the border of Kansas.

Soon after, the guerrilla operations culminated in the fiendish massacre of defenseless people at Lawrence. There was no longer any question what must be done, and you promptly issued the order which had before been contemplated and discussed. A few days thereafter, I visited you at Kansas City and west to Independence. I spent several days in investigating the subject and in conversing with the people who had left their homes in obedience to your order. There was left no room for doubt of the necessity of the measure that had been adopted. Hence, after a comparatively unimportant modification, I approved your order and thus assumed the whole, or at least my full share, of the responsibility for it.

Upon returning to St. Louis, I made a full report of the matter to President Lincoln, explaining the necessity of what had been done, and assuming the responsibility therefor. Neither that humane President nor any other officer of the government ever uttered one word of dissent as to the wisdom, justice or humanity of that policy.

And I now repeat that the responsibility for that policy was fairly shared with you by the President and by me, in proportion to our respective rank and authority.

You understand that I have no desire in this to throw responsibility on President Lincoln nor to defend myself. I have never regarded that act as one requiring exculpation. On the contrary, it was an act of wisdom, courage and humanity, by which the lives of hundreds of innocent people were saved, and a disgraceful conflict brought to a summary close. Not a life was sacrificed, nor any great discomfort inflicted in carrying out the order. The necessities of all the poor people were provided for, and none were permitted to suffer.

A few unthinking people have no doubt supposed that order was an act of retaliation for the massacre at Lawrence. Nothing could be more absurd. The farmers of Western Missouri were not regarded in anywise responsible for Quantrill's acts. Whether they were willing or not, made no difference. If they raised crops his men would live upon them, as did also our troops which they had occasion. A large portion of these citizens who were in good circumstances had voluntarily ceased this unprofitable purveying and had gone elsewhere. It was simply an act of dispassionate wisdom and humanity to stop it altogether.

To call your order an act of inhumanity or retaliation upon the people of Missouri, is like accusing the Russian Commander of similar crimes against the people of Moscow, when he ordered the destruction of that city to prevent its occupation as winter quarters by the army of Napoleon.

For my own part, I have been and am still entirely content to leave to impartial history, the approval or condemnation of each of my official acts during the late war. But it is simply justice that you, who have been censured by some, for your celebrated order, have this statement of the facts in regard to it, for such use as your just vindication may require.

I am, General, very truly your friend and obedient servant,
J.M. Schofield, Major General

Enforcement of General Order No. 11 resulted in the displacement of thousands of civilians within the four counties affected—many of whom were in fact loyal to the Union. Countless homes and towns were burned, devastating the area. There is still debate today on the effectiveness of the order, but there were no further invasions into Kansas by guerrillas. The order was replaced by General Order No. 20 in November which was less harsh, and rescinded completely in January 1864 when General Egbert Brown replaced Ewing.

Colonel Van Horn did not see Plumb often during the War. He was Colonel of one of the first Missouri regiments and fought the first battle of the war, in July 1861. He was away from Kansas City much of the time. Soon after the Quantrill raid and the issuance of Order No. 11, when Van Horn was at Cape Girardeau, Mo., he received an order from Schofield to report to Headquarters at St. Louis forthwith. When he went there General Schofield sent him to Kansas City as Provost Marshall of the District of the Border, which included Kansas City. He succeeded Major Plumb. The only reason for his appointment was that he was familiar with the country affected by Order No. 11, and knew many of the people of that district personally. It was believed that he could, therefore, enforce the order with less difficulty than anyone not known to the people, and perhaps mitigate much of the evil such orders entail always. He says the order was the order of Schofield and that General Ewing would have preferred not to have issued it. There was great pressure in Kansas for such an order, and General Lane was very insistent. Col. Van Horn formed a high opinion of the ability of Major Plumb from the papers and records received from him when he turned over the office of Provost Marshall.

Thomas Barber recalled guerrillas constantly raiding Kansas City.

> Before the Quantrill raid, the guerrillas were constantly harassing Kansas City and closing in on it. Ewing did not have sufficient troops to protect the country around him and patrol the State line. He did not lack much of being a prisoner in Kansas City. Plumb once directed Barber to take a guard and round up everybody that could not give the counter-sign–beginning at the levee and coming up Main and Delaware Streets to the camps or headquarters at 11th and Walnut–and put them in the storeroom of T.M. James, on Main Street. This was because of some expected raid by guerrillas. Barber met and arrested T.M. James the first man (Thomas M. James) but he was soon released by Plumb and allowed to go home.

As with every historical event, there are criticisms. Reading through the abundance of firsthand accounts of Plumb's pursuit of Quantrill, it is evident that although unsuccessful, he made every effort physically possible to catch up to him. He was thwarted by exhausted horses, insufficient manpower, inaccurate intelligence, and fatigued men–including himself. He and the 11th Kansas were not done with bushwhackers and would continue to face Quantrill and those of his ilk in the coming months.

Chapter 8

Bushwhackers

Fall of 1863

George Plumb continued to be on detached service with his brother, and had his fair share of encounters with bushwhackers. At this time, he went with Major Anderson from Lawrence, Kansas to Independence, Missouri to be near operations.

> I was at one time with Captain Green and got after some guerrillas. There were three or four companies of us and a lot of rebels. One of them had gone into a house,–some of the boys had seen him, so they went up and asked the woman if there was a soldier there; she said no and they could search the house. They looked but did not find him; later saw him outside; had changed his uniform for a butternut suit. Captain Green had two big pistols and followed the man down the path firing and calling after him to halt but he got away. A woman came out of the house and started over the stile, she had the man's soldier clothes concealed under her dress but they dropped out as she went over the stile.
>
> After we got Quantrill out of the hills here came Stanwatie [Stand Watie] a Cherokee Confederate officer with 1500 Creeks, Chickasaws, and Cherokees, up the Neosho Valley. Some of the 3rd Wisconsin were with us. I went down and stayed a while and then got permission to go on the Red River Expedition but the others stayed four or five months till April or May. The thing that made me mad was that my brother had orders from the commanding officer not to let me do scout work anymore but to keep me in line.

Fighting with bushwhackers was an entirely different sort of combat than federal troops were used to when engaging with the regular army. They did not form into companies and march out to meet each other over open fields. Instead, they fought in short engagements in small groups often in dense vegetation obscuring their movements. This type of guerrilla warfare is similar to what American troops faced in the dense jungles of Vietnam. It was rare to take prisoners of bushwhackers, and it was rare for bushwhackers to take prisoners of Union soldiers. Fighting was brutal and merciless on both sides.

In his diary, 11th Kansas Sergeant Sherman Bodwell described many horrific scenes with a cold demeanor. A perspective such as that is often necessary to cope with the brutality of combat. Note that these entries take place only a month and two months after Quantrill's attack on Lawrence.

> Saturday 26th Sept. [1863]
> Spent in the brush. About noon having command ("E" & "G" 11th Mo "B" & "H" all under command of Maj. Plumb), divided taking position in, above, and below Sibley. Maj. Ross [11th Missouri] drove 10 guerrillas up from bottom below and Co. "B" firing on them took two of their horses. A little later Maj. Ross struck a camp taking three horses. A little afternoon being with Maj. Plumb "H" having separated from "B" struck a horse track following it for a mile or two through timber. Maj. and Lt. dismounted, went to the fronts, and soon sent back for six or eight men dismounted, then for more. I went up with them and found we were at a creek crossing heavily tracked. Horses heard neighing near. Moved forward on the trail (some 15 of us) till we came in sight of a fellow sitting above on the steep hillside reading. On picket apparently. Feared to move lest he should see us, and give alarm, and feared to fire for the same reason. Four men fired by order, rather to his surprise judging by his movements. We dashed up the hill, and as we done it found ourselves in camp one fellow firing both barrels of a shotgun at the Lt. at about 20 steps. I lost my two shots by caps failing. Took eight horses, seven saddled. Toward evening, while following down a ravine to the Blue, came on a foot track. Word sent back for half the men. Busily sending them up which threw me in the rear. Came down into valley of Blue firing in front and then a foot race up the timber after the party (supposed) we had driven from camp three being mounted. They fired back, and the hindmost especially used his shotgun with good grit. Race lasted for about ¾ of a mile, the boys firing after them as they ran. Lt. R. finally bringing down the last. I came up, just as the Lt. finished him with a shot through the head. Took supper, and

moved on to Franklins, threw out pickets and watched roads till late daylight.

Thursday Oct. 1st/63
Marched early, halted for breakfast, when command divided. Maj. Plumb taking his com. ("B" & "H"), and moving toward Napoleon. About 10 the Maj. Lt. and the advance came suddenly on two guerrillas mounted. One dismounted and took the brush, but the Maj. [Plumb] brought him [down] with his holster pistol. I rode up. Lt. stood over him, his pockets having been searched and papers taken. Among them a discharge from the rebel service signed by Captain, Gen. Rains, and Gen. Price. He was talking, claiming to be a prisoner, etc., Lt. asked Maj. [Plumb] are you through with him? Maj. [Plumb] nodded assent. Lt. said to men standing about "mount your horses" and as they drew off, aimed and fired the revolver ball striking just back of the eye, and he was with his judge, with all his imperfections on his head. Lt. stood between us so I did not see his face. [Sergeant Amos] Custard says he instinctively raised his hand to shield himself and "an ashy paleness overspread his face as when a cloud passes over the sun."

As we came from the brush found the boys taking a horse from the woman at whose house they were about eating. She cursing (almost) the men and wishing she had a revolver to blow brains out, etc. In the affair she dropped from under her clothing a man's calico shirt and what seemed to be some bushwhacking uniform. Coat gaily trimmed.

Reached Napoleon, and in evg. Wellington. Clogston & Houston (9th K) were in blue and butternut in advance, and one man they found in the wood committed himself as a guerrilla before the command came in sight to show his mistake, arrested him.

Took supper in town, men being apportioned to the various houses. As we were lying down, heard firing, and should have known the prisoner was "attempting to escape," if I had not heard his cries as the first bullets struck him. Rest of command came in evening.

Sabbath Oct. 4th
Cloudy and quite cool. Marched about sunrise. Came soon on trail and followed to the camp in which the guerrillas had probably most of them gathered. A dog was heard barking before reaching camp and was found at the feet of a man hung in camp to a small sapling. His trousers had been taken and he left hanging in his hat, blouse, shirt, and boots. So hung seemingly as not to strangle. On his back a paper written, "This man was hung last evening, in revenge for the death of W. Haller. He says his name is Thomas and that he belongs to the Kansas 9th." Buried him in the ravine near where he hung. There seems to be something of the deathlike brooding over these camps. Always hidden where hardly more than a horse track points the road, in heavy timber and creek bottoms, offal lying about, cooking utensils cast-off clothing, when we steal in upon them carefully watching lest a crackling stick alarm the expected occupants, the very air seems thick with the crime with which so lately they seethed. A woman's shoe here; a child's cradle used as a feed box there; how strangely out of place.
A little later came to the camp where we killed as it is said "W. Haller" and captured the 40 horses. Sept. 16th. Quantrill has evidently gathered bands and left, maybe for Kansas, maybe for the South, and we were fooling away our time under Col. Weir about Blue Spring when we should have been here, doing the Lord's work on the fiends. Too late now. Marched back to Morg. Walker's, 10 m from Ind, Finding bal. [balance] of command. Letter from Mary Sept. 28. Ed married. Com. marched at evg. Reaching Pleasant Hill 15 m. at 10 P.M. 25 M.

In December of 1863 Plumb was ordered to Humboldt, Kansas in command of a sub-district headquartered there. Lt. George Walker was with him and described some of the conditions in Humboldt:

> Walker does not remember what troops he had, but knows he had Company C Eleventh Kansas, Company K, same regiment,

he had stationed at some town west of Humboldt. Had troops at Osage Mission. This District extended into the Indian Territory (now Oklahoma). The Eleventh Kansas had then been made a Cavalry regiment. At Humboldt Plumb had Walker detailed as quartermaster and commissary.

Plumb found at Humboldt that some of the officers were securing forage by commutation–that is, getting their forage and rations from whomsoever they pleased and charging the cost of them into their accounts with the quartermaster at Fort Scott. There was nothing in the form of a contract to govern the price at which they were charged. The quartermaster remitted the prices charged. (This was for supplies for all the forces). In many instances, Plumb found that the supplies had been taken from loyal citizens and not paid for. Other officers, sometimes all officers, bought two or three times as much as they were worth. Plumb stopped the commutation plan at once, and directed Walker to buy the supplies in the open market at the lowest price he could get until a contract could be entered into by authority of the quartermaster. Walker got the supplies for about half that had been paid to Thurston. Thurston had been to see Plumb before Walker arrived and had been told that nothing would be settled until Walker got there. Plumb was at Humboldt from December 1863 to July 1864, when he was sent to command the District of which the headquarters were at Olathe. The 15th Kansas was sent to Humboldt and the 11th Kansas sent to Olathe.

At Humboldt, many herds of cattle were brought in by soldiers. There were contraband cattle from the Territory or from the Osage Country. These cattle were all turned over to Walker, who killed for beef all he needed to supply the District, and the remainder were sent to the quartermaster at Fort Scott. After Plumb was sent to Olathe Walker remained at Humboldt about a month. There were about 300 head of cattle then at Humboldt. Soon after Plumb left two orders came to Walker. One directed that he turn over to Indians named in the order 200 head of cattle. The other directed him to turn over to the Indians 90 head particularly described by marks and brands. There was a third order directing that the cattle be turned over to Thurston as the representative of the Indians. Walker turned over all but six head of the cattle, and these he killed for supplies.

The Pin Indians [derogatory term for Native Americans who swore allegiance to the US government and were given pins] were the full-blood Cherokees and were loyal to the Union. The mixed bloods were almost all in the Confederate army. General Grant had issued orders that none but dog tents be issued to soldiers under penalty of dismissal from service without trial. While Plumb was absent from Humboldt Major Hawes of the 15th Kansas requested Walker to issue what was known as an "A" tent or shelter tent to private so and so for a laundress attached to the 15th Kansas. Walker replied that he had no authority to issue any such tent. Hawes sent them a formal order to have the tent issued. Walker said if Hawes would send a detail he would go to Fort Scott and get the tent. Then Hawes sent a peremptory order that the tent be issued and Walker issued it. He made out his report about the tent and mailed it Saturday, but no mail went out until Monday. When Plumb returned Walker reported to him what had been done about the tent, saying that the matter would get him (Walker) into trouble as well as Hawes. Plumb told him to take his letter and report to the post office, and he sent for Hawes. Hawes arranged with Plumb to keep the tent by making the issue a temporary loan of the tent to be returned on demand. This protected Walker and Plumb allowed it to stand.

When Plumb went to Olathe he found the commutation practice in full blast, and he soon stopped it. He regarded official business of the government as sacred as any private business, and he had it transacted with as much care and honesty. Walker says Plumb was absolutely honest in all the relations of life.

1864

Plumb had been promoted from Major to Lt. Colonel in April 1864, a decision that was made with some resistance. Plumb's reputation had suffered among some Kansans stemming from his pursuit of Quantrill. The blame unfairly laid at his feet had continued to haunt him. Plumb did not let the disparaging remarks hold him back, and he was determined to continue to do his duty to the utmost of his ability.

For some time, Plumb was assigned to the post at Humboldt, Kansas. His duty there was to attempt to track down and stop marauding bushwhackers who were attacking federal troops. The following is an incident of that time as recalled by Asher S. Childers of Company C of the 11th Kansas Cavalry.

> During the war, there were two roads leading south from Fort Scott, Kan. One ran almost directly south to Fort Smith, Ark., and the other a little southwest to Fort Gibson, I.T. From Baxter Springs south between these two roads is a hilly country, mostly covered with timber and dense undergrowth.
> After the massacre at Baxter Springs, this part of the country was infested with a bloodthirsty band of bushwhackers, and it was almost impossible for any but large bodies of troops to pass over these roads without being killed and robbed, for they took no prisoners.
>
> In February 1864, the commander at Fort Scott fitted out an expedition to drive the bushwhackers out of that country. At that time Col. Preston B. Plumb, of the 11th Reg. Kan. Cav., was in command at Humboldt, Kan., a post 40 or 50 miles west of Fort Scott, on the border. Col. Plumb was ordered to take Co. C, 11th Kan., and a company of Indians from the Osage Mission. The Osage Mission is about 40 miles south of Humboldt, on the Neosho River, and from there south there was no feed for man or beast except what we took with us on our horses.
>
> After we got near where the Fort Scott and Fort Gibson Road crosses the Neosho River Col. Plumb thought best to keep in the timber as much as possible and as the Fall and Winter had been dry the Neosho River was dry for several miles above its junction with Spring River, so we traveled in the river bed. After passing Spring River our course lay on the west side of Grand River, where after 40 or 50 miles we camped for the night.

Col. Plumb sent me and another man to ford the river and see what we could find on the other side. After going about a mile we found a place where men had camped a day or two before. We returned to the command a little after dark and reported. The Colonel decided to go back 20 or 30 miles to the ford, where the road from Neosho, Mo., crosses the Grand River, and look the country over on the east side.

We found out that the bushwhackers never traveled on the roads, but always kept in the woods. After crossing to the east side the company of Indians was ordered to go four or five miles east before turning south, while our command kept close to the river. A several miles jaunt brought us to a log cabin, with no one but a woman and a small baby in sight, although hanging on the side of the cabin were the carcasses of a deer and a hog.
Col. Plumb asked the woman if there were any men around. She said she had not seen a man for six months, and the Colonel replied, "Madame, I believe you lie."

From there we went down a path toward the river. A short distance from the cabin we found a saddle and a gun in the bushes and fresh horse tracks pointing toward the river. We followed the tracks across the river and saw a man ride out of the canebrake within a few rods of us. Col. Plumb started after him on foot, while the men followed, some on foot, some horseback, but the brush was so thick we could not follow fast. We expected to be attacked. George Plumb, a brother of the Colonel, got thru faster than the others and shot the bushwhacker through the head.

From there we continued on down the river until we crossed a beautiful stream, Cowskin Creek, and came to a little prairie a mile or two wide and several miles long. Just as we came to the edge of the prairie we saw some men with a drove of cattle. They were bushwhackers. The whole command charged after them. One of them turned to one side, so as to get into the timber along the creek. As soon as he got to the timber he jumped off his pony and got behind a large oak tree, and raised his gun to shoot. By that time three or four of us were closing in on him. His gun failed to go off, and we rushed up to the tree, only to find the man had disappeared. An old Austrian rifle lay by the tree, and the pony was standing nearby.

A rod or so beyond the tree was a ledge of rocks 20 or 25 feet high, running up and down the creek for a long ways. We could not think the man had jumped over the ledge, and as there was no brush or anything in the way, so the man could hide, we were puzzled to know where he had gone. Others of the men had come in from the chase. They searched up and down the creek but could find no trace of him.

On the edge of the ledge was a large rock. I climbed up on it to rest. Al Brandley tried to get up, too, but somehow in getting up he lost his balance and fell. He caught himself just at the brink of the ledge, but I thought he had gone over. Just then I heard the report of a gun under the rock and saw smoke come up in my face. I saw Brandley's feet below me. At the same time, the bushwhacker came up and said: "Don't shoot me anymore. I surrender."

Before I could get him he fainted and went headlong to his death over the ledge to the bottom below. Brandley had shot him thru the body while he was under the rock. The man had a double-barreled shotgun with him under the rock loaded with buckshot.

The company of Indians had found the camp of the other bushwhackers on the other side of the creek, and killed several of them, and scalped everyone they killed.

After the fight with the bushwhackers, a cold rain and snowstorm came upon us, and we got lost in the woods and wandered around for three days without anything to eat until we found some wild hogs. After the storm was over we found our way back to Baxter Springs, and at the end of two days more we arrived at the Osage Mission, a few hours after the Indians had got back.

That night the Indians had a scalp dance over the scalps they had taken while on the expedition. They divided the scalps up in little locks of hair, so each one would have a lock, and men and squaws danced around in a circle, all chanting their doleful cry of "Au-wa, au-wa." Although the weather was close to zero, I saw old gray-headed squaws dance until they were so exhausted they would drop down in the snow. After our horses and the men got filled up and rested up we went back to our camp at Humboldt, and that was the last we heard of that band of bushwhackers.

There are numerous stories of Plumb's character and personality as a military officer. J.W. Logan served in the 11th Kansas and related the following short stories while they were stationed in Humboldt.

I knew Senator Plumb before he went into the War. When I went into the War he enlisted me. He was Recruiting Officer, ranked Second Lieutenant at the time. I saw him at Emporia, Lyon County, Kansas. He treated his men good. Was a kind officer to his men. He was brave as any of them, no one braver than Plumb. His ability as a soldier was first-class. He was good and kind in every way to his men, but he exacted discipline.
I remember once when we were camped at Humboldt, Kansas. He was Major in command of the Post. The Company of the 15th Kansas relieved our Company. Our quarters we had built ourselves and spent our own money for them. We tried to sell them to this new Company, but they would not buy it. We thought it was our property to do with as we pleased, we the last night we were to remain there, we decided to destroy the property. We tore it down and were burning it. Plumb arrived on the scene about that time, and he stopped it, and told us not to do that; rather than to destroy it or burn it up, we should give it to the poor or to the country. He showed his humanity there. That was not all we did. We had dug a well at our own expense, which on leaving we filled up with rock. When we got on our way, and he [Plumb] found out that we filled up that well, he sent an order and brought us back and made us take the rock out

of the well. He was kind and generous, and yet he wanted discipline.

Plumb had a strong sense of justice and fairness which directed his service in the military and followed him for the rest of his life. He treated others with respect and expected the same courtesies to be shown to him. When they were not, his temper could flare. Although these instances were rare, they did happen, and they happened throughout his life. The following letter from September 1863 illustrates this point very well. The man who evoked Plumb's ire was Mr. J.W. Furman. Unfortunately, his exact name and title have been lost to history, but given the information in the letter, it is very likely that he was some sort of politically appointed agent within Plumb's district in Missouri. Given the lack of any reference to military rank, it is likely he was a civilian. Furman seems to have inserted himself between Plumb and his soldiers and gone so far as to try to usurp his authority, and worse, insult his character in front of the men. This, of course, is a serious grievance to any military officer. An officer's authority with his men is paramount, and a civilian attempting to degrade that could not be tolerated. The graveness of this offense explains Plumb's tone in the letter:

> Independence, Mo, 28th Sept. 1863
> General,
>
> Col. Wier advised me to write a short statement about a difficulty I had with Furman.
>
> F. told the men whom he took with him to Lexington that he ranked me and could order me where he pleased,–told it in a way to bring me into contempt with them. This, too, when I had cordially proffered him all the assistance in my power and had detailed the men for him against my judgment. He went to the Q.M. at Lexington and asked for a horse. The Q.M. declined. Furman then ordered him to consider himself under arrest! Yesterday he went to the quarters of Co. B and ordered a detail of nine men to get ready to accompany him at once! The sergeant reported the fact to me and I went to Furman and told him that such things were played out; that I would not allow him to bring me into contempt with my men, nor make details at all. He impudently told me that he had more authority than I had and could turn the whole District upside down–run the

whole thing, &c, &c. Afterwards in the presence of officers and men he denounced me as a liar.

I will kill him, if he is allowed to come around me, if it breaks me of my commission, I am thoroughly satisfied he is playing me false and shall never trust myself within his reach. I believe that our safety lies in his death.
I have told you just how the matter stands. I have no concealment from you; neither do I claim any immunity on account of our friendship. But I have my own honor and responsibility as an officer to look after as well as the welfare and safety of the men under my charge.

J.W. F. will be killed if opportunity offers by men whom he has robbed. I prevented it yesterday, told the men that there were matters of which they were not judges and succeeded in allaying the feeling somewhat.

All I ask is that he shall not serve around me; that I shall not see him; that the men of the 11th shall not be bodyguard for him, and shall not risk their lives in his hands, or on his plans.

Col. Wier will tell you of the very suspicious circumstances of yesterday, other than these I have narrated.
    Very Respectfully,
        Your obedient servant
            P.B. Plumb
            Maj. K.V.C.

Future Senator Stephen Elkins served on the Union side during the war, while his father and brother enlisted in the Confederate Army. He later described the following incident which illustrates Plumb's sense of justice very well.

I remember well when a detachment of his regiment came into Kansas City. I was a captain at Westport in the Missouri Militia, and this detachment had gotten so close to Westport that they strapped their carbines on their saddles and were marching along in irregular order when Quantrill and his men, who knew of their movements, and who had intended starting towards Westport to take the town, but who, instead of attacking

Westport, got behind the stone walls of what was known then, and I think now as John Wornall's near Brush Creek, and secreted themselves behind the walls and waited until the detachment was opposite them and fired on them from behind the wall, killing from fifty to seventy-five men. I don't remember the exact number. This infuriated Plumb, and he always called them murderers, because of the way his men were attacked. He never showed the intense hatred of the Kansas people for the Missouri people, but always tried to be just and fair.

Plumb's experiences hunting bushwhackers in Missouri stayed with him his entire life. A feeling that is shared by all combat veterans the world over. Many years after the war, Plumb recalled one particular instance from Missouri and shared it with a couple of friends:

> Plumb was with a scouting party of his men in western Missouri, looking for bushwhackers. It was at a time when the border struggle was as merciless as Indian warfare. The bushwhackers were looking for the scouting party. Late in the day Plumb and his men went into camp in a ravine full of brush. They were well concealed. They had lain there resting for some time when suddenly the bushwhackers, from whom they were looking, came into view on an elevation within gunshot range. The Kansans kept very quiet, and the unsuspecting bushwhackers proceeded to make themselves comfortable in camp. In numbers, the parties were about equal. Plumb, in whispers, instructed his men to pick his bushwhacker and wait for the command. There was one left when the scouting party had been told off to cover the bushwhackers. Plumb took his gun and leveled it upon that man. To his hearers, he described the terrible sensations that went through his mind as he lay there with his rifle upon the unsuspecting enemy. The bushwhacker who had fallen to Plumb's lot finally took his seat on the ground with his back to a tree, drew from his pocket a letter, and began to read it. He sat with his face full toward Plumb. It seemed like murder, but the alternative of the situation was kill, or be killed. Perhaps the wait was only a very few moments, but it took the senator much longer to describe the

conflicting emotions which he passed through. At length all was ready. Plumb gave the command, in a whisper, to fire. The volley rang out. The bushwhacker Plumb had aimed at fell forward, dead, his hands still clasping the letter. The scene was described by the senator with awful vividness. Mr. Plumb may not have been a sentimentalist, but every minute detail of fact and every swift operation of the mind pertaining to that shooting of the bushwhacker remained with him all of his life.

Chapter 9

Price Raid

By the Fall of 1864 things were not looking good for the Confederacy. Abraham Lincoln's reelection seemed a sure thing, General William Tecumseh Sherman was marching through Georgia leaving a trail of destruction, and Lee was bogged down in Richmond. The Confederacy thought this was the time to strike in the western theater and retake Missouri from Union control while severing Union forces from their supply lines. For this task, Major General Sterling Price was given command of roughly 12,000 cavalry troops and 14 pieces of artillery. Price's forces were ill-equipped and lacking in many basic necessities. They did, however, gain the additional support of about 6,000 pro-Confederacy guerrillas within Missouri. This brought their force to about 18,000 men (all mounted) facing a Federal army of about 35,000 men. This force included cavalry, infantry, and Missouri militia forces.

Second Battle of Lexington

The Price Raid, or Price's Missouri Expedition as it is alternately called, consisted of several battles throughout Missouri and Kansas. Plumb and the 11th Kansas Cavalry fought hard in these conflicts. Many of the men were veteran soldiers by 1864, but there were a few new recruits who had just joined the ranks. Private Walter Wellhouse was just such a man, and recalled some of the events of this campaign:

> February 22, 1864, at Pleasant Ridge, Leavenworth County he enlisted in Company A, Eleventh Kansas. His Captain was H.E. Palmer. Wellhouse joined his Company at Shawnee Mission. In April or May he was moved (with his Company) to Olathe; and soon afterwards to Aubry, where the Company remained until about the 10th of October, when it was ordered out for the Price Raid and rendezvoused at Hickman's Mills.
>
> The great scout to define the position of Price was sent out, and Company A. was part of it. It went by Lee's Summit, Pleasant Hill, Warrensburg, and Lexington. At Lexington, Company A was sent out two miles on the Dover Road to Hinkinson's house as a picket. Late the next day the Captain had bad news. Shelby was in or very near Lexington and the Union forces gone on

towards Kansas City. Captain Palmer led his men through Lexington and came up with his command. Wellhouse remembers that Plumb was in this scout.

Corporal Fairfield described this same scouting party to Connelley:

> When it was known at Kansas City, that Price was coming up through Missouri it was necessary to keep fully informed of his movements. General Curtis sent Companies A, K, and a part of D on a scout. Fairfield did not tell me who commanded the detachment, but Captain H. E. Palmer, now of Omaha was along. The route was via Harrisonville, Pleasant Hill, and Warrensburg. Plumb joined the scout at Pleasant Hill and was in command some of the time after that point was passed. Warrensburg was found barricaded and fortified, and it was supposed that it was held by rebels. As it was the object to discover the position of the enemy more than to try to fight, the troops were passing the town by. Captain Palmer asked permission to take 25 men and go into the town, which he did and found it held by Union troops.

> The scout found the rebels—Price—at Knobnoster. To that point it had been the intention of Price, Fairfield thinks, to go straight into Kansas in imitation of Quantrill's raids. The Confederacy hated Kansas as much as Quantrill hated Lawrence and wished to devastate it as a closing act of the rebellion. But at Knobnoster Price turned towards Kansas City. At Holden, the scout struck for Lexington and beat the rebels into the town. Price forced the little command out of Lexington and it took a position on a high hill to the west of the town. The rebels attacked, but the men could not be driven out. Then Marmaduke was sent west on the south of the position to flank it, seeing which the Union command was forced to retreat. Captain Palmer had been cut off when Price occupied Lexington. He said to his men that Price's army was full of guerrillas and a Union soldier's life would not be worth a snap of the fingers when captured and asked his men to draw their pistols and follow him. They did so, and all rode through Lexington at full

gallop and were not molested. The rebels were busy with the men on the hill, and those who saw Captain Palmer move through the town thought it was some part of their own force—for many of the rebels wore Union uniforms.

When the scout retreated from Lexington it stopped at Wellington and thought to make a stand and destroy the bridge over the Sni, but found it could not effect this. It got out of Wellington only thirty minutes ahead of the rebels in strong force.

The next stand was made at the bridge over the Little Blue. The bridge was heaped with combustibles ready to be set on fire at a moment's warning. There other Union troops were found. A hard battle was fought there, the Colorado troops losing heavily. The bridge was burned, but the rebels crossed at fords. The Union forces were driven on and through Independence. At the Big Blue, they found the Kansas Militia, "their tents looking like a camp of the Midianites," as Fairfield put it. That was Friday night.

Ben Simpson, of the Kansas State Militia, and lifelong friend of Plumb's, recalled being with Plumb during the fighting at Lexington:

> Simpson says that the battle with Price at Lexington, in the Price Raid, was at the Fair Grounds. The rear guard, under Moonlight, formed in the timber on the hill west of Lexington. The fence at the foot of this hill was thrown down. The Confederates formed beyond the foot of the hill, and Moonlight said he was sorry the fence was down, for he saw that the Confederates were going to charge in force and were much stronger than the rear guard. Moonlight rode rapidly along the ranks and ordered the officers to see that all the men had their guns loaded. Moonlight's men carried repeating carbines which shot seven times without reloading. Moonlight called out to some officer to know how the road down the hill was, for the hill was rough on that side—to the west. The officer addressed said he did not know. The Confederates then came in range and

Moonlight opened fire on them and emptied many saddles. But he could not hold the hill and had no intention of trying to do so. He did not retreat until the Confederates were almost on him when he took his men down the west slope in good order. Plumb and Simpson were about the last to leave the field. The road down the north side of the hill was cut down into a limestone ledge which cropped out there. The road was sunk three or four feet into this ledge in some places, and had steep or perpendicular banks on the sides. About halfway down the road there was a square turn toward the west, the road having passed more to the north to that point. At the turn, there were walls five or six feet high and straight up from the road, which at that point was cut into the solid rock. As Plumb and Simpson reached this turn a caisson came up on them on the run and tried to make the turn and pass. The caisson cramped and almost turned over, the wheel pressing Plumb, Simpson, and another man against the rock wall at the out angle or corner, and they were unable to extricate themselves; the caisson pressed heavily against them and pinned them to the wall. The Confederates were following down the hill, and they were soon in revolver range and opened fire on the men about the caisson. Every minute they came closer and Simpson heard the bullets striking on the tires of the wheels of the caisson and rebels were all around them. Moonlight in some way learned of the condition of things at the turn of the road and wheeled about and charged up the hill, driving the rebels back and holding them long enough to take the caisson out and release Plumb, Simpson, and the other soldier from their dangerous position. [At this juncture of the interview, Connelley made a note that the official reports say the tongue of the caisson carriage was broken off.]

Simpson and Plumb rode together the last men back of the rear guard. Simpson is of the opinion that it was not at Wellington that Plumb tried to burn the bridge, but at a creek (Sin-a-bar) only two or three miles west of the stand made on the hill. At the bridge, which was an old-fashioned wooden structure roofed over with shingles, a boy who had a lead horse was with them. They had overtaken him, as he had fallen behind riding one horse and leading another. When they came to the bridge Plumb said it ought to be burned, to which Simpson assented. Then Plumb said they must try to burn it. They had matches and they cut shavings from the timbers and tried to start a fire. They had dismounted and given the bridle reins to the boy. Soon the rebels came near enough to open fire on them. After a few shots, the boy could not hold all the horses, and Plumb told Simpson to take his and Plumb's horse on through the bridge and keep them there in readiness until he got the fire to going. Simpson led the horses to the west end of the bridge and down a depression out of reach of the bullets which were now coming through and around the bridge pretty thick. The boy with his horse followed Simpson and did not stop at the end of the bridge, but hurried on after the rear guard and they did not see him again. The fire was so heavy now and the rebels being almost up to the bridge, Plumb could not stop longer without being killed or captured, and he ran through the bridge to Simpson. They mounted and followed the command. The small fire Plumb had started did not burn the bridge, and it was probably extinguished by the rebels.

General Blunt's division was heavily outnumbered by Price's division, forcing Blunt to withdraw. This then led to the subsequent Battle of Westport.

Sgt. Sherman Bodwell recorded the events of October 1864 very clearly in his diary, which is included below in full:

Tuesday 18th
About 10 P.M. (17th) saddled for Warrensburgh, but receiving orders from above moved North East. Price reported at Lexington. Rested an hour or two before daylight, reaching Lexington about 4 P.M. Some fifty guerrillas in town just before our arrival. (Shooting of prisoner). Halted in Mulligan's old works awhile, then went into bivouac for night.

Wednesday 19th
Price reported in force, below at Dover and Boone Conscripting, etc. Capt. Huntoon detailed in morning to repair Mulligan's works, using citizens but had no time to commence. About noon

reports of enemy advancing in force, forage details taken in, pickets engaged, etc. About 2 P.M. Brigade moved rapidly out south of town some 4 miles. Firing in front. Dismounted and laid down fence. Skirmishing in edge of timber a half mile in front. Mounted, moved on a good distance, and "prepared to fight on foot." A round shot struck near as we moved in, but no enemy in sight. Mounted "four right, column right" and up lane to Wire Road, the other regts. moving in advance rapidly. Took position on a high hill overlooking the field just left, the enemy moving in force in three lines across the open country in full view. Our howitzer opened upon them. The Col. dissatisfied with their work took hold himself, sighting and watching the shells as they went home. We were formed just back of the crest of the hill, we chiefs of platoon seeing fairly over a shot occasionally passing over. A squad of our men coming up halted in front of us. One of them falling dead, shot through, they moved out of the way. Maj. Anderson comes rushing in from the right. "Col. they are flanking us on the right." Double the skirmishers the Col. shouts. A line of their skirmishers moved up coolly on our left, some fifty yds on the opposite slope. Custard with this platoon sent down, skirmishing sharply with them. The flanking process in full view. Howitzers withdrawn. We changed front to face the enemy's skirmishers on the left to gain time and get off [remove the] broken down howitzer. Corpl. Woods horse wounded. Moffet wounded in shoulder. "To the left" moving off leisurely toward Wire Road. Soon doubled the gait the enemy following hard.

Where the road passed house with orchard on left, turned left into orchard and formed facing up road. "I" Co. on the other side. Enemy's advance came up, one sings out "Come on boys, here they are" and their bugle sounded a call not in our tactics. We were in readiness and fired a splendid volley, leveling low, the flame flashing in one sheet in the early twilight. Having delivered fire, moved out again and up the road. At Sni bridge passed another Battalion formed for another stand, but none was needed. Brigade marched west to near Little Blue.

Thursday 20th
Marched a little beyond Blue, Company sent 5 miles above, to picket Crenshaw's Crossing of Blue. A rainy night. Horses kept saddled and men on the alert.

Friday 21st
Orders in morning, to remain till the enemy appeared, fire upon them and come in. A heavy column reported advancing on Wire Road and bridge burned by Cols. order. Felled trees in the crossing. Firing in direction of camp through forenoon, seemingly retiring toward Ind. About 10 A.M. supposing we were cut off from communication with Col., moved out leisurely on Ind. Road expecting to come on the enemy's rear, but entered town to find our forces were still in front. Moved out on Wire Road, meeting wounded coming in in ambulances and mounted. Met Gen'l. Curtis and staff. Some five miles out, found the regiment in an open field to right of road in line. Col. Moonlight issuing ammunition. Took our place in line. 55 men present. Took their names on back of Mother's letter rec'd last night. Dismounted. Firing in front. Reg't. mounted and moved toward Ind. Co. sent to Spring Branch Road to watch left flank. Rejoined regiment in Ind.

Cos. "B" and "H" left to cover retreat. Took our position near our old quarters facing the hill by Mrs. Dodgions house. "B" at right angles with us, on Wayne City Road. Enemy's skirmishers opened fire from the timber, we returning it. The men behaved well, keeping line as well as horses would let them. One of their sharpshooters struck the hill a little in front. Some of the boys sung out "more powder." Shot struck curb stone at my horse's feet. Then came one with its heavy thud into the shoulder of William's horse just in front of me. I on the sidewalk in rear, superintending my platoon (2nd). Col. M [Moonlight] with us watching our behavior. Followed the regt. (now well out of town), moving at the walk. Another stand at R.R. Bridge, then on to and across Big Blue passing through the militia camps in the darkness found corn and lay down.

Saturday Oct. 22nd/64

Mounted about sunrise. Moved down on Blue to watch against the enemy's crossing. Firing above at Byram's ford. Ridgway sent to open communication with Jennison, reported falling back. Hard riding here and there. Late in afternoon moved rapidly through and south of Westport, finding the enemy in force moving from the timber into open prairie, and toward the State Line. All the Cav. Regts. present I think. Company sent out as skirmishers. Shot from enemy's battery passing over, and falling short. Skirmished with them till they fell back. But few of their balls came up while our Gallagher's [carbines] kicked up the dust all among them. Rejoined regiment command moved to rear and we in the dusk to Shawnee Missouri where we lay for the night. We felt that Kansas was doomed. Col. said, "Price will go through undoubtedly. I ask leave to use my regt at will." A rebel Lieut. taken at evening said they had been skirmishing in their rear that day for the first time. Pleasanton might be within reach yet.

A trying position. Company deployed as skirmishers on a low swell of prairie in obedience to Jennison's order's, the Capt obeying, his ranking officer because he felt as we naturally felt; averse to backing down in presence of the 15th that sweet outfit being in a nice hollow in our rear and safe, or nearly so. At about ¼ mile distance the Rebs threw about 600 men on right into line, then opened with their two pieces. Sitting in line, in full view of the guns, seeing the smoke, hearing the shell, coming up seeming by this for one, with a general sense of relief as each went safely by us or burst in front or rear, and all in obedience to a fool order of C.R. Jensen, neither a man or soldier was trying to discipline but the men stood splendidly, and I was more proud than ever of the "best company, for work" in the best regiment Kansas furnished "or any other State" (Every soldier felt about that way I suppose throughout the armies). [William] West, a fine soldier, but a little excitable, (Poor fellow, he has wife and children at home and was at last killed at the Red Buttes [Battle of Red Buttes July 1865]) on the right of my platoon, or left of the 1st reined his horse to the right starting to the rear, saying "We better be getting out of this." I remarked quietly, guess we'd better wait till we get orders, West." He looked for an instant as if an old idea had struck him, reined his horse back front to the music.

Battle of Westport

The Battle of Westport took place October 23, 1864, and is often referred to as the "Gettysburg of the West" as it involved approximately 30,000 men, making it one of the largest battles west of the Missouri River. Bodwell's diary continues below with his account of the fighting that day:

> Sabbath, October 23rd, 1864
> Mounted at daylight. To Westport and out again skirmishing sharply and at close quarters in wheat and cornfields south, then fell back to Westport. Regt. moved west and took position behind stone wall. Co. sent on hill in front to observe movements of enemy and report. Could see a heavy force close in to where we had been fighting in morning. Ordered to skirmish on left flank of Regt which would move southward. "To the Left" and away. Rising next hill the field of battle lay before us, or line of battle and the enemy's in full view in the open prairie. Our artillery playing upon them beautifully; Our line advances, theirs then moves to the rear and becomes a mob rather in growing confusion. "Pleasanton" was "up" and Kansas saved. Away we went southward on their flank coming upon a body of them at ford of Blue above Santa Fe where we and the stragglers with us left five of their dead, then on their track scattered with saddles, blankets, etc., through Santa Fe. Some 8 miles south, came on flank of a heavy column supposed to be Pleasanton pressing on the rear. A scout sent out returned reporting having been fired upon when close up. It was the enemy and we had "flanked Price." Slowly and sullenly the heavy column was pressing southward on its long retreat.

> No flag but one (a large black one) to be seen over it. A force (supposed to be our regt., but turning out to be Jennison) came up in rear when we deployed while a strong body of the enemy

halted and formed line, then opened fire. Bowman's horse wounded by bullet. The Parrotts or Brooks [artillery] shells came rushing through and over in a very uncomfortable manner bursting in front and rear, one wounding Lt. R. slightly. Command moved to rear a solid shot knocking a limb overhead as we descended into the timber. Rejoined regt at Aubrey about 10 P.M.

Private Walter Wellhouse of Company A described an instance of fighting during the Battle of Westport involving Plumb's command. The following story is possibly referring to an incident in the battle when a local farmer named George Thoman sought out General Curtis and led him to a gulch which allowed the Union forces to cut through the Confederate lines. General Curtis took a portion of the 11th Kansas with him to the ravine.

In the battles to check Price, he saw Plumb but once. On the 23rd of October, the Eleventh Kansas was formed just west of the State line, west of the present Country Club grounds. Colonel Veal's forces were at the McAbee farm and had been cut to pieces. Darkness was coming on. Jackman's Brigade was marching through the lines through the gap made by crushing Veale, and had to be stopped else the Confederate army would pour over the State line into Kansas.

To check this advance was now the work of the Eleventh Kansas. If it should fail the gravest consequences would follow. The Confederates marched steadily northwest until they came in view of the line of the Eleventh Kansas. At that instant, Lt. Col. Plumb with four Companies of the 11th was beginning his advance toward the Rebels. Seeing this the Confederates stopped short and formed a line of battle facing Plumb. Plumb marched his men across the State line to a little valley running parallel with the rebel line and there turned up the valley and when his troops were directly opposite the enemy he halted them, faced them about, formed his line, and marched up the hill, his line firing at will after the first volley. Wellhouse says he never saw a finer sight. The flashes of Plumb's guns were like fireflies on a damp summer night. The advance was irresistible

Illustration of Plumb's dismounted cavalry charge during the Battle of Westport. Drawing by Andy Robbins. Author's collection.

and Jackman's brigade was swept from the field and rolled back with such loss that no further attempt was made in that quarter by the enemy. This was the first maneuver that Wellhouse saw in the War and the most effective.

This maneuver was especially dangerous for Plumb and his men. He was tasked with stopping Confederate forces from crossing into Kansas. If Plumb failed, there would be no one in a position to check the Confederacy's advance. Plumb's valiant dismounted cavalry charge uphill into the Confederate line, pushing the rebels back and thwarting their attempt to push on into Kansas, was a key moment in the regiment's history, and owed its success to Plumb's bravery and tenacity.

Fairfield also described Plumb's involvement in the fighting on that Saturday and Sunday:

> Then came the real battles on Saturday and Sunday. On Saturday the rebels tried to get into Westport by a flank movement, and the Eleventh Kansas (or a part of it) under Plumb went into a cornfield and checked them after hard fighting. Plumb was in all the battles of Saturday and Sunday – in the front and thick of it. On Sunday morning he led the Eleventh (or a part of it) into the battle along Brush Creek. He led his men gallantly all the time in these fights.

Bodwell's diary continues and describes the aftermath of the fight as well as where the regiment moved.

> Monday, Oct. 24/64
> Marched south at daylight. At Cold Water came again on enemy's flank. Co. [H] and Co. "I" out again skirmishing while Col. formed regt. in line. Enemy repeated yesterday evening's operation, except the firing. A little firing by a few of their skirmishers in the Grove. Reached Mound City at midnight. Rained before morning.
>
> Tuesday 25th
> Enemy near. Two alarms in morning. Marched for Ft. Scott. Near Lincoln saw to our left the beginning of Battle of Osage. A messenger soon bringing news of capture of Marmaduke, 4

guns, and 400 men. In timber at Lincoln, found the enemy in front, and in line of battle on our left, the main column beyond moving south. Crossed Osage above and reached Ft. Scott about sunset. Price's rear is marked at night by the light and in daytime by smoke of the prairie fires kindled with an object doubtless.

Wednesday 21st
Commands of Curtis and Pleasanton marched early in forenoon. About 4 P.M. came upon Price's trail. Enemy moving in four parallel columns of fours. Burned wagons and abandoned horses all along road. Marched till midnight when regt fed and rested in cornfield, then moved into prairie and lay cold and miserable till morning. Gen Blunt, we are told wished to strike the enemy at daylight, but Curtis spoiled all.

Thursday, 27th
Via Rooks Point to Carthage (burned) arriving at midnight. Fairfield tells me of capture of our Topeka Militia. Feared Col. and McV might be among the killed or captured. Met in afternoon Miller of Tecumseh, escaped who tells me Howard, Flanders, Green and the Williams are prisoners with their Capt. Huntoon, and suffering severely.

The Battle of Westport was a loss for the Confederacy, contributing to the eventual failure of the Price Raid to retake Missouri. Estimates of casualties are varied among historians, with losses at around 1,500 men on each side. The Battle of Westport featured many future prominent men aside from Preston B. Plumb. Those who fought alongside him included: Buffalo Bill Cody in the 7th Kansas Cavalry, Wild Bill Hickok who served as a scout, future Kansas Governor Samuel Crawford, the mountain man John "Liver Eating" Johnson of the 2nd Colorado Cavalry, and future Kansas Senator Edmund G. Ross also of the 11th Kansas Cavalry.

Food and rations for the men following the battle were scant, and hard tack became a precious commodity. Captain John G. Lindsay of Company F later recalled the following story in a letter to Plumb. The orderly he is referring to is Plumb, who served as an aide to General Ewing when the regiment first started.

Twenty-two years ago today we were on the march following old Pap Price and went into camp near Webbers Falls, cold wet, hungry and out of "grub." You will remember that terrible march from Kansas City to Webbers Falls on to Fort Smith and return, and as you remember who this orderly was (I think he was from Lyon County) who refused to sell me a cracker (hard tack) for $5 but said "I'll give you half of it" and did so.

On a humorous note, Captain Alfred C. Pierce of Company G relayed the following story, which was printed in the *Leavenworth Times*:

Capt. Pierce of the Eleventh Kansas, is six feet six inches in his stockings. During the Price raid, he lost his uniform and was returning in citizens' clothes. While seated at the dinner table at Monticello he heard a little fussy military individual heaping abuse upon the Eleventh Kansas. He listened silently till the abuser had subsided, and then mildly told him that he would have to take back everything he had said. The little man said he would take back nothing. At this, the Captain was slightly "riled," and began to rise up out of his chair, and take the folds out of his body. The little man watched his ascent in alarm and amazement, and exclaimed in terror: "Hold on, Mister, don't go up any higher! I take everything back!"

Chapter 10

Headed West

Winter of 1864-65

Following the end of Price's Raid, the 11th Kansas did not see any more hard fighting in the area. Price's army had started with approximately 13,000 men and was left with 3,500 by the end of the fighting in December. To the War Department, a more serious threat was brewing in the western territories.

Walter Wellhouse recalled that the 11th Kansas was stationed at Olathe in January 1865 until the regiment rendezvoused near Olathe to march to Fort Riley:

> On this march the Regiment camped one night at Tecumseh. William Wellhouse, the uncle of Walter, lived near where Berrytown now is. Wellhouse was without a horse and was marching on foot. At Tecumseh, he sought his Captain and could not find him. He wished leave to go and spend the night with his uncle. He found Lt. Colonel Plumb standing by a fire and approached him and made his wants known. Plumb gave him permission to go and did it in a kindly way that made Wellhouse his friend ever after. The next camp was at Indianola northwest of Topeka, and Wellhouse came up with the command there. The army crossed the Kansas river on a pontoon bridge at Topeka. The 11th Kansas remained at Fort Riley a month. In February it started for Wyoming.

The regiment had been ordered to the Dakota Territory to protect the telegraph lines from hostile Native American attacks. This order was especially grievous to the men as they had enlisted in the army to fight to preserve the Union and protect their homes from the ongoing border hostilities with Missouri. For many Kansans, they had been fighting since the mid-1850s, and they wished to continue fighting for their state, not be sent westward to guard telegraph lines. The federal government was not sensitive to this, however, and saw only a regiment with a good fighting record that could be easily sent west to fill a personnel shortage following the discharge of many men of the 11th Ohio Volunteer Cavalry regiment who had been stationed there for some time prior. According to

Plumb's diary, the regiment left Fort Riley on February 20th to begin the arduous trek to present-day Wyoming. The regiment also headed westward with ten Black undercooks who had enlisted in 1864.

> Monday, February 20, 1865.
> Left Ft. Riley at 9 a.m. for Kearney, Nebraska, with Companies B, D, F, H, I, K, L, and M of the Eleventh. Had 2 wagons to each company, one for Hospital, one for Hd.-Qr., one for non-Coms. & Band & 2 for Q.M. stores. Rained heavily at time of starting,–arrived at Bachelder, 12 miles distant on Republican, about 3 P.M. Hd. Qr. team got in about 5–about half of the Co. teams got in during the night. The remainder stuck in the mud and the men stood up in the rain all night. Met Mr. Barry at his home near Camp. First time I had seen him for several years. Took dinner with him. Q.M. bought hay and corn of him.

Along the way to the regiment's post of Platte Bridge Station in present-day Casper, Wyoming, Captain Palmer received devastating news from home.

> Captain Palmer married Betty Houck, of Westport, Mo. When the 11th Kansas was ordered to the Plains he made an effort to be allowed to remain at home until the birth of their first child, which occurred in January 1865. But he could not secure that leave. He left home on the 16th and the child was born the 18th. A messenger was sent after him to Fort Riley, but did not come up with him. He had left for Fort Kearney, Nebraska, with his men. The weather was frightfully cold and roads blocked with snow and ice. He did not get to Fort Kearney until about the last of February. There was then a telegraph line to Fort Kearney and beyond. He had told his wife to telegraph him at Fort Kearney. From a point on the Little Blue he rode to Fort Kearney ahead of the troops. The weather was awfully cold and he had been compelled to wrap himself in blankets and to wrap a blanket about each leg to avoid freezing to death. He went into the telegraph office and was handed a telegram from his father-in-law saying both his wife and baby were dead. The shock was awful. He went out, and soon met Plumb and Colonel Mitchell.

Plumb knew something had happened for Palmer was weeping, and asked him what it was. Palmer handed him the telegram. Plumb read it, steadied himself a minute, and then burst into tears himself; and he did not try to conceal his grief. Palmer said he was going to the stage office and take the stage home even if he were hung for it. Mitchell told him he must not do it, as the Secretary of War had ordered that no man have any leave–but Palmer was crazed and went on to the stage office. Plumb went with him and did not try to dissuade him from going home. At Leavenworth Palmer found an order for him to aid court martial boards there, and this order was perhaps the result of Plumb's efforts on his behalf–but Palmer does not know.

Had that order not been waiting for Palmer when he arrived, he himself would have been facing a court martial. After some time, Palmer was ordered to the plains and rejoined the regiment there. Meanwhile, Plumb and the rest of the regiment continued on their treacherous journey west. Walter Wellhouse described the terrible weather of the journey:

> Only a brief stop was made at Fort Kearney. The march up the Platte was a hard one. The line faced blizzards most of the time and there was much suffering. At Cottonwood Springs some of the men dislodged from the trees some Indian corpses found in them. Crossed the South Platte at Julesburg. There it rained three days and then followed a blizzard which kept the men in their tents 48 hours. The Government had some pitch pine wood there hauled from such a distance that it cost $75 a cord but the 11th Kansas burned it.

The following is a letter written by Thomas Barber to his father in Emporia, Kansas, dated at Ft. Laramie June 8, 1865, which describes the trek from Fort Riley to Platte Bridge Station.

> We left Ft. Riley for Ft. Kearney, Feb. 20-65, a distance of about 200 miles with 9 companies of the 11th Kansas Cav. and a large supply train with Col. Plumb in command. On the 24th rain commenced in earnest turning to snow and sleet covering everything with sleet, the wagons with rear guard under Com'd

of Major Anderson were stuck in the soft ground and compelled to stay on the open prairie and take the storm until daybreak on the 25th and Col. Plumb with the advance guard were bunched up on the prairie 3 miles in advance. About daybreak, the sleet stopped and the Colonel ordered the bugler to Call Retreat but the bugle being full of ice failed to work. When by his verbal order we fell in line to help get the wagons out of the mud onto a place where we could feed our animals some corn and get a hard tack for ourselves. This was accomplished by the aid of Cav. ropes with 50 men on their horses pulling ahead of the mules. By 12 o'clock we were on higher ground and all eating corn and hardtack but still covered with ice, before dark we got to wood and water where we melted some of the ice from our saddles and clothes. That was the worst storm I was ever in.

Early morning of the 26th the Col. with 100 men with axes and spades struck out to build a bridge across a creek with steep banks on each side, four long trees, two feet thick and forty long were cut and dragged across, then poles across them, then brush and prairie grass carried by the men ¼ mile. Then dirt on top and Col. P.B. [Plumb] threw more dirt than any of us and proved himself a real bridge builder.

Our guide told the Col. [Plumb] that the crossing of this creek on the old road had much low ground on each side and would necessitate doubling teams for over a mile. The Col. Says, "Can't we find a better place further up the creek?" The guide says the banks are all steep and 60 feet across from bank to bank. [Plumb asks] "Is there any timber on the creek?" [The guide replies,] "Yes. Plenty of it." Then says the Colonel, "We will build a bridge and save ten miles travel and a better road." The bridge was completed in 6 hours and ready for the train before it got there...

We arrived in Ft. Kearney on the 5th of March. On the 6th we were ordered to prepare for the march to Ft. Laramie on the 9th. All went well with us for four days, then came rain, sleet and high winds – many times were our tent ropes broken and tents

Portrait of Lt. Col. Preston B. Plumb taken January 12, 1865 in Paola, Kansas. Image courtesy Mollus–Mass Collection, United States Army Heritage and Education Center, Carlisle, PA.

blown heavenward so the rain could get closer to our bodies. After three days of miserable weather, we camped in a cedar thicket after marching 20 miles before breakfast through sleet and snow. That night about 200 men lined up before the Colonel's [Plumb] tent and begged him to let us rest a full day in this sheltered spot as many of the men were without horses and had to walk. His reply was "My beloved soldiers a good soldier will always obey orders and mine were received yesterday by telegraph to continue our march to Julesburg at the best possible speed, and while I truly sympathize with you in this the hardest most cruel march of your life, I beg and implore you to help me to fully obey the order from our Commanding Officer, Gen. Conner, and I will let those on foot ride my two horses while I walk to Julesburg." One man says "Col., I can't ride your horse and see you walking. God bless you!"

Major Anderson one of the principal petitioners for a day of rest in this quiet spot replied to Col. Plumb as follows: "Colonel the Lord is going to give us a fine day tomorrow and to please you we will have reveille at three in the morning and resume our march by daybreak – God bless you!"

We crossed the river at Julesburg and remained there till our 198 horses came from Leavenworth to remount our boys, who lost their horses in the Price raid. Col. Plumb and I were at Julesburg when the horses came in with 20 of our men driving them which had to be crossed over the river immediately to get corn and be delivered to the men who were to receive them for duty. The river was high and lots of slush ice running which made it a fearful looking stream to cross and thirty below zero and strong north wind and twelve inches of snow on the ground, only ten bags of corn for the twenty-five cavalry of Capt. Murphy at Julesburg station the Col. says these horses must be taken across–I will give $50 for a pilot. Murphy's men had crossed many times but not one of them would try it now for $100. The Col. says to me, "You and I have the best horses in the world and both accustomed to swimming Kansas rivers, let's try it," turning to Capt. Murphy ordered him and all his men to help our men drive the horses in after us, which they did in good shape and bade us goodbye. The first plunge was about 100 yards from the shore but keeping our horses headed upstream they were carried to a shoal about 50 feet when the Col. motioned boys to go farther downstream thus avoiding the hole we got into, then we got along very well till we got almost to the north bank where a deep channel had recently been cut out about 100 feet wide this took us and all the loose horses into swimming water but the drivers escaped it by going lower down. When we got to our camp we were all covered with ice and no fire to thaw us. Col. and I were pulled from our horses carried in his tent and covered with all the available blankets, etc. till we were thawed enough to get our boots and clothes off and the other men were similarly treated.

The next day we started for Ft. Laramie 200 miles up the North Platte. Here the Command was distributed to different points from Ft. Laramie to Sweet water on the California road.

Their destination of Platte Bridge Station was established in 1862 as a military post, although the bridge crossing itself was established in 1859 by French-Canadian Louis Guinard. The bridge was a strategic point to cross the Platte River and was utilized by countless pioneers following the California, Oregon, and Mormon Trails. Thousands of settlers crossed the bridge each year; 25,000 in 1865 alone. The wooden bridge itself was about 1,035 feet long and eighteen feet wide. It was briefly a Pony Express stop, and then became a major telegraph station in 1861. The sheer number of travelers and its position on the telegraph line made it a target of Native American attacks. Keeping the telegraph lines operational was crucial to relay information back and forth from the coasts, which meant having a military presence at the post was a high priority.

Upon reaching Platte Bridge Station in April 1865, Plumb chose to establish regimental headquarters about five to seven miles distant at the base of Casper Mountain. The camp was set up in a "V" shape giving each wing a view of potential threats to the fort. This location provided ample timber, a freshwater spring, and good grass for grazing their horses. Plumb named this location Camp Dodge, and it consisted primarily of tent quarters, but there were three wooden buildings constructed on the site. From there, Plumb dispatched companies of the 11th Kansas along the telegraph route. The 11th Ohio Volunteer Cavalry was also stationed along this route, and the arrival of the 11th Kansas to the area put the Kansas soldiers in command of the district. Colonel Moonlight of the 11th Kansas was stationed at Fort Laramie, while Plumb managed the day-to-day operations of the telegraph stations.

When not busy with camp duties, the men often wiled away the time by readings. Books were hard to come by this far from civilization and the scant books and magazines the men had were passed around throughout the companies. Now promoted to Lieutenant, Sherman Bodwell wrote in his diary April 25, 1865:

> Warm, with wind northerly but light. Emptied revolver and cleaned it. Wagons returned from Sweet Water and we start in morning. Read L. Maria Child's, Madame de Staël, and Madame Roland. Have lately appropriated from Col. "Martin Chuzzlewit" and "Little Dorrit" and much interested in both. Such characters as Little Dorrit and Clennam make one better by looking at them. Dicken's best are too good to be of this world unless Christ were in them, and that is left to be thought so or not, at the pleasure of reader.

While at Camp Dodge, Plumb received word of a caravan of Mormons headed westward who were in distress. He recalled the following story many years later:

> While thus engaged they camped one night not far from a band of Mormon converts on their way to Salt Lake. The soldiers learned that small-pox had broken out in the Mormon caravan; that the people had remained in camp some days. There was a suspicion that the party might be in some distress. Plumb left his soldiers and went down to the Mormons. He met an Elder in charge of the converts. After he had looked at the sick, and had arranged to supply their immediate necessities, Plumb entered into conversation with the Elder.

> "I found him," he said, "a plain, simple man, and I drew him out. I got him into conversation about his religion, about the motives which prompted him to go on a mission to these people, to labor with them, and to start with them across the plains for Salt Lake. We sat there talking well into the night. I finally left the

Illustration of Camp Dodge established in April 1865 near present-day Casper, Wyoming. Drawing by Andy Robbins, author's collection.

Elder, satisfied in my mind that his motives were pure and good, and that he was honestly trying, in his own way and according to his own light, to do the best he could for humanity. That was the first time I had ever had an opportunity to study these peculiar people. I made the most of it; and ever since then, while condemning some of their practice—as all of us must—I have felt that they were at least entitled to be credited with a certain honesty of purpose."

Thomas Barber's letter home also described some of the fighting the regiment was involved in with the local Native American tribes.

Then came the hazardous task of repelling the numerous Indian raids on the white man and his property. On the 2nd of May, Col. Plumb with a squad of men got after about 200 Indians and drove them north about 100 miles killing several and captured 40 ponies. By his determination and daring in this raid, we gave him the name of Prince Boneparte as he is certainly the best and most effective Indian fighter I was ever with, even Joe Gail, Sam Bean, and Kit Carson with whom I was in Arizona in 1858 against the Apaches in command by Mangos [Mangas] Colorados. On June 3rd about 200 Indians made an attack on an immigrant train near Platte Bridge and as soon as we heard the firing the Col. took about 50 of us and went for them driving them 20 miles, killed 7 horses and 12 Indians and some 20 or more wounded. Our loss was W.T. Bonwell killed and one of the 11th Ohio wounded. This is another time that our Colonel proved a daring, shrewd but cautious commander, and had Bonwell obeyed the Colonel's orders he would not have been killed. This was a band of Cheyennes commanded by White Eagle. After this fight, we were convinced as Capt. Green of B Co. said that our highly esteemed citizen and lawyer was also a good soldier.

Colonel Moonlight had been respected by the men during their service prior to reaching the Dakota Territory. However, by May of 1865, relations between him and the men of his regiment were strained. On May 2, 1865, he organized the Powder River Expedition in an attempt to track down a tribe of Cheyenne rumored to be in the Wind River area. He brought with him about 500 cavalry soldiers including men of the

11th Kansas and 11th Ohio, as well as famed mountain man and guide, Jim Bridger.

> Thomas Barber was in the Powder River Expedition with Colonel Plumb. They started from the Platte Bridge and went along the California Road to the Sweetwater. They left the California Road (about four companies of cavalry) at either the South Pass or Wagon Wheel Gap on the Sweetwater and went directly north to Lodge Pole Creek and along to Powder River. It was more than 150 miles from Wagon Wheel Gap to Powder River. Our guide was James Bridger and Colonel Plumb had Raphael Montoio, a Mexican, who was captured at Sonora, Old Mexico, by Apaches and by the Apaches sold to the Cheyenne Indians, who lived about the Black Hills and roamed over that country for years. Bridger was at that time very old–rather superannuated. We were three days without fresh water–only had very strong alkali water, which was not fit for man or beast. Bridger took them to a creek and when they got there the water had dried up until there was just a little alkali water (a strong solution of alkali) in the bottom. Major Anderson took a drink of that and burned his mouth.
>
> Col. Moonlight was along and it was at this place that there was a threatened mutiny against him. The moon was shining very brightly and one of the men took advantage of that fact to say "Moonlight we are not going to follow you; there is too much Damn moonlight here." Some of the men were desperate with thirst and hardship and refused to obey the commands of Col. Moonlight. Moonlight was exhausted and gave up and in a manner relinquished the command to Plumb. Then Plumb asked Barber if he could not lead them out of the difficulty and take them to water. Mr. Barber told them to go due east towards the range he saw, which he supposed to be mountains, and that they would find water. They came to a little steep cove in which snow had drifted during the winter and which had not melted. The horses rushed in and ate this snow–some of the men also got some of it to eat. Barber went up the mountain over the range and came down to a beautiful stream of clear, pure water on the other side. The horses were unmanageable and plunged into the stream–they could not be controlled–and some of them went in over their heads–Barber's horse did this. They camped there

about forty-eight hours. Some of the men had a little hardtack and Plumb had a can of tomatoes. Barber had a can of condensed coffee. Colonel Plumb intended his tomatoes for Maj. Anderson, who had been burned by the alkali and a few of the other soldiers. He told Mr. Barber to rake out a few of the coals from the fire and Barber did–Plumb put his tomatoes on these coals and was busy talking to Barber and the tomatoes got too hot and just as he was about to open the can it exploded and threw the tomatoes up in a big cottonwood tree. Colonel Plumb ran around and picked up little bunches of tomatoes and put them on crackers and gave them to the sick men. It was at this place they used up the two quarts of condensed coffee of Mr. Barber's. This condensed coffee had sugar and cream in it and had a screw-topped can. There was also a silver-plated spoon–a nice one.

They went back to Sweetwater to the garrison or station at Independence Rock, it was also a stage station. They did not find any Indians although they had followed their trail up, but the Indians had scattered going way north. From Independence Rock, they went back to Platte Bridge.

This expedition spelled the end of any real respect the men had for Colonel Moonlight and stoked the fires of jealousy that Moonlight held for Plumb. It also served to increase tensions between the 11th Kansas and the 11th Ohio regiments.

On May 28th, Private William T. Bonwell had started to write a letter home to his mother, wherein he described the situation at Camp Dodge:

This is one of my lonely eavnings [evenings] and I will try to while away time for a while by conversing with you through the silent agency of the pen. We ar [are] in camp it is Sunday and oh how lonely all tho there is some excitemente [excitement] in camp aboute [about] the Indians they have our ration train coreld [corralled] aboute 50 miles below here. We have sent reenforcements to them and now the telegraph is cut on both sides of us and we ar looking hourely for an attack but still the thoughts of a battle field or the war howls of the red savage fails to drive away the thoughts of home and friends to the soldiers.

The Indians have bin [been] hovering around our camp for time two days. Last night we discovered two of their pickets a watching our camp. The colonel dispatched myself and one other man to go to them. It was just getting dark and they was laying on a high ridg [ridge] and when we got in aboute [about] a quarter of a mile of them thay [they] fled leaving us in the dark. They have the mountains on us and we cannot go to them withoute [without] there pickets finding us oute [out] then they travel.

Mother our litle [little] camp looks like it was almost diserted. [deserted]

It is so warm through the middle of the day that the boys all strik [strike] for the pinery only those that ar [are] on duty. I can se [see] our pickets on the hill to the east and the north of camp and now and then se [see] a soldier of move up from some part of camp with a long look to the east and a sigh. He will through [throw] himself down in some shade to dream of home and friends long left behinde [behind].

Private Bonwell never got a chance to finish that letter. On June 3rd, a small band of Native Americans fired on Platte Bridge Station in an attempt to draw out the soldiers into an ambush. Plumb was the ranking officer in the area and responded with a detachment of 11th Kansas soldiers. He submitted the following report to headquarters at Fort Laramie summarizing the Native American attack.

> Headquarters
> Eleventh Kans. Cav.
> Camp Dodge, near Platte Bridge, Dakota
> 4th June 1865
>
> I have the honor to report that on Saturday the 3rd instant about 3 P.M. a party of ten Indians dashed down to the river bank opposite and fired upon Platte Bridge Station. The garrison returned the fire, wounding a pony. The Indians then fell back. Learning of this by messenger from the station, I took 10 men

from Co. "B" 11th Kans. Cav. & leaving word for 20 more of Cos. "A" & "F" to follow speedily as possible proceeded to the station and taking with me from there 10 of Co. "G" 11th Ohio Cav. Started in pursuit. A hard chase of five miles brought us up within shooting distance of the Indians & a running fight ensued—which resulted in one Indian pony being killed and his Indian being wounded. Over one-half of the detachment had fallen behind, on account of their horses not being able to keep up, and the Indians made an effort to turn the scale by suddenly wheeling about and charging upon us but failing to induce a corresponding movement on our part, they scattered and ran off at a rate of speed that showed that their previously comparatively lagging gait had some ulterior purpose in view. This purpose was quite apparent immediately after, as a party of about 60 Indians came charging down the bottom of Dry Creek half a mile to our left with the apparent purpose of getting between us and the station & cutting off the stragglers. But at this time the detachment of Cos. "A" & "F" appeared in sight & the Indians wheeled about and we pursued as rapidly as possible. A small portion of the party being able to keep within shooting distance of their rear guard for a mile or two. Some 6 or 7 of "A" & "F" Cos. & one of Co. "G" 11th Ohio pursued a party to the right & considerably in advance and were ambushed by about 30 Indians, front & rear, & being somewhat scattered & having exhausted the charges of their revolvers in the long chase, were unable to hold their ground until assistance could come up & Privates, William T. Bonwell Co. "F" 11th Kans. & Stahlnecker Co. Co. "G" 11th Ohio were killed. The former was scalped. The latter was saved from mutilation by the bravery of Private Martin of Co. "A" who threw himself into a ravine close by and drove the Indians off with his carbine. These men would probably have escaped if their horses had not been shot & fallen with them. Private Bonwell's falling on him binding him firmly to the earth. This advance party had shot an Indian, killing him & part of them were catching the Indian's horse when they dashed upon them making a complete surprise. After this, the Indians went off more rapidly than ever & I recalled the men and ceased pursuit. The men all behaved with their usual bravery.

The Indians were mostly armed with firearms—some having both rifles and revolvers. They were well-mounted and had besides about 20 extra ponies. The consequences of lack of corn for our animals were painfully apparent after the first two miles of the chase. They cannot compete with the Indian's horses even for that distance on rough ground. One Indian is known to have been killed and from four to six wounded severely. The bodies of our men who were killed were brought to camp & buried today with military honors. The affair was the first experience of the kind most of the men had ever had and was of value to them. It will also serve to show the Indians that they may expect to fight often as an occasion is presented.

      Very Respectfully,
      Your Obed. Servt.
      P.B. Plumb
      Lt. Col. 11th Kans. Cav.

Insufficient supplies and rations for the regiments out west were ongoing issues. As Plumb referenced in his letter, lack of feed for their horses had a detrimental effect on their ability to pursue the Native Americans for any length of time. In addition to food shortages, the soldiers also dealt with a lack of ammunition. The 11th Kansas was armed with a variety of carbines (Smith, Starr, Hall, and others) as well as revolvers. Some men did not have carbines and only carried revolvers. Each carbine took a different type of ammunition, which made completely supplying the regiment difficult.

Plumb did not always remain at Camp Dodge. He was often called to Fort Laramie or rode out to one of the smaller telegraph outposts under his command. These trips were often fraught with danger, as Thomas Barber later recalled to Connelley:

> Here [at Platte Bridge Station] Plumb got a telegram to report to Fort Laramie and Plumb and Barber went to Fort Laramie. Plumb said to Barber, "Tom I want five or six good men and I want you to pick them out for me." Plumb knew that Barber would know what he wanted, good men with good horses.
> On the way down, about forty miles east of Platte Bridge they came to a point in the road where a Cedar thicket came from the river right up to the road on the left, and on the right had a

deep ravine on the mountainside full of timber. Colonel Plumb halted his men and instructed them to look to their arms and have them ready for business and told them if they would have any trouble it would be at this place as the timber would thoroughly cover the hiding place of the Indians and they could come close to the road. They started on a gallop to get past this part of the road and every man had his pistol ready to shoot. They went in double file [two abreast] and the men on the left side were to watch the left of the road and those on the right to look out for the right side. Colonel Plumb saw the first Indian and fired the first shot, and every man on the right side of the command fired in that direction. They learned from the old Frenchman [Louis Guinard], who was married to a Squaw and was Station Agent and toll man at Platte Bridge, that there were nine Indians killed, that is counting those that were wounded and died afterwards. Colonel Plumb who fired the first shot, from the command, said the Indians fired before he did—they did not hit anyone. The trip to Fort Laramie was a record-breaking one—Plumb said the trip could not be again made in so short a time. The horses were good and the one ridden by Plumb was a beautiful roan given him by Raphael [Montoio]. At Fort Laramie Plumb and Barber separated—the escort of Colonel Plumb went back to Platte Bridge and left Colonel Plumb at Fort Laramie and Barber did not see him again in Wyoming.

Plumb's diary confirms Barber's timeline and also gives mention of a friendly-fire incident that luckily caused no harm.

Monday June 5, 1865.
Leave Platte Bridge at 12 M with Barber, Barnes, Rafail [Rebfield], Leighton [Letcher] for Ft. Laramie. Arrive at D.C. [Deer Creek] at 6:30 & take supper with Lt. Green, Co. K having camped there on its way to La Prelle. At 9 start for Box Elder 12 miles distant where Maj. Adams battalion is camped. Approached camp at 12 am. Fired on by picket no damage done. Camp until daylight.

Tuesday June 6, 1865.

At daylight leave camp and go to La Prelle 8 miles distant. Maj. A's battalion got in soon after. Wait until 9 when leave for Boater accompanied by Maj. Adams. Arrive at 1 P.M. make acquaintance of Capt. Lefelt & Lt. Foid 3 U.S.–part of command garrisoning post. Leave at 3:30 for Horse Shoe 25 miles distant. Cross Elkhorn 15 miles out & arrive at H. S. at 8 P. M. Get supper at station. Lt. Van Antwerp & detachment present.

Wednesday, June 7, 1865.
Leave at 4 A.M. Go 3 miles to spring & graze an hour. Go 7 miles further and stop an hour on Little Bitter Cottonwood. Go to 9 mile Ranch on Platte & stop 30 minutes to graze–& go on to Laramie arriving at 1:30 P.M. 38 miles from H.S.

While at Fort Laramie, Plumb received orders to go to Fort Halleck and remain there. His orders were to protect Ben Holliday's Overland Mail route from Native American attack, while still overseeing the telegraph route.

Before leaving Fort Laramie, Plumb penned a letter to Governor Samuel Crawford of Kansas petitioning for the discharge of the men of the 11th Kansas. In his view, and the view of the vast majority of the regiment, they had enlisted for a term of 3 years or the duration of the war. A war that was now over, and had been for nearly two months. They had not enlisted to go west and fight Native Americans, they had signed up to preserve the Union and their free state of Kansas.

> Fort Laramie, Dakota, 10th June, 1865.
> Gov. S.J. Crawford,
> Topeka, Kansas.
> Dear Sir:
> You are undoubtedly aware that by a recent order the War Department has directed the muster-out, immediately, of all Cavalry whose term of service expired on or before the first day of October next. This order, if carried out, would enable the men of the Eleventh Kansas to get to their homes about one month before the expiration of their service–which ends the 15th day of September next, though most of the enlistments date one month earlier. But General Connor, Commanding District of the Plains

has directed that there shall be no present action taken under this order and there is now every prospect that the men will be detained here until fall, unless this order of Gen. Connor can be modified.

The Eleventh is composed largely of farmers, whose pecuniary interests have suffered materially during the time they have been in the service. It is of the utmost importance to these men that they get home as early as the middle of August. Two weeks in August is worth more to them than a year's wages. Having served the Government faithfully for nearly three years this class of men, at least, have a right to claim immediate discharge, now that the war, for service during which they enlisted, is ended. It is stated that Gen. Connor has authority from the War Department for his order.

Now, Governor, I think I can reasonably ask you, on behalf of the men of the Eleventh to use your influence, at once, to have this exception removed, and the men ordered home with the remainder of the troops of the same class.

> Very respectfully yours,
> (Sd) P.B. Plumb,
> Lt. Col. 11th Ks. Cav.

It is not known what efforts Governor Crawford may have made on their behalf, but the men of the 11th Kansas were not discharged along with their fellow cavalry soldiers of other regiments. Plumb was a strong believer in fairness in all dealings, and the fact that his regiment was neither treated squarely by the federal government nor received the same treatment as other regiments angered him greatly. Later in life, while on the Senate floor, he referred to this incident and the callous disregard the War Department seemed to have for the lives and livelihoods of the common soldier.

The following letter dated June 15, 1865, was published in the *Leavenworth Times*, by an anonymous soldier of Company H. It was written from Horseshoe Station and describes the conditions in the area as well as the morale of the men.

Dear Sir: I notice that other Kansas regiments occasionally ventilate their whereabouts through the columns of your paper, and I propose to do the same for the 11th Regiment Kansas Cavalry.

We left Fort Riley February 20th, arriving at Fort Kearney, March the 4th. From there we continued our march until we passed Fort Laramie, when the dividing up of the regiment commenced, with headquarters at Camp Dodge, near Platte Bridge, D.T., April the 18th, since which time we have been employing ourselves in scouts, escorts, carrying mails, &c. Some of us have been out as far as Three Crossings, and one detachment is now on escort to South Pass. The regiment has lost two killed, one near Deer Creek and one near Platte Bridge. Our trip out was an exceedingly hard one, on account of the severity and inclemency of the weather, which does pretty much as it pleases here. It snows, rains, freezes, blows, is calm and hot; all these changes occur so rapidly that you are led to believe that they all exist at once. I believe that if the Government would fence this country in that it would make a good Botany Bay for rebels and other criminals, and prove more efficacious than capital punishment. In speaking of the regiment, Companies E and C, who were ordered to Fort Larned from Fort Riley, and Co. G, which was left at Fort Leavenworth, neither of which have been with the regiment since, are not included.

As to the Indians, their main object seems to be plunder. It seems to be an utter impossibility to make any movement against them without their receiving information thereof in due time to make good their escape.

The majority of the men are becoming much dissatisfied with being made an exception to the order from the War Department discharging volunteers. They consider that they have performed their duty, and the object for which they enlisted (the crushing of the rebellion) having been attained, those who have families are anxious to return to them, and those who have none yet are on nettles to get back to make arrangements for having them before cold weather sets in. I should think that under these circumstances we should have the sympathy of all the Kansas fair sex—more especially of those who wish to procure good husbands (I'm supplied myself). But seriously, why is this outrage being perpetrated against a regiment which, in time of direct need, stood unflinchingly at their post, without a murmur, and to which Kansas was wont to point with pride. I refer to these matters not as a boast, but it seems that the willing horse is being rode a little too far. The indications now are that we will be called upon to go on the Powder River Expedition. This will, in all probability, take until the time at which, by limitation, nearly the whole regiment should be mustered out and at home. Why embitter, by misuse men's feelings who were ever ready and willing to perform their entire duty, and more, so long as the necessities of their country required it?

No officer ever had the respect and confidence in a deeper and fuller sense than has Lieut. Col. P.B. Plumb, commanding the regiment. Company H feel especially favored also in their Company Commander, Lieut. Sherman Bodwell.

We, in times gone by, have grubbed, piled, and burned brush, dug wells, &c., for the benefit of somebody, and now I would suggest that if some honest, enterprising individual would only get a Government contract for furnishing hay out here, and manage so as to have the 11th detailed to put it up for him, he might make a nice thing of it.

We have all sorts of wild beasts, vermin, and insects out here. Some are shy and distant, whilst others are quite sociable, and seem inclined to form our acquaintance. Among the most tenacious and impertinent of these are the mosquitoes, of which, in places, there are a million to the square foot, (it's a fact,) and were it not for the rich and nutritious wittles [food] that we get, their long bills and oft-repeated draws would prove most disastrous to our well-being.

As to reading matter, we occasionally get the CONSERVATIVE, Missouri Democrat, State Record, and Christian Advocate. When these are worn out we fall back upon our library, which consists of one songbook, a dilapidated Harper's Monthly, a dream book, and the "history of the four kings' (several copies). In conclusion, ladies of Kansas, if you feel any interest in our welfare, and expect ever again to see our weather-beaten phizes [faces], we implore you to come to our rescue; and, with the hope that your efforts will, as they always should, prove successful, I will for the present bid you and Mr. Editor adieu.

   E, Co. H, 11th Kan. Cav.

On June 11th, Plumb set out from Fort Laramie to Fort Halleck, situated between the current cities of Laramie and Cheyenne in present-day Wyoming. Plumb's diary entries give insight as to the timeline of his movements:

> Sunday, June 11, 1865.
> Order from Gen. Conner for me to go to Camp Collins, Colorado with 4 cos. of 11th.
>
> Monday, June 12, 1865.
> Bamer, Barber, Cowan & Leighton (Jr) start with [blank] for P. bridge.
>
> Tuesday, June 13, 1865.
> Order from Gen. C so changed as to send me to Halleck with two cos. Two to go to Collins, Co L. arrives from Horse Shoe.
>
> Wednesday, June 14, 1865.
> Sioux Indians being taken to Julesburg wheel & kill Capt. Foutz & three men. Dispatch received at about middle afternoon.
>
> Thursday, June 15, 1865.
> Command gets across river easily in the morning.
>
> Saturday, June 24, 1865.
> Arrived at Halleck at 2 P.M. accompanied by Lt. Booth & 20 men under Lt. Thornton. Met Col. Potter & Capt. Humphrey Mills.

Plumb's service at Fort Halleck was largely without incident, and while he was in command of protecting the Overland Mail Route, it suffered no disruptions. Owner, Ben Holliday, was so impressed with

Plumb's work that he offered him a position with his company to continue to oversee the route. Plumb politely declined the offer.

While Plumb was at Fort Halleck, companies I, K, L, and a few men from Company H were still up at Platte Bridge Station when the post was attacked on July 26, 1865. The resulting Battle of Platte Bridge claimed the life of a young Lt. Caspar Collins of the 11th Ohio, son of Colonel William O. Collins of the same regiment. Platte Bridge Station was later renamed Fort Caspar in his honor (there already being a Camp Collins in Colorado). Collins led a detachment of 11th Kansas soldiers across the bridge in an effort to escort the wagon train of Sgt. Amos Custard, also 11th Kansas, to the post safely. Unbeknownst to all of the soldiers, a large party of Native American warriors consisting of members of the Lakota, Cheyenne, and Arapaho tribes had congregated and were laying in wait to ambush them. In the ensuing fight, four men of the 11th Kansas were killed.

Later that morning, Custard's wagon train came into view of the post and was surrounded and attacked by the Native Americans. Custard's detachment of Company H held off the attackers for about four hours, all in plain view of the men at the post who were unable to aid them in the face of such overwhelming numbers. Custard and his men were brutally tortured with hot irons and killed and mutilated viciously.

Lt. George Walker had led a small detachment out to try to repair the telegraph lines to send word for reinforcements and ammunition, and was also attacked. The total casualties at the end of July 26th were one officer and one enlisted man of the 11th Ohio killed, 26 11th Kansas soldiers killed, and nine or ten men wounded. This was the largest loss suffered by the regiment in a single engagement, and by Plumb's feelings, a fight that they should not have even been in.

Also in July, Plumb was promoted from Lt. Colonel to Colonel, but as he was leaving the service, he was never mustered in at that rank. On August 13, 1865 Plumb and his men began the arduous month long trek back to Kansas, to Fort Leavenworth to be mustered out of the service. On September 13th he was discharged and on September 29th he finally returned home to Emporia. He wrote in his diary:

> Friday, September 29, 1865.
> Home from the wars <u>forever</u>.

Chapter 11

Back to Civilian Life

Plumb had made plans with his brother to start a cattle ranch prior to the close of the war. George recalled:

> Before we left the army my brother and I went into partnership. I followed him up to Fort Riley when the regiment was going across the plains. He said, "George, come go along." I said no, I had had enough, I was going home. He said it was the only legitimate business as long as the war lasted. I said father and mother were getting old and I was going home. They had already sold the old home place to Preston and bought one nearer town. He said then for me to go back and put up some feed on that place and in the fall we would buy some stock. I had already bought some horses and sheep and father was looking after them for me. Preston said, "let's enter into an agreement," and we wrote out a very detailed partnership agreement. I came back and raised the feed; in the fall he came home. We bought sheep and horses and cattle and I took care of them.
>
> We had a family living on the place and Preston was there with me some of the time and we boarded with them. We would work thru the day and at night we would talk our plans over. He would say how this is something like living, being independent, and having one's freedom. I have been working for the public all my life and paying my own board. He had unloaded every care and was just as happy as a boy. He had a fine gray mare he got while in the army and got to going to town nights and would be gone pretty late. One morning he said he was awful tired, and had not got in till two o'clock. Finally, he told me he had spent that night with Judge Ruggles, a brainy fellow. Preston had gotten word from a cousin named Loofborrow in Iowa that had taken a law course and he went to Judge Ruggles to see if he would take him into his office as the fellow was looking for a place to locate. Ruggles said "Why wouldn't you come in with

me?" and before morning they had decided on a partnership but Preston kept on with me on the farm for a while.

Following his discharge in September 1865, Preston Plumb had kept in touch with young Carrie Southwick whom he'd met in Ohio before his service. Carrie was now 18 years old, and for Christmas of that year, he gifted her a beautiful engraved leather photo album adorned with semi-precious stones and with the inscription, "To my darling wife." The matter of engagement and the terms "fiancé" and "fiancée" were not commonly used at that time, and it is likely that his reference to her as his "wife" meant that they were engaged.

Plumb returned to his law office, but did not immediately marry Carrie. The reason for the delay is unknown, but it is possible he waited until he had a proper home for her to live in. Prior to his service, he'd been living at the newspaper office, on the family farm, and in his law office. None of which would be suitable to bring a new wife to, let alone start a family in. Emporia was still a new town, only 8 years old after the war, and although it was growing, it was not an urban sprawl with housing readily available. Structures needed to be built and that took time.

In 1866 Plumb was reelected to the State Legislature and began serving in January 1867. He was also elected Speaker of the House for that term and led the state legislature through several important issues. Kansas was beginning to boom with the influx of new settlers and businesses following the close of the Civil War. Establishing the necessary infrastructure was important, and a number of public buildings needed to be financed and built. There were also new amendments to the state constitution to consider, as well as numerous claims for damages resulting from Confederate General Sterling Price's raid into Kansas. Plumb kept the session on track and focused, and it accomplished more in that single session than it had in many previous years.

Following the close of the state legislature on March 3rd, he began his return trip to Ashtabula, Ohio to marry Miss Caroline Southwick, traveling with his friend, Milton Reynolds.

> At the close of the Legislature in 1866 [sic 1867] Senator Plumb, then speaker of the house, had important business east, as far as his old home in Ohio. He had left his best girl behind him. I was going east that spring myself on a little matter of business to bring a wife and baby back to the blooming prairies of the Sunflower State. Mr. Speaker Plumb and myself traveled together. I was not aware of his mission. We got water bound up

We find the following in the Ashtabula, O., Telegraph, of the 9th inst:

"MARRIED—On the evening of the 8th inst., at the residence of the bride's mother, in Ashtabula, by Rev. Mr. Tuthill, Col. P. B. PLUMB, of Kansas, and Miss CARRIE SOUTHWICK."

From the above it will be seen that our gallant friend, hitherto invincible in battle with the Confederate States, has been fatally wounded by the young archer, of the United State, and Carrie—d off the field. The fair bride was certainly fortunate when she took her chance at the matrimonial lottery, and, like little Jack Horner, "stuck in her thumb and hauled out a PLUMS." We hope that Fortune may treat the Colonel as generously as he treated the printers.

Above: Wedding announcement from the Emporia News for Preston and Carrie Plumb, March 22, 1867, Newspapers.com Below: Wedding portraits of the couple. Courtesy Carrie Clarke and Kenneth Spencer Research Library, University of Kansas.

in Illinois by the excessive and unusual spring floods of that year. We camped in a little country town and slept together in the second story of a little rickety country hotel. We were expecting a train along about daylight. In the middle of the night, a train was switching on the side track; Plumb being naturally a little nervous under the circumstances and annoyed at the hindrance to his eastern trip, supposed our train was coming and jumping out over myself, raised the window hurriedly and was about to jump as I grabbed him by some useful article of apparel, I don't think it was his pants, and probably saved the life of a future United States senator. When I learned a couple of weeks after, he had got married down in Ohio, his nervousness and anxiety to travel eastward was readily explainable.

Mr. and Mrs. Plumb, aged 29 and 20, respectively, returned to Emporia, arriving April 1, 1867, and lived in "a one-story, three-roomed house at the corner of Merchant and Second Streets. It was a box house–that is built of boards put on upright and the cracks or joints covered with battens. One of the rooms was a lean-to kitchen." They lived at this location for a few months before moving onto Plumb's property and new farmhouse, where they resided for the next three years. Almost immediately, the Plumbs started their family with the birth of their daughter Mary in 1868 and their son Amos Hinsdale "Dale" in 1869. Friend of the family, Mrs. Abigail Morse said:

> He [Plumb] was a believer in thorough and effective work everywhere and had no patience with the slovenly farming which many of the settlers did. He moved onto his farm to show them how a farm should be run. "And," said Mrs. Morse, "When he got on the farm he found that Mrs. Plumb was the better farmer." She was always his true helpmate and when her health failed he was in such distress as few husbands undergo. He depended on her counsel and advice in all things.

Carrie Plumb was plagued by ongoing health issues her entire life. It is not known exactly what illness she suffered from, but it often left her weak and bedridden. She was the youngest of her family—her brother Alfred Southwick, twenty years her senior, would go on to gain notoriety for inventing the electric chair. She came from a family of outspoken abolitionists, and like her husband, enjoyed serving her community and working on projects for the benefit of the town of Emporia.

> Mrs. Morse relates that once these four women [Mrs. Perley, Mrs. Plumb, Mrs. Storrs, and Mrs. Morse] were out in the country when a settler desired to dig a well. He was uncertain as to where to dig it, fearing that he might miss the subterranean spring or vein of water. He was trying to locate the water with a divining rod, which was the forked branch cut from a peach tree. This would not "work" in his hands, nor would it do any better in the hands of any of the women except Mrs. Plumb. In her hands, it would turn towards the ground at a certain place, and all the women could not grip it with sufficient force to prevent this turning while Mrs. Plumb held it. The well was dug at the spot indicated and a good well it proved. Mrs. Morse told Senator Plumb that his wife would prove the salvation of that part of Kansas as she could discover water on the dry prairies.

Plumb was again reelected to the state legislature in November 1867, but did not serve as Speaker during the 1868 session. Meanwhile, his law firm of Ruggles & Plumb quickly became one of the most successful and lucrative firms in the state.

> The firm of Ruggles and Plumb was at the head of the bar of the State. Johnston recalls that they always had many cases before the United States Courts at Leavenworth, and he saw them try cases there. They were both good lawyers, and they tried their cases hard–for all that was in them. "And," said Judge Johnston, "they were hard fellows to beat in a lawsuit." Plumb was a fine real estate lawyer. The firm had all the good business in the counties around Emporia–Morris, Osage, Marion, Greenwood, Lyon, Woodson, and others. They also had business for men to the southwest of Emporia in the country where counties were unorganized. Their business was said to be worth more than that of any other law firm in Kansas. They had a heavy business from stockmen–all the cattlemen employing them. In this business, Plumb rode over the country in buggies and on horseback. He rode all over that part of Kansas where the business of his firm

took him, and also far to the south and southwest. And he was a hard rider. Plumb argued his cases closely and was a ready talker.

Working as a lawyer following the close of the Civil War was a much more rough and tumble enterprise than the legal profession is nowadays. A story about one of Plumb's court cases printed many years after the fact illustrates that point well.

> When Plumb was in El Dorado on a county seat case, he got up and said: "May it please the court"–but the court was not pleased, for the judge noticed that [Plumb] had an eight-inch navy revolver strapped around him. Calling the sheriff, he whispered to him to find out how many revolvers the lawyers had on. The sheriff in a few minutes reported seven. The judge got down off the bench, cleared his throat, and walked into the adjoining room. Opening his grip [bag], he took out a black bottle and took a drink. Then he strapped a pair of navy revolvers around him and returned to the bench. Colonel Plumb caught on in a minute, and wondered what was up. The judge, after smacking his lips to get the whiskey taste off them, said: "This court thinks it understands itself; Colonel Plumb you can go on with your arguments.' And he did without further interruption.

Even though his law firm was at the head of the bar in the state, Plumb never stopped being that enthusiastic pioneer who had walked to Kansas nearly a decade before. Senator Stephen Elkins of West Virginia met Plumb when he first arrived in Kansas and remained close with him. "I stopped off in Emporia once in returning from New Mexico to make Plumb a visit and talk over some business matters. I remember very well Plumb's fondness for swimming and his going out barefoot in his shirt sleeves to the stream near Emporia to swim, and returning to his law office, sunburnt, the very picture of health."

Plumb's work as a lawyer required him to travel often and this created a strain on the young family. Carrie Plumb recalled that "he wrote [Carrie's] mother that he should quit the practice of law and stay at home and try to get acquainted with his wife. This letter was not mailed when written and Carrie saw it lying on the table. It was the first intimation she had that he would quit the law, and she was much pleased. He went downtown and before he came back had accepted the Presidency of the Emporia National Bank."

Emporia National Bank

While President of the Emporia National Bank, Plumb proved to be generous and fair with its customers and stakeholders. His leadership guided the bank through the financial crises of 1873 when many banks within the United States went bankrupt and dissolved. He was always eager to help however he could. Accepting this position also reunited him with Captain L.T. Heritage, whom he'd served with in the 11th Kansas Infantry and rescued at the Battle of Prairie Grove in December 1862. Heritage had been severely wounded during the fight and discharged from the service not long afterward. He walked with a limp due to his wound and had found work as cashier at the bank.

> "Mr. Plumb was very kind to the Welsh people," said Mr. L.W. Lewis. In 1871 Lewis was taken sick with typhoid fever. He had been contracting and had built a bridge over the Cottonwood River. He was wishing to go to the Atchison Branch, between Topeka and Atchison, to continue contracting. This was unfortunate, for Lewis had very little money and owed some to workmen. He had ordered his tools sent to the Atchison branch, but someone having a claim of $132.00 brought suit and attached the tools, so they could not be removed. The foreman came to Emporia and told Lewis how the matter stood. When the physician came on his call he saw that something had disturbed Lewis and inquired what it was. Mrs. Lewis explained it to the physician who went out after saying that Lewis should not worry about the matter–that he would bring in a man who could attend to the matter. He soon returned with Colonel Plumb. The physician told Lewis to tell Plumb all about the matter, but in doing so to take his time and not get excited. This Lewis did. When he concluded Plumb said. "Mr. Lewis, do not trouble yourself about this matter. The sale is tomorrow. I will go to Cottonwood Falls and attend to the matter better than you could if you were well. You do just what the doctor tells you to do and leave this matter to me." Plumb went the next day as he said he would. He could not prevent the sale, but he paid all the bills–judgment, costs–everything, and said to the foreman that he could send the tools to Atchison at once.

When Lewis got well enough to get around he went to see Plumb and asked him how much he owed him. Plumb showed him the bills he had paid and said that was all Lewis owed him. He would not accept a cent for his services, nor would he take any interest on the money he had advanced.

In 1877 Lewis came back to Emporia from Colorado. He had no money, but went to work in a lumber yard for $1.50 a day. A bridge was to be built at Hartford and Lewis put in a bid on it. He got the contract and the Commissioners required a bond. He could give no bond, as he supposed, but finally thought of Plumb. He took the bond to Plumb and explained the situation. Plumb looked at the bond and told Lewis to sign it, which he did. The contract was immediately closed up when he presented the bond with Plumb's name. But he had no tools and again went to Plumb and told him he had nothing to build the bridge with. "How much do you need for tools," he asked Lewis. "About $250.00," replied Lewis. Plumb filled out a blank note and Lewis signed it. Then Plumb endorsed it and paid Lewis $250.00. Lewis said he thought the interest was taken out in advance. Plumb said to wait and see how the matter turned out. When the bridge was completed, Lewis was paid for it and went in to see Plumb, and to pay his note. Plumb said the amount was $250.00. Lewis said there ought to be some interest in addition, but Plumb would take no interest, Lewis was not permitted to pay any interest. "I have a warm place here," said Lewis, placing his hand on his breast, "for Senator Plumb that will last as long as I live."

Mr. George Newman of Emporia recalled two instances to Connelley regarding Plumb's work with the bank:

Mr. Newman came to Kansas in 1867 and says that he had a limited capital with which to begin business in Emporia. He engaged in the general merchandising business. A short time after he engaged in this business, he purchased an undivided half interest in the building where he is now located. In this purchase, he entered into a contract with the owner of the other interest in the building to make certain improvements on the premises. These improvements were such as were required in the building to be used for a general store. The man from whom he purchased the building seemed not to know very much about Mr. Newman. The purchase was completed in the bank, of which Col. Plumb was interested. When they were turning over the deed the seller demanded of Mr. Newman that he furnish a bond conditioned that he carry out the contract and Mr. Newman said that he was a stranger in town and did not know of any person to whom he could make application to furnish a bond, when the other party became excited and talked loud, saying the deal was off. Col. Plumb heard the conversation and came out of his office in the back part of the bank and demanded to know what was the trouble in closing up the deal. When it was explained to him, he said to the seller of the property that he might make out his bond and bring it to the bank and he would sign it, and the bank would sign it if that was demanded. The bond was made out and signed by Col. Plumb. Mr. Newman said that was the first real acquaintance that he had with Col. Plumb and his action gave him great confidence in Plumb and made him like him very much. It was the beginning of a friendship which lasted as long as Col. Plumb lived.

Another instance that came under the observation of Mr. Newman was in relation to the purchase of seed by the farmers for planting one year (1872) when the grasshoppers had destroyed all the crops and these farmers were compelled to replant. The country was new and the farmers were poor. They really had no money with which to buy these seeds. They came to town to see a man who kept seeds for sale, but he could not afford to sell them on credit as he was not financially able to do so. Some of these farmers talked to Col. Plumb about the situation, as all the people always did talk to him about any business they had in this part of the country. Col. Plumb told the seed man to take notes from these farmers for the seeds they required and bring these notes to the bank and he would personally see that the bank carried them until they could be paid. The farmers in this way procured the seeds they needed and did pay all the notes, except possibly one note. Mr. Newman believes one note was not paid.

T.H. Lewis settled in Emporia in 1870 and needed Plumb's help to save his homestead.

> Lewis took a homestead near the present town of Burrton. He could not be there all the time, and his friends there wrote him a settler was going to jump his claim and that he had better pre-empt it and save it. He concluded to do that, if he could raise the money. He had fifty dollars and needed one hundred and fifty more. He went into the bank and saw Captain Heritage, who wanted to know whom he could get for security. He could not get security. He went back to work and watched for Plumb to go by to his home for dinner and when he passed Lewis followed him around the corner and explained his needs. Plumb said for him to come into the bank when he got back from dinner, which he did. When Lewis went in Plumb told Heritage to let him have the money. Lewis saved his homestead and later sold it for $300 – all through the friendship of Plumb.

Plumb's generosity at the bank extended beyond the town of Emporia. John Maloy who came to Council Grove, Kansas in 1870 recalled:

> Plumb was always alert for the people, and he was the friend of the people. Many of the first settlers of Morris County borrowed money from him in the early days when times were hard. If his bank could not let them have the money, Plumb would loan them his own money. There are many well-to-do citizens about Council Grove whom Plumb tided over from year to year in the early days and carried until they could get on their feet.

In 1871 the Plumbs had welcomed the birth of their third child, Thomas Ewing Plumb. Thomas was named after Brigadier General Thomas Ewing, Jr. who Plumb had served under for a time during the war and who he knew well from his time as a state supreme court reporter before the war.

In February of 1873, tragedy struck the family. Little Thomas died of pneumonia, although the exact circumstances are unknown. There had been a major cold spell through the area just prior to this date, and shortly after, the family moved from the farm into town. It is possible that the case of pneumonia was brought on by some sort of accident involving the farm and the water nearby, which is why the family was quick to move into town taking up lodging in a townhouse building shared with Mrs. Abigail Morse.

Portrait of Senator Preston B. Plumb taken shortly after his election to the U.S. Senate in 1877. Image courtesy the Library of Congress.

Chapter 12

Mr. Plumb Goes to Washington

Although Plumb had kept busy at the Emporia National Bank and with his many business investments, he desired more. He had run unsuccessfully for U.S. Senator in the previous election, but in 1876 he tried again.

In December of 1876, Plumb wrote a letter to Leslie J. Perry, a fellow veteran and newspaperman in Paola, Kansas:

> The fact is, Perry, I want to be where I can <u>work</u> and help somebody else as well as myself. Doubtless I have seemed <u>weak</u> in sticking so tenaciously to the one ambition, when I could have gone off on to a bypath, and had what, and <u>more</u> perhaps, than I deserved. But I have felt that unless I was where I could accomplish something tangible I had better remain in private station. My ambition may have been too great–but it has been sincere–and in the main unselfish for I have really cared more to have a chance to do for the friends who have so tenaciously stood by me than for myself.

Elections for senators at this time were done through the state legislature. It was not until 1913 that the general public voted for senators directly with the adoption of the 17th Amendment to the U.S. Constitution. Judge Tom Ryan gave an interview with Connelley in 1910 in which he described the senatorial election in the Kansas state legislature and the political atmosphere at the time:

> I knew Senator Plumb from 1866 on, but not intimately until 1876, although Plumb, during all the period, was a very prominent man in Kansas. We were brought together in '76 more closely because of the political situation. I was nominated for Congress, and he was a candidate for the Senate. My District at that time was new,–there had been but one representative from that district before I was nominated. The incumbent, Brown from Hutchinson, was serving his first term. He was a good man. Kansas had three representatives at that time. Plumb was at the convention that nominated me,–I think he was a

delegate. He was very active in that campaign. I remember he made a speech that night at the convention in Wichita. I heard him make a good many speeches but I think that was the finest one I ever heard him make.

We were then, and ever after, close friends, politically and personally. There were several candidates for Congress at that time but I think there was but one ballot,–they began to change before the ballot was finished, and I was nominated on the first ballot.

Plumb was a candidate for the United State Senate at that time–that is to say, it was generally understood that he would be,–that was his political ambition, to go to the Senate. He had been a candidate once before. He was engaged in the banking business in Emporia at this time, and associated with others, I think, in the cattle business. He was a very active business fellow, and was connected with a good many public enterprises in those early days in the development of Kansas, because of his business ability. He was a good lawyer, and his law firm, Plumb and Ruggles, stood at the head of the bar of the state.

Connelley: Do you recall anything of the contest for the Senate the winter after you were elected?

Yes, I do. I was very much interested. Harvey was the incumbent and was a candidate for reelection. Governor Tom Osborne was a candidate. These with Plumb were the three principal candidates. Simpson of Paola was a candidate but he was a friend of Plumb. In those days he was a very shrewd politician. Osborne was a good politician too and a very good man. I think there was not a bit of bitterness engendered so far as the candidates were concerned. If there was any feeling at all it was on the part of Harvey who thought he should have been returned. So far as Simpson was concerned he had quite a following and Tom Osborne was strong but there was no bitterness at all. I don't recall any particular issue on which the election turned. There was the highest respect for Senator

Harvey but he was regarded as a little slow, while Plumb was like lightning. The others were all a good deal more active than Harvey, but the latter was an excellent man, clean reliable in every way, and made a creditable Senator. My active association with Senator Plumb began after that election. My support of Plumb for the Senate at that time, was perhaps, in a sense, the logic of the situation. Although Harvey and Osborne both had a good many friends in my county, still Shawnee was radically for Plumb. The Topeka people at that time felt very keenly the fact that the Congressional representatives of the State had never secured any public building for the capital, and they thought they were entitled to it. In these times there would be no doubt about getting such things, but that was in '76, and Kansas had been struggling to get public buildings ever since she became a State in '61. Now it would be a great surprise to find a community like that so intensely interested in so small a matter.

As I was going into Congress, I very much desired the support and cooperation that I felt sure I would have with Plumb in the Senate, and so I was interested from that standpoint. We got our public building the first session. It was a pretty hard job though to get it because Leavenworth did not want Topeka to have one until she could have one herself. Phillips was the representative from the Leavenworth District and he had been in Congress two or three terms, and so we had that sort of opposition to overcome right there. Besides, it was a Democratic House, and not very much interested in states like Kansas.

Colonel John C. Carpenter recalled the same election to Connelley in 1910:

In '77 there were four candidates for Senator,–Judge T.C. Sears who was General Attorney for the Missouri, Kansas Texas R.R., with headquarters at Parsons, and strongly urged by that element. Then there was Ex-Governor T.A. Osborne, and James M. Harvey, the incumbent in the office at that time. He had been elected to succeed Caldwell. Osborne had appointed Crosier after Caldwell's death to fill the vacancy till the

Legislature met and they elected Harvey. Then there was Walter T. Simons of Fort Scott,—at that time he lived at Osage Mission in this county. They were pretty equally divided in votes: I think if anything Harvey had a few the most. Plumb came next and then Sears and Simons were about equal with 28 or 30 votes apiece. In that day there were no party caucuses to nominate the Senatorial candidate. Each member of the Legislature, regardless of his party, voted directly for the man he desired to be elected. The result was after they started in to ballot, they balloted for several days without any change. This condition might continue for a whole session. Through the instrumentality of Sam Wood, a caucus was convened for the purpose of nominating a candidate. That was the first caucus that was ever held for Senator. That caucus was convened and everybody was invited. It was held in Union Hall in Topeka on Kansas Avenue. I think that J.J. Mohler of Salina was the chairman, but of that, I am not certain. There was still difficulty in deciding who should be the candidate. The followers of the four prominent candidates stuck to them at first in the caucus. Then they commenced to inject new names, and I think they voted on nearly every name in the state,—everybody got some votes. The caucus dwindled away until after midnight. At that hour the caucus did not have to exceed 35 present and they agreed on Judge Low of Fort Scott for Senator. With only 35 votes he did not stand any chance at all, when on joint ballot it required 82 votes to elect. The next day at 12 o'clock after meeting in joint convention Plumb was elected Senator on the first ballot, I think. The caucus had had the effect of eliminating and condensing so it was the means of making possible an election the next day. Plumb's forces were swelled by the majority of the Harvey men. After they left Harvey they were for Plumb,—Plumb knew that all the time. The Sears forces after they left him were for Plumb. Plumb's trouble was to keep Harvey from gathering strength,—to have Osborne and Simons stand firm, to hold their men, in order that the Harvey men might get discouraged. Plumb came up from the Tefft House and made his talk to the Legislature, and a very short one it was. I would not want you to say this, but he was the worst scared man you ever saw,–pale as a ghost. He realized it was a crisis.

Crisis though it may have been, Preston B. Plumb proved victorious and was elected as a U.S. Senator from Kansas. He would serve as senator alongside John James Ingalls, who had taken office in 1873. Plumb's first session as a Senator was a new experience for both him and his fellow senators. His personality was not that of the typical politician. He was there to work and had no interest in wasting time on any of the social aspects of being a senator. Judge Ryan continued:

> Plumb was a man who was not very much disposed to lay down and go to sleep in the Senate until he got a little old. You know there has always been a feeling in the Senate that the new Senator should be a listener and a spectator for awhile: must go through a sort of an apprenticeship. Plumb was not built for that sort of thing. I always thought the following was done to discipline him though I don't know. Plumb was very active in a certain measure and made one or two speeches on it in his vigorous forceful style, and although he did not have any help at all, he fought it to a finish, and my recollection is he insisted on an aye and no vote, and I guess Plumb voted alone, but he was right, absolutely right. The Senate soon learned that Plumb was a useful man. He was active right from the first. He was thoroughly informed regarding all subjects he handled and especially on those matters that came up in his committees. In all committee work he was a tremendous power, –almost the controlling power. Later he became a great power in the Senate in all matters of a financial character, including matters of revenue and expenditures and all constructive work. He was a marvelous senator and consulted on many matters. He wielded a tremendous influence in the Senate for years.

The bill Judge Ryan referenced wherein Plumb voted alone, was a bill for the relief of Dr. William A. Hammond. Dr. Hammond had been the Surgeon-General of the Army during the Civil War and was found guilty by court-martial of corruption and fraudulent purchases with government money. He was removed from his position and dismissed from the service. The bill to expunge Dr. Hammond's record originated in the House and was based largely on the fact that Dr. Hammond had become well respected in his profession since the war and was earning roughly $60,000 per year annually (roughly $1.8 Million in 2023 values). This bill came to the Senate on March 12, 1878, and although Plumb knew it would pass, he was fundamentally opposed to it. Plumb intimately knew the workings of military court-martials, as he served on them during the war. He stated:

> I was in hopes that someone of the Senators in favor of this bill would vouchsafe to the Senate an explanation of the reasons why it should pass. For myself, while I have no hope that the bill will fail to pass, I feel that I have a duty to perform which will not permit me to remain silent…It is, I think, an unwarrantable interference by Congress with the affairs of the Army and with the action of courts which it has established for the purpose of administering justice in the Army…It is in effect saying to persons aggrieved by the action of courts-martial that Congress can be induced by the operation of social and political influences to set aside that action. This inevitably weakens the authority and destroys discipline. I say no one certainly can impugn the justice, the good faith, or the kind-heartedness of Abraham Lincoln. He knew every single step of that trial which was taken. He was as well advised as any man could possibly have been of any ulterior purpose which might have been had in view by the Secretary of War,…After a patient and careful examination of the proceedings, he certified to them, and directed that the sentence of the court-martial be carried into effect.
>
> What do we find as a basis for this proposed action? This report is based upon the fact that this man is eminent. Congress, therefore, puts its action upon the ground that he is eminent…We are proposing here a way to reinstate this man alone in his former position in the army because he is eminent in his profession.

Following Plumb's speech, a vote was ordered resulting in 55 Yeas and 1 Nay. The single Nay vote coming from the new senator from Kansas.

Colonel O.E. Learnard echoed Judge Thomas Ryan's comments about how Plumb's unusual outgoing personality clashed with the expected meekness of new Senators.

When Learnard first went to Washington after Plumb's election to the Senate, Senators there accosted him, with, "What kind of fellow is this you have sent us from Kansas? He makes motions and sustains them with speeches and then alone votes for them! He acts like a wild fellow." "Just wait," said Learnard "and you fellows will be voting for his motions. He is all right in what he is doing and you will see it soon." And so it turned out. Plumb's manner of doing things, saying things, as well as his gestures and movements, were new to the Senate. They denoted an intensity and strenuousness not seen before in that body. It took the Senate some time to find out that there was method and force and power and strong personality in all that Plumb undertook to do in the Senate. The senators soon became his friends–many of them–and his followers–or if there ever was a leader in the Senate Plumb was one. Plumb was strong with the element that wished to do things, strong with people high in the financial world who wanted to build railroads and develop mines and improve states and territories.

Although Plumb was relatively well known within Kansas, this was his first foray onto the national stage. His fellow Kansas senator, Ingalls, had risen through the ranks and had made a name for himself in current affairs. Many remarked that Plumb and Ingalls made a good team as their personalities tended to play well off each other and provided a good balance. Rather quickly, Plumb also made a name for himself among senators with his innate grasp of facts, figures, policies, and laws. Judge Ryan added:

> In all public affairs, he was active, well-informed, and usually aggressive. His colleague, Ingalls, was a very different type of man. He was exceptionally brilliant but he was a man who was disposed to tear down or destroy. He was a feature of the United States Senate. Whenever Ingalls was to speak the galleries would be crowded, and generally, the House was pretty well represented over there because it was understood that there would be something interesting. With that representation in the Senate Kansas was made quite conspicuous and exerted a great influence. Plumb and Ingalls made a good team, so to speak. The representation in power and brilliancy was not exceeded by that

of any other state in the union, and that is saying a good deal. Each occupied his field fully. One was a powerful orator,–along his line of oratory Ingalls has never been equaled. On the other hand, Plumb in all other fields was away to the front. While Plumb was not a brilliant man, he was a man who talked with great force and clearness; he was logical and convincing, and he always had something to say,–he never talked unless he did. He had the capacity for all the practical fields of legislation. He was a constructive man,–he would tear down a shanty and construct a palace. Because of these qualities, he had become a tremendous power in national politics, consulted by all the leading men; shaping campaigns, from the matter of the details of the organization throughout the whole country, to the raising of the necessary funds to carry it out. He was a man of wonderful tact. He knew how to organize forces to secure the best results whether in business or politics. I speak of that in the broad national sense, not merely locally. He could make a rattling good campaign speech too. It was not a high grade of oratory but was pungent, clear, and convincing, - the kind that would make a fellow get out of his chair and throw up his hat.

The election of Plumb to the Senate thrust him into the spotlight, and to a certain extent, the family as well. Carrie Plumb was concerned that her health issues would burden her husband, and that she would not be able to fulfill her obligations socially as a senator's wife. She later recalled that, "He said that he did not want her to wear herself out in any such way. That his wife and children were more to him than any office in the world could be, and that if he could not hold his office without his wife's sacrificing herself in social work in Washington, he did not want it and would resign and come home to Emporia." Plumb never purchased a home in Washington, rather, he rented furnished rooms for his family. His children at the time of his election included Mary, Dale, and Ruth, ages 9, 8, and 3 respectively. Plumb himself was rather young, being only 39 years old when elected.

Chapter 13

A Thorough Kansan

Plumb spoke the Kansas language. In fact, he invented it; he did things; there was always a Kansas breeze about him; he blew in with a breath of the prairies on him. Plumb was Kansas.
– "Curley" Harrison

Plumb was new in Washington, but quickly found his footing. He was determined to better Kansas's situation in the union, and he wasn't going to change who he was to do it.

Once a Newsman, Always a Newsman

Plumb subscribed to nearly every paper in Kansas and read them all each week. He made it his business to know what the people of Kansas wanted before they even knew they wanted it. E.J. Edwards, a Washington D.C. newspaper correspondent, wrote about his visit to Plumb's office:

> I had occasion to call on Senator Plumb one evening at his rooms. When I opened the door in response to a loud and hearty summons to enter, I at first saw no one. But I had never before seen such a collection of newspapers and unbound documents as the room contained, not even in the office of a newspaper exchange editor.
> They were scattered about everywhere; the floor was literally carpeted with them and they were stacked up in the corners and on shelves placed against the walls. For a few moments, I gazed about me in silent wonder. Then I heard a rustling in an alcove of a room, as if someone turning over a newspaper and I discovered Senator Plumb all but hidden behind an opened newspaper and dashing through it at a breakneck speed, seemingly taking in an entire column at a single glance.
>
> "Well, Senator," I said in my surprise, "This is somewhat unusual."

Illustration of Senator Plumb at his desk in Washington, overflowing with books and letters. Drawing by Maria Rose Wimmer, author's collection.

He smiled. "This is where and how I keep in touch with my state," he said. "I have every newspaper published in Kansas, daily or weekly, sent to me here. I read every one of them faithfully. I do not look at the Associated Press reports or at the reprint matter but I read carefully the local news."

"I also read the editorials very carefully. I am especially careful to read the editorials of the Democratic papers. In this way, I am able to keep abreast of the latest twist in Kansas thought, just as from the local news columns and the letters of the country correspondents I learn of the latest happenings to and the views of John Smith and John Jones."

"They say in the Senate I believe, that I know everything worth knowing about Kansas. Well, I try to learn all about it that is worth knowing; and it is only by taking and reading thoroughly the papers of the State that I have been able to keep in touch with it, its people, and its prevailing opinions. But it's a job. It keeps me busy evening after evening. It turns my quarters into an old newspaper scrap heap." And the junior senator from the Sunflower state looked ruefully at the mass of discarded papers hiding the carpet completely.

Plumb made it a point to be as informed on all issues relating to Kansas as possible. To this end, he was second to none in the senate. All senators took subscriptions to newspapers from their home states as well as the larger national papers, but Plumb subscribed to every Kansas paper he could. He was well known among newspapermen throughout Washington and received hundreds of newspapers each week to read. And he read them all.

Mr. Scott said he was the correspondent of the *Topeka Capitol* for some time while Plumb was Senator, and that he put in much time at his office and Committee Room. When Senator Plumb was looking over the Kansas papers one day he stopped and said to Scott, "It frequently happens that I get good ideas from the very smallest newspapers published in Kansas–valuable ideas–these I find in both editorials and in contributions. A few days since I found in a small paper a commentation on the money question. The writer was a farmer. His position was right and his ideas original and well-stated. I wrote him a letter commending his article.

John M. Carson was a special correspondent of the *Philadelphia Times* and the *New York Ledger* for thirty years and met with Plumb many times over the course of his work.

He says Plumb was a favorite with the newspapermen stationed at Washington. Senator Plumb never ceased to be a newspaperman in the broadest and best sense of the term. He knew what was news and what might be properly published and what should not be.

In that day newspaper work was not done as it now is. Then the Associated Press was not the institution it now is. It sent out about four thousand words daily from Washington, and all the important news went by way of special correspondence. Every newspaperman had to have some Senator to whom he could go and from whom he could secure information of what was done in important Committees and in Executive sessions. Plumb was a good judge of men and knew that an honorable representative of a good newspaper was one of the most trustworthy men in the world. Any such man could always get an audience with Senator Plumb and get all the news anyone was entitled to. Plumb was the "stand-by" of a number of these correspondents. He was never annoyed by the call of a newspaper correspondent, –he was never too busy to see and talk with him. His office was the headquarters for the correspondents.

Carson says Plumb was the greatest worker he ever saw. He would throw off his coat and vest, and sometimes his collar, and attack a pile of work big enough to last an ordinary man a week and never stop until it was done. He has seen a wagon load of newspapers in Plumb's office through which the Senator had just gone and thrown aside. He was a great walker, rarely riding about the City of Washington. Plumb was always informed about everything. Carson said that newspapermen could size up public men quicker and better than any other men in the world, and that they knew a public man through and through. They all admired Plumb and recognized his sterling qualities. They knew he was a sincere, hustling, genuine man.

It has never been definitively determined, but Plumb likely had a photographic memory. He could read and retain facts and figures with computer-like accuracy. He seemingly only skimmed newspapers, yet knew their entire content. He was also well known for being able to do multiple tasks at once. William Miller, who worked at the Library of Congress, recalled, "[that] he had often been in Senator Plumb's rooms here [Washington D.C.] and had seen him work. Once he went in and found him looking over papers and dictating to two stenographers. He was at the same time talking to some Kansas visitors. When Miller went in he was included by Senator Plumb in the conversation. Plumb kept both stenographers busy and looked over the papers and talked to his two visitors without any confusion or apparent effort."

Lawyer A.B. Browne once met with Plumb to discuss legal business and was surprised at Plumb's ability to hold multiple trains of thought. "Browne said that Plumb could read two columns at the same time and fully comprehend both. He is the only man Browne ever saw, or knew, who possessed this dual ability—power. Once Browne was sent to see him. Entering his office he found the Senator reading a newspaper. He told Browne to sit down and talk to him about whatever business he had on hand, and it was some of Plumb's business. Browne thought his reception rather cool and Plumb indifferent to the matter he was sent on. He said to Judge Britton on his return to the office, that he believed Plumb had not heard a word he said "for", said the discouraged man, "he read a paper all the time." But afterwards, he heard him repeat all that he had been told when he was discussing the matter with Judge Britton."

Plumb's Connection to the People

While serving in the Senate, Plumb maintained his position at the Emporia National Bank for several years. But a trip home from Washington didn't mean a break from his political duties. His office in Emporia was often busy with Kansans vying for the opportunity to air their concerns with their senator.

> On the 29th of May, I called to see W. H. Brooks who moved to Emporia about the year 1872. He is a grocer and when he came to Emporia opened a grocery store on the first floor of the

building in which Senator Plumb had his office. He recalls that when Senator Plumb was home from Washington a perfect stream of people poured into his office during his stay in Emporia. It seemed to be composed of people of all conditions and Senator Plumb was patient with everyone. He never refused to hear even the most trivial complaint anyone might make against any department in Washington and made note of it and agreed to give it his attention and did give it his attention.

Despite now being on the national stage, the politics of his home state still occupied the greatest space in Plumb's mind. "Plumb would become frightened about political conditions in Kansas–uselessly frightened," Ben Simpson, who had served with Plumb during the war, said. "I could not understand why he did so, for he had both moral and physical courage in a high degree. I have seen him lead his men into places where it looked like neither he nor they would ever come out alive. And sometimes he voted alone in the Senate."

C.R. Rice, Methodist Presiding Elder of the Emporia District, recalled the following instance after Kansas had elected a Democratic governor:

> I learned as the years went by to esteem Senator Plumb very highly for what I thought to be his sterling worth as a man and citizen. I was never disappointed in him; always knew where to find him. Sometimes I thought he might be too conservative, but he was always as true as steel to his party and state. To illustrate: In November 1882 Kansas turned a complete political somersault and elected George W. Glick governor and a number of Democrats were elected to the Legislature. We, Republicans, were pretty blue over the election. The next morning I went to see Plumb and found him in his office in the bank all alone, and said to myself, "now I am going to have a good talk with him", but he was looking out the window, whistling low, and hardly recognized me. I sat in silence for some time as he continued to look out on the street and whistle. After a time of, to me, embarrassing silence, I ventured to ask the question, "what do you think of the election, Colonel?" He faced me and Yankee-like returned the question, "what do you think of it"? I felt for a time as if I was in the wrong pew, but he eventually said in measured terms, "it is too early to say much, but I think it will

work out all right. I have faith in the people yet." I soon made up my mind that he did not want to talk, and left him whistling and meditating. I ventured to see him a few days after, and the smoke had blown away somewhat and he talked quite freely for him, and said more than once, as he had said before, "it will work out all right; the dear people will learn something that may do them good. Two years of Democratic rule can't hurt us very bad."

Plumb was well known for keeping appointments and obligations to others, and no person was more important than any other. The following story is told through Plumb's son, Dale, in a letter to William Connelley in 1910.

Yesterday afternoon I was introduced to Mr. Richard Cramer, 1320 R. Street, N.W., City, formerly of Rush County, Kansas. Mr. Cramer was appointed to a position in the Treasury Department and afterwards transferred to the Pension Office by my father. He was born in Germany and came to this country when he was 19 years of age, running away to escape military service. He settled in Indiana at Elkhart, afterwards moving to Kansas. He said that my father was the best friend that he ever had and he remembers particularly a favor which he did for him. It seems that some people in his section of Rush County wanted something done at one of the departments and he went to father's office one evening and father asked him when it would be convenient for him to go to the department. He replied, "name your own hour, I will be there." "All right, 10 o'clock tomorrow morning." He was there in the hall at five minutes of ten and as the clock struck 10 he went into the office and found my father dictating. Congressman John A. Anderson, of Kansas, followed him into the office and asked my father to go to the department with him. He replied, "no Anderson, I made an appointment with you at 9 o'clock and I now have an appointment with Cramer and I am going to keep my word with him." This impressed Cramer, as he held a minor clerical position.

Plumb maintained a strong base of support within Kansas throughout his senate career. A major reason for this is illustrated in the previous story, and countless others—he was never too busy to stop and help one of his constituents.

Francis A. Brogan, a respected lawyer in Omaha, Nebraska recalled two incidents that give great insight into Plumb's personality:

> My acquaintance with Senator Plumb was slight; I was a student in college when I first knew of him, and from '85 to '88 I practiced law in Emporia, Kansas, in the office of the attorney for the bank, there, with which he was connected, but he was seldom in Emporia during that period, and I saw him very little. It so happened that the senator had a very high opinion of my father, whom he had known in his early days in Kansas, and he expressed his opinion in very flattering terms to me, regarding my father. For that reason I felt on better terms with him than a boy in my position would naturally have felt towards a man holding the position of United States senator.
>
> I recall one incident while I was a student at Georgetown College in the City of Washington, in 1883. I had been appointed to represent my college in a debate on the subject of the advisability of territorial expansion by the United States, a matter which was then purely academic, but which, as you know, has since become a great national question. I was on the affirmative of the question, that is, I was advocating the policy of territorial expansion, under proper conditions. We were at liberty to inform ourselves in any way we could, and I availed myself of that permission by calling on Senator Plumb. I found him disengaged at his home one evening, stated my situation to him, and asked him to help me. He promptly lifted one leg up on the other knee, and hugged it in that position, while he proceeded, for nearly an hour, to tell me what he thought on the question I had in mind. He said, this country should not extend its sovereignty over an alien people, like the Mexicans, or those of the South American republics, neither should it take in outlying islands, such as Cuba, (naturally neither of us thought to apply the test to the Philippine Islands). But he proceeded with much enthusiasm to tell me of the possibilities of Canada, especially

the Northwest country, which was then scarcely heard of in the United States. He said the country directly North of these Western states, Manitoba and the country West of it, was destined to be one of the great wheat granaries of the world, and it would be settled by a people homogeneous with those of the United States, and he laid down the doctrine that the extension of the sovereignty of the United States should only be over those people who were homogeneous with the American people, and who would fit into its political and social structure. He concluded, that if a peaceful opportunity should present itself, to unite the states and Canada, it should be embraced by all means, but further than that we should not go. Naturally, his familiarity with the details of what was then a little-discussed subject was a surprise to me. His talk impressed me so, that, having a good memory, I simply embodied it into my argument. The debate was held before judges consisting of Senator Morgan of Alabama, Samuel J. Randall of Pennsylvania, and a congressman named, Waite, from Connecticut. I think they were surprised at the maturity of thought which I displayed on a subject in which the public at that time had little interest. Anyway, they decided that I had won the debate, and I was awarded the gold medal. I always thought that it was Senator Plumb debating through me, and that I ought to have given him credit for it.

I am able to recall only the hazy outlines of an incident that I think is well known to many Emporia people. When I was in the office of C.N. Sterry, an attorney for the Santa Fe Railroad, and also one of the attorneys for Plumb & Hood, and the Emporia National Bank, there was an old soldier named, Elijah Moore, living on a small farm near Emporia, a cattle dealer, and a customer of the bank, that is, a borrower from Emporia National Bank, of which Hood was then president. Moore got in wrong with the bank, in some way. He had borrowed money, giving chattel mortgages on cattle, and renewing them from time to time. Finally, he absconded, and when the bank looked up its security, it found that he did not have all the cattle which he had mortgaged. Major Hood became very angry, claimed he had been cheated, and insisted upon prosecuting Elijah Moore.

A detective was sent after him, and found him hiding in the Panhandle in Texas, and brought him back. He was prosecuted for some little offense connected with the giving of the mortgages and saw the penitentiary before him. He must have written an appeal of some kind to Senator Plumb, and Plumb recognized him as a fellow soldier who had been with him, either in the Civil War or in the troubles preceding it, and wrote to I.E. Lambert of Emporia, then recognized as one of the leading criminal lawyers in Kansas, and urged him as a special favor to him, to defend Elijah Moore, against the prosecution which was being pushed by Senator Plumb's own bank. The situation was rather complex, not to say a little comical. Lambert was intimately connected, both in business and in politics, with Plumb and Hood and the bank, but he responded cheerfully, and succeeded in bringing out, upon the trial, the intimate personal relations existing between Senator Plumb and this old soldier, and the fact that Elijah Moore had performed some political service for Senator Plumb at a critical time, and wound up by assuring the jury that Senator Plumb was, "on his knees in Washington praying to Heaven that this jury will acquit Elijah Moore." I think the jury actually believed in this reverential attitude on the part of the Senator; at any rate, they acquitted Moore.

Elijah Moore had served in Plumb's regiment, the 11th Kansas Volunteer Cavalry, and was a member of Company C, recruited by Plumb in Emporia. Plumb felt a strong loyalty to his brothers in arms, perhaps to a fault, but it was a bond that he would not allow to be broken for any reason. It is more likely that this is the reason for his aid to Moore, rather than any political favors. As much as Plumb cared for his former soldiers, they seemed to reciprocate the same care. Major Martin Anderson, who had served in the 11th Kansas with Plumb organized a surprise reunion of the men at a Topeka train station for Plumb.

> He got all the Eleventh Kansas soldiers into line and marched to the railroad station and formed them in line. Plumb got off the train in a hurry, as he always did, and ran against the line almost as soon as he could distinguish it in the crowd. There stood his old regiment. He knew personally every man there. He was

overcome with emotion at the friendship shown him and he burst into tears. It was some time before he could utter a single word. No man ever loved his men more than Plumb loved his regiment. "And," said Major Anderson, "they worshipped him."

Plumb was generous by heart and often took the time to give thoughtful gifts to friends and strangers alike. He donated to various churches and social causes, and gave away twice his Senate salary each year. Judge Graves said General J.K. Hudson told Connelley this story:

> Plumb was visiting some Virginia planter and was well entertained. He observed that the planter had a poor pocket knife. He asked to examine it, and when he had looked it over he said, "You should have a better knife than that; when I get back to Washington I will send you one." The planter did not expect him to remember the knife, but he did remember it, and one day the planter was surprised to receive a fine knife by mail from Senator Plumb.

> Plumb came one day into the office of Judge Graves and looked over his law library. He observed that his set of U.S. Statutes was not full. He told the Judge that he would send him from Washington the missing volumes. Graves supposed he would not think of the matter again, but he did. In a few weeks, the volumes were all sent to him.

Although Plumb had risen in stature from his time as a pioneer in Kansas Territory, he never forgot his roots or failed to find time to visit with an old friend from those days.

> Nobody who witnessed the evident pleasure with which Senator Plumb greeted a friend he had not seen for twenty years would say he was without sentiment. And a number of these old acquaintances who hunted up the Senator was further proof that he was not as cold-blooded as he sometimes seemed. In his busiest hours, the Senator welcomed the partners of his pioneer days. He would leave the company of fellow Senators under almost any circumstances to "have a talk with a man I haven't seen since the war." He used to say to those old friends that it

felt real good to "see 'em, and rub noses awhile." One morning he laid down a letter with an ejaculation of pleasure and turning told this story: "In 1857, before we had a Post Office at Emporia, we used to leave messages in the cleft of a tree at the ford of the Neosho above town. A letter left there would in time reach the person to whom it was addressed, for everybody crossed at that ford and looked in the cleft of the tree. One day I found a note there for me. It was from a man who had left it to inform me he was tired of Kansas and was going back home. From that day to this I never heard from him. I didn't know he was living until this morning I received this letter from him in Oregon." Then the senator smiled, reread the letter and put it away.

Gifts and Charity

Charity was a subject Plumb engaged in constantly, with most people remaining unaware of his efforts. He did not advertise or promote the causes he gave to, or the projects that he worked on for the benefit of others. The only record of many of these efforts is through the stories shared with Connelley and a few surviving letters referencing them. O.E. Learnard of Lawrence, Kansas recalled the following story.

> Plumb was very thoughtful of his family and friends. He was much troubled and suffered much anxiety because of the poor health of Mrs. Plumb, and often spoke of the matter to intimate friends. He was extremely liberal to his friends. Once Learnard took a watch from his pocket to see what the hour was. It was an English hunting-case gold watch. Plumb inquired what kind of watch it was and looked it over. Learnard said that when he got another watch he intended it to be a good movement, but that the case should be of plain silver and have an open face, so that it would not have sufficient value to tempt thieves or pickpockets to steal it, while it would be handy and convenient to see the time by. He came home, and was much surprised (and gratified) to receive by express a package from Plumb a few days later, which, upon being opened, was found to contain just such a watch as he had described to Plumb. Plumb had had Learnard's monogram engraved on the case and sent it as a

present. Learnard yet carries the watch, which he exhibited to me with evident pride and it is one of his most valued personal articles.

The following letters are from Plumb to Mary Perley in Emporia. She was a friend of the family and worked with the poor in the community. The last remark indicates how he truly felt, that even though he had done so much, he did not seem to see the impact he had made.

Nov. 28, 1886
Dear Mrs. Perley:
A day or two before I left Mr. Perley came with the usual subscription paper for the benefit of the poor of Emporia and that he led me to think of something in the same connection, to-wit, A Christmas dinner for the same poor people. My idea is that a good wholesome square meal be furnished them on that day—or rather the material out of which they could make it, and out of which they should make it. Is the idea practical and worthy of being carried out? To how many families should it apply; and what would be the cost of the plan if carried out? I found Mrs. Plumb in New York rather better than I had anticipated, and have no doubt of her recovery. The process will be slow but I believe it is sure.
Very truly yours,
(Sd) P.B. Plumb

Washington, D.C. Jan. 28, 1888
Dear Mrs. Perley:
This cold weather makes me think of those who are or may be insufficiently supplied with fuel, shelter, clothing and food – and especially those of Emporia and vicinity. I had intended to provide a Christmas dinner for a number of such, the same as last year, but forgot it at the proper time. I will however add to your fund for the uses of the needy whenever you report the necessity or desirability of it.
Mrs. Plumb has been up and down – but I think I can see that she gains some strength. She gets lonesome and that puts her

back. If she could see you and one or two of her other friends every few days it would be helpful.
Very truly yours,
(Sd) P.B. Plumb

No date
I often think of what I have accomplished, or rather of what I have not accomplished–with discouragement. But your cordial words of commendation incite my too willing belief to a conclusion that perhaps I have not been wholly a failure. With sincere friendship for you and all yours,
Very truly yours,
(Sd) P.B. Plumb

Mrs. Perley later recalled:

Mr. Plumb always gave double the largest subscription on the list and a Christmas dinner etc. besides. He has told me many, many times if there was any need to let him know for his hand and purse were always open. I have a number of letters from him in regard to helping the poor, I presume I received twenty or thirty but I did not keep them all,—many went on record in our books which the Secretary kept. We had a charity ball every year for benevolences and he gave us a hundred dollars always for that.
I know there was never a church built in Emporia that he did not contribute to liberally. At the time the Congregational Church was built he gave a thousand dollars; he subscribed five hundred, gave three hundred Dedication Day and later gave two hundred more. He was always giving.

J.M. Cavaness was a longtime friend of Plumb's and also a minister. Plumb donated to various churches, regardless of their affiliation, because he believed in their work to help others. This letter he sent to Cavaness on Senate stationery in 1886 illustrates his feelings on that matter:

> United States Senate,
> Washington, D.C. July 27, 1886
> Dear Cavaness:
> I have yours of the 21st. It was the first information I had ever had of your ministerial inclinations. No doubt you did well to follow them as thereby you have satisfied your conscience. While I have never envied, —as I suppose no one ever did, —the worldly estate of a minister, I have never ceased to admire their self-sacrificing zeal for their Master's work. The world owes them a debt it will never pay. Their reward must be found in a consciousness of duty done. They are the great conservative and still the truly progressive force of society.
>
> All this you know better than I and I will not weary you by repeating it. But I will put it into practical shape by crediting you with the interest due next month on those notes. That is about my share. Am glad to do it and know that the money will do more good in your hands than in mine.
> Sincerely Yours,
> (Sd) P.B. Plumb

Besides charitable donations, Plumb also regularly performed small acts of kindness. His longtime friend Ben Simpson told Connelley the following story:

> There was a merchant at Chanute who had prospered in business to the point where he went to New York to buy goods. On one trip he stopped in Washington. He had never been to Washington and arriving at an early hour in the morning he felt so forlorn and lonesome that he wanted to see a Kansas man. Plumb had been at Chanute sometime before and had gone into the business houses of the town, as he always did in every Kansas town, and had met this gentleman in his store. The merchant remembered Plumb and succeeded in finding his apartments. He got to his door as the Senator was getting up and getting dressed. Plumb invited him in and inquired if he had had breakfast. The merchant had not so Plumb took him to breakfast, then following his usual habit, Plumb proposed they

walk about the city. In doing so they passed a new brick house, which was not quite completed. The merchant stopped to look at the house saying he intended to build a brick house in Chanute and that house just suited him, and he believed he should like to build one like it. They tried to get into the house but were not able to and so looked all around the premises from the outside. Plumb went to the next door and got information as to who was building the house, the architect, and all other information the neighbor could furnish. The merchant went on to New York but when he got home, he found a letter from Senator Plumb which contained complete plans of the house made by the architect. This man was a Democrat but he became a strong partisan of Senator Plumb. He told Simpson in Topeka once just after an election that he had voted and worked for the representative for the Legislature on the Republican ticket from Chanute because he understood that that member was to support Senator Plumb.

Plumb's gifts also extended to the President. In a somewhat cryptic letter, President Benjamin Harrison thanked Plumb for a gift that was likely a "thank you" for some efforts made on the behalf of Plumb and Kansas.

> Washington, April 7, 1890
> Dear Senator:
> I am much obliged to you for the elongated package which I found in my room on Saturday. Its medicinal virtues will be proved on occasion.
> Very sincerely yours,
> (Sd) Benj. Harrison

One can only imagine what was in the "elongated package," or what liquor was a favorite of President Harrison's.

Personality

Like any person in the public eye, Plumb had his share of critics and enemies. While he was a sensitive man and could be hurt deeply by harsh criticisms, he was quick to recover and did not hold ill will against those who had wronged him. Judge Tom Ryan who served in the Kansas House of Representatives recalled:

Senator Plumb had a great many enemies; he was maligned terribly, so was Senator Ingalls for that matter. Some people thought Plumb avaricious, selfish. While it is true he was a close and energetic businessman he was in many respects charitable, generous and benevolent and I am inclined to think that he contributed more for such purposes in Kansas than any other representative the state ever had. While that sort of a close aggressive businessman might naturally be expected to be steeled a little, the conduct of Senator Plumb not infrequently attested that he had a heart as gentle as a woman. He was full of sympathy. He was tolerant of the faults of others. I bring to mind instances where he spoke kindly of those who were bitterly attacking him and attributed their bitterness to their ignorance of facts or to distressing conditions that soured them against the world.

I recall an instance that strikingly illustrates this quality of Plumb's temperament. A man who had occupied considerable prominence in the state, had some ability, but was thought by many not to have much character or manhood, sought the senator's support for an important appointment. At that time there was a little coterie of conspirators in Washington engaged in the work of villainizing Plumb in the newspapers, and during the entire campaign for that appointment, the applicant was associated with this coterie and co-operating with these conspirators in putting out through the public press the most brutal attacks, yet he was a daily visitor at Plumb's office for the purposes of consulting with the Senator regarding his interests in the pending appointment. Although Plumb was fully advised from day to day of this man's treachery he continued to faithfully support his application until the President turned it down. When some of his friends reproached him for it he replied that misfortune had embittered the man against the world and that he was in a frame of mind to have no confidence in anybody and that the people he had been associating with found it easy to mislead him and once he could get on his feet again he would be alright, loyal and useful, and he felt that he ought not to drop him and that if he should drop him it would serve to confirm in his mind the bad things those fellows had been telling him about himself.

Politics can often turn to mudslinging and dishonest backstabbing. Plumb was averse to anything of the sort and made that clear to anyone who worked with him. Senator Henry Blair of New Hampshire recalled two incidents of Plumb's strong sense of decency and honor:

> Plumb was a man of courage and very quick of action. In his Committee Room one day was Governor Ordway of Dakota Territory, who had taken issue with Senator Pettigrew about public land matters and county lines and county seats. Pettigrew and others were present. Governor Ordway said something very discourteous to Pettigrew. Plumb ordered him to withdraw the remark and apologize. Ordway did not do so, and Plumb sprung from his chair reaching for him. Ordway was at the opposite end of the table, but it seemed that Plumb was halfway to him reaching for him with both arms before he left his chair fairly. Plumb did not wait to call a guard to put him out, but was in the act of doing it himself when Ordway apologized and the episode was at an end.

> Plumb had a strong sense of justice. Blair had a bill to authorize the establishment of schools in the South for the poor. Plumb opposed it, saying that each state should provide its own funds for schools largely, as Kansas did. He took a strong stand against the bill. Senator Morrill, of Vermont, prepared a bill designed to aid the State Agricultural College and believed he could get it through if Blair's bill was out of the way. He professed to be for Blair's bill, but secretly worked against it. Some Senators came to Blair and told him what Morrill was doing. The course of Morrill came to the ears of Plumb, who resented it. He said he was not in favor of Blair's bill before, but now he was. He was indignant and enraged in an instant at Morrill's course. The Blair bill was finally defeated or withdrawn.

No state had any better friend than Plumb was of Kansas.

> He was always a friend of the old soldier–had been a soldier himself. He abused the fellows we sent abroad for aping the foreign ways and doing un-American things and being extravagant, saying that as long as the Government had a dollar the old soldier should have something to eat and wear.
> Plumb was American to the core–democratic and cordial in manner and despised affectation and sham of any kind.

Although Plumb had risen steadily through the ranks of Kansas, and even national society, he remained as down to earth as ever. An article from the *Atchison Globe* described Plumb and fellow Kansas Senator Ingalls, who were both in town for the funeral of John A. Martin.

> A central figure of the scene was United States Senator Preston B. Plumb. Mr. Plumb seldom comes to Atchison, and yesterday attracted a good deal of attention. He is a plain sort of a statesman, and dresses like a man who buys his clothes by chance. A brown suit loosely covering a figure inclined to corpulency, and a slouch hat, completed his attire. He shaves clean, except a billy-goat bunch of hair at the end of his chin. He looked yesterday more like a cattle baron on his way to market with a carload of steers than a senator of the United States. But odd as he looked, and plain as he was, he got in his graft in great shape, and was in continual demand by smaller statesmen. He carried his hands in his pockets, and lounged over the radiators and tables in the hotel corridors in an easy and approachable manner, and the way he had of calling the fellows "Bill," or "Jim," and his friendly way of arming them about it was captivating. Our John J. Ingalls was also in the crowd, with his clean-cut visage, tailor-made clothes, eyeglasses, and critical, yet smooth and friendly air. He always had a crowd around him, and when he stalked away it was only to be the center of another caucus.

Walter Stevens was a great friend of Plumb's and had occasion to write in the *Globe Democrat* some stories relating to his character and temperament:

> It [the conversation] related to the candidacy of ex-Governor George T. Anthony for the interstate commerce

commissionership. The scene was a typical one for the senator's room. Mr. Plumb sat at his tall desk, without any vest, and without a shirt collar. A great gray dressing gown, without ornamentation, plain as any army blanket and of not much finer texture, was thrown around him. He had not had time to go to breakfast. The hour was an early one for Washington. On the desk was a heap of type written answers to correspondents. Two ladies sat waiting in one corner of the room. Private Secretary Flenniken stood behind the senator, taking memoranda of various department matters to be attended to. Colonel Manning sat at the window waiting for a conference on a matter of business. A telegram was shown to the senator. It prompted him to lay aside all other matters and enter into a confidential conversation. Only when he was greatly interested did he give his mind to a single line of thought. He talked for ten or fifteen minutes, going over the matter of ex-Governor Anthony's candidacy and the opposition of Congressman Funston. There was no trace of anger in his manner. But in most earnest language the senator expressed his regret that such personal differences had occurred. He told how a state's influence was crippled at Washington when representative men of the party fell out, as in this case. He described the effect of Mr. Funston's hostility toward Anthony at the White House. The question was not as to the truth of what Funston had charged. The fact that he had gone to the president and had protested showed the lack of harmony in Kansas and prompted the president to ignore the state in the matter of this appointment. The senator deplored the action of Mr. Funston on the latter's account. He said that it could not but hurt the representative in his district. He could not see how a man could so permit his personal resentment to injure himself.

This talk illustrated a phase of the senator's character. His intensely practical nature enabled him to see the folly of anger, and it was very seldom that his temper got the best of him.

Plumb seemed to have only one weak point, attacks that chided him on his poor upbringing in an attempt to discredit or humiliate him.

Senator Nelson Aldrich of Rhode Island discovered this when his joke at Plumb's expense brought explosive results.

> There are not many people in Washington who ever saw Senator Plumb really angry. Once in a party of senators a practical joke was played upon him. The time was being whiled away with a social game of cards. There were no stakes worth mentioning. But one of the party sent out and got an extra pack of cards. At a convenient stage in the game, he slipped an extra king or two to a New England senator, a man of irreproachable morals and habits. And this New England Senator, carrying out the joke, played a hand which betrayed the fraud, but not the humorous phase of it, to Senator Plumb. In an instant, the great frame of the Kansan towered above the card table. His face was pale with anger. He denounced the trick, seized his chair, and had it raised high in the air when the others at the table seized him. It took all of their strength, for Plumb was powerful, to prevent a tragedy. The senator who had planned the joke tried to explain it, but he could not make Mr. Plumb see its harmlessness. His contempt for fraud and hypocrisy was too strong. The New England senator said afterward that from that time he had played no cards. It was nearly a year before even speaking relations were resumed between the two men.

There are several accounts of the preceding card game story, and a running theme between those accounts was the fact that the trick was done in an attempt to mock Plumb and humiliate him. Hence his strong reaction to the cheat.

Though often portrayed as being upright to a fault, there are rare instances of Plumb's wit and humor shining through. Connelley told the following story in a speech given in Topeka, Kansas in 1910:

> Barney Sheridan tells this political story on Plumb: "Uncle Dick Blue and Congressman Funston had taken sides against Plumb in some Kansas matter. There was no break in the friendly relations existing between the parties, for all of them, together with W.C. Perry, were walking along some street in Washington. Blue needed to get some money. If any of you ever tried to draw money from a Washington bank on drafts or checks on home

banks you will recall the many requirements made of you. Complete identification must be made and an endorser good at that bank furnished. The amount secured is charged to the account of the endorser until the draft is paid. Plumb had lost much by such endorsements, no doubt. And the financial reputation of Uncle Dick was not quite equal to that of J.P. Morgan anyway. As the bunch of Kansans were passing the Riggs Bank, Blue said, as though the matter was not an important one and had just occurred to him–"Oh, yes, Plumb, here is a bank. I want to get some money. Come in and identify me and endorse my paper."

"Ah," said Plumb, throwing up his head and stepping a little quicker, "you see [Congressman] Funston? He can write better than I can!"

Appointments

Plumb was famous in all the departments within Washington D.C. for exerting his influence to have Kansas men appointed to jobs. He often carried around a "blue book" full of statistics on the state of Kansas to support his claim that he was only after the state's fair share of government employees. If someone approached him and asked for a position, and if he felt them qualified, he would advocate for them.

Many of Plumb's friends found themselves offered jobs that they did not realize they were even being considered for. George W. Finney of Neosho Falls, Kansas was offered positions at an Indian Agency in New Mexico and as a receiver at a land office in Topeka, Kansas. Finney was unable to take the positions but remarked, "Plumb was always looking out for his friends. Often a man would find himself appointed to an office for which he was not an applicant if Plumb believed him well qualified for the place.

While Plumb could always be counted on for this type of service, Kansas's other senator, Ingalls, was not nearly as reliable. Plumb's brother, George, told the following story to Connelley:

> While on a trip to Muskogee, I met a man, whose name or residence I did not learn, who told me a story about Preston. He had gone to Washington, about the time Preston had first gone there, to get an appointment for some land office in the western

part of the state, probably at Kirwin. He had stayed around Washington a week or two waiting for the case to be called up before the Interior Department. Mr. Ingalls had promised to attend to his case, in fact, had asked him to come to Washington to be there at the time, but as it was so long before the case would be called, he went to Senator Plumb and told him he was there as an applicant for the appointment; that he had spoken to Mr. Ingalls and Mr. Ingalls had told him he was attending to it and that it would be all right. Senator Plumb told him he was sorry he had not known it as he had a man there for the same place, but that it was Mr. Ingalls' place to make that appointment (but he did not believe he would do it) and said you go to him and tell him to be there to attend to it. He said he would not be there if Mr. Ingalls came—that he would keep his man away, but if Mr. Ingalls was not there that he, Senator Plumb, would be there with his man. When the time came the man hunted for Mr. Ingalls but was unable to find him, so Senator Plumb got his man appointed. The man told this story as though it was one of the things he wanted to remember about Senator Plumb. He said Senator Plumb said to him "I am very sorry this had to be, but I knew Mr. Ingalls would not attend to it and I had a man I wanted in. If at any time I can serve you I will do it."

Chapter 14

A Big Winning

Garfield Presidential Nomination

The 1880 Republican convention held in early June in Chicago, was only a few short years after Plumb's Senate election, yet his influence had grown to the point that he played a major role in the nomination of James A. Garfield for President on the Republican ticket. The three leading candidates for the nomination were Ulysses S. Grant (for a third presidential term), James Blaine (U.S. Senator from Maine), and John Sherman (brother of William Tecumseh Sherman). Plumb and the Kansas delegation were for James Blaine and the "half-breed" faction of the Republican party he represented.

By this time, party politics were increasingly influenced by corporations, which Plumb detested, and who supported Grant's candidacy. Blaine was for civil service reform and against "cronyism" which Plumb also supported. Another member of the "half-breed" wing of the Republican party close to Plumb included Senator Justin Smith Morrill of Vermont; the namesake of the Plumbs' youngest child, Preston Morrill Plumb. Rutherford B. Hayes, and fellow 1880 presidential candidate, John Sherman, were also members.

The nominating votes were deadlocked and no clear victor could be determined. It became clear that without finding a candidate who could pull votes from at least two candidates, the nomination process would essentially be stuck. James A. Garfield was an Ohio senator who had served effectively as a Major General for the Union Army in the Civil War and was also an unexpected dark horse candidate for the presidency. Unbeknownst to many at the time, and even today, Plumb played a major role in the nomination of James A. Garfield by the Republican party for President.

The following is a previously unpublished account of exactly what happened behind the scenes of the convention to secure the nomination for Garfield. Ben Simpson had served in the Civil War alongside Plumb (although not in the 11th Kansas) and they had remained close personal and political friends. Simpson, who gave this interview to Connelley, was present throughout the convention and was at Plumb's side for much of it. This story serves as just one example of Plumb's growing influence in United States politics:

The Convention at Chicago was long drawn out. On Sunday there was much talk and speculation as to who would benefit from the break in the ranks of Sherman and Blaine, for it began to be the opinion that neither could be nominated. There was a majority against Grant, but this majority was not so hostile to him as to make it impossible for enough to go to him to give him the nomination. Garfield was frequently mentioned as a possibility. From the very first a Pennsylvania delegate living near the Ohio line and not far from Garfield's home, had voted for him for President. A voice in the Convention had cried, "Nominate Garfield" while he was delivering his speech nominating John Sherman. And of the thirty-six ballots cast by the Convention Garfield had votes in all except six. There was a feeling that he might be the nominee of the Convention.

Sunday afternoon James F. Legate, at the Kansas headquarters at the Palmer House, told Simpson that Powell Clayton, of the Arkansas delegation, wanted to see him. Simpson went with Legate to the headquarters of the Arkansas delegation, at the Grand Pacific Hotel, and there either Legate or Clayton placed hands on his shoulders and pushed him into a room beyond the one occupied by the Arkansas delegation. In that room, Simpson saw Senators Conkling, Cameron, and Logan. Conkling said, "Mr. Simpson, we understand that you are very influential with your delegation." Simpson replied to the effect that the Kansas delegation was made up of the personal and political friends of Senator Plumb, and said, "If you desire anything from the delegation you will have to get it through Plumb." Conkling leaned forward, put his hand on Simpson's knee, and said, "I like to see a man who is faithful to his Senator." Then he asked, "Who is your personal choice for President?" Simpson replied, "My choice, and that of a large majority of those from Kansas is James G. Blaine." "What if Mr. Blaine cannot be nominated?" asked Conkling. Simpson said there had been no consultation of the delegation and he could not say for whom the delegation would be. "For whom would you be," asked Conkling. "I would be for Senator Plumb" replied Simpson. "For Senator Plumb for President?" asked Conkling. "No, but for whomever Senator

Plumb was for President," Simpson said. "Your delegation would probably follow Plumb?" inquired Conkling. "I think so," said Simpson. Then either Logan or Cameron asked, "Mr. Simpson, would you be willing to enter into any arrangement to place your delegation under some other condition?" "Certainly not without consultation with Senator Plumb," said Simpson. There was silence. Simpson thought the interview was over and rose to go. As he was about to say, "Good Day Gentlemen," Senator Cameron said to his associates, "Let's consider Wisconsin now." Then Simpson went out of the room.

Simpson returned to Kansas headquarters and there saw Plumb and told him of his interview with Senators Conkling, Cameron, and Logan. Plumb asked him if the Kansas delegation could be transferred to General Grant. Simpson said to do that they would have the most trouble with John A. Martin.

The leader of the Wisconsin delegation, as Simpson believed, was Keyes of Madison. The delegation wanted to make an arrangement by which one of their number, Mr. Cassiday, should be appointed to the first vacancy which should occur in the Supreme Court of the United States. This became generally known to the delegates to the Convention. The Wisconsin delegation were in an attitude to be dealt with, being for none of the leading candidates, but were supporting Washburn of Illinois and voted for him at least a part of the time.

After Simpson saw Plumb, Senator Conkling visited the Kansas headquarters. This was before the delegation had eaten supper. Plumb was not then at headquarters and various members of the delegation went out to find him, but without success, and Conkling went back to the Grand Pacific.

Sometime on Monday, and it must have been in the forenoon, Plumb told Simpson that he had seen Senators Conkling, Cameron, and Logan on the previous night; and that they wanted him to be for General Grant. Senator Conkling took up a sheet of blank paper from the table and tendered it to Plumb, saying, "Senator, write on that sheet of paper anything you want of the Administration and we will sign it. And if you do not regard that as sufficient we will have it signed by General Grant who is in Milwaukee, and returns here by tomorrow noon. We want Kansas for General Grant as it is an enthusiastic Blaine State." Plumb replied that before he could do that he would have to consult with the members of the Kansas delegation. He did not tell Simpson that he had seen any of the others, but it is possible that he had and that he found it difficult to interest them in the candidacy of General Grant. Simpson said, "Plumb, I don't think it can be transferred to Grant." Plumb looked up with the old toss of his head and said, "If we are to have trouble with you, I know it cannot be done." Simpson said, "No trouble with me, but you will have with others." Plumb seemed impatient and dissatisfied about the attitude he found toward Grant.

At supper Monday Plumb said to Simpson, "I want you to go with me." They did not go up to the Kansas headquarters, but went directly from the dining room to Garfield's room in the Grand Pacific Hotel. Garfield was there when they arrived. Others present were Mr. Sherwin, Postmaster at Cleveland, Ohio, and a Major Swain, Judge Advocate in the Army, and who had been in Garfield's regiment in the war. Garfield was evidently expecting Plumb, for he met him at the door, and took him by the hand, and led him to a corner of the room where they sat down on Garfield's large canvas-covered trunk. Simpson, Sherwin, and Swain seated themselves at a table about the center of the room. This diagram will show the positions: [See Fig. 1]

Simpson thought it seemed as though Swain was trying to hear the conversation between Garfield and Plumb. Simpson and Sherwin talked a few minutes about the result of the break which all knew had to come soon. There was a knock at the door, and Swain opened it, and A.W. Campbell, editor of the Wheeling (W.Va.) *Intelligencer*, a delegate to the Convention came in, shook hands with Simpson, and asked about his brothers who lived on a farm in Miami County and whom Simpson knew. Soon another knock was heard at the door, and Benjamin Harrison a delegate from Indiana, came in, and at once joined in the conversation about the break. Harrison disliked Grant and wanted everything possible done to prevent his nomination. In a few minutes, W.D. Bickham, a delegate from Ohio, editor of the *Dayton Journal*, and regarded as Sherman's Manager, came in. He joined in the conversation about the break. After that, others came into the room, but Simpson does not remember their names. It is safe to say that there were at least a dozen in the room in addition to Garfield and Plumb. At the table sat now Harrison and Campbell, as shown here: [See Fig. 2]

The condition of the Wisconsin delegation was being discussed, and it was rather an exciting conversation. Cassidy, of Wisconsin, was mentioned. Harrison said, "I know Cassidy well. I will get him in." and went out to bring him in. Someone asked, "What will we give him?" That is, what should be given to him to go with those there against Grant. Simpson spoke out and said, "Give him any d—d thing he wants." Everybody in the room laughed and looked at Garfield. Simpson feared he had expressed himself too plainly, and said so, but Garfield spoke up and said, "No, Simpson, you are in earnest." By this time there were twenty to thirty people in the room. Plumb rose suddenly and said to Garfield, "General, I will see you later," or "General, I will see you in the morning." Simpson is not certain which expression he used.

Plumb and Simpson went back to the Palmer House, and went from the bar into the lobby, where Plumb disappeared. It was not later than eight o'clock, and Simpson does not know where Plumb went. Simpson went to Kansas headquarters, where he found Bent Murdock in charge. From there he went to the room of Jim Merritt, who was not a delegate. In Merritt's room, Simpson found a poker game in progress–bought chips and took a hand. About midnight Plumb came in and said he wanted in the game, bought chips, and took a hand. He continued in the

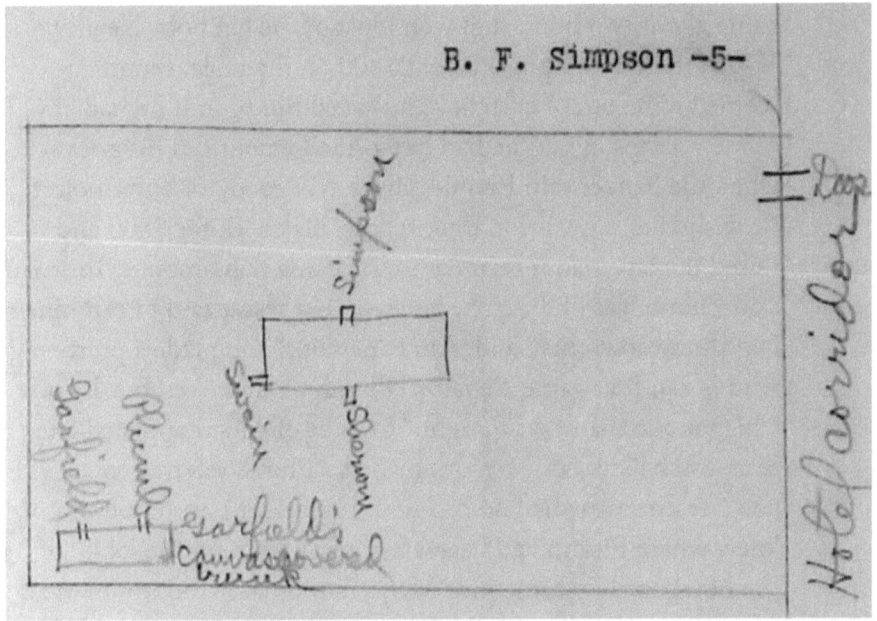

Above: Figure 1 illustrates the seating arrangement of Garfield, Plumb, and Simpson with Plumb and Garfield discussing the nomination on Garfield's trunk. Below: Figure 2 illustrates the same scene after additional senators had entered the room. Both drawings were done by Connelley in the presence of Simpson and are taken directly from Connelley's notes. Images courtesy Lyon County History Center.

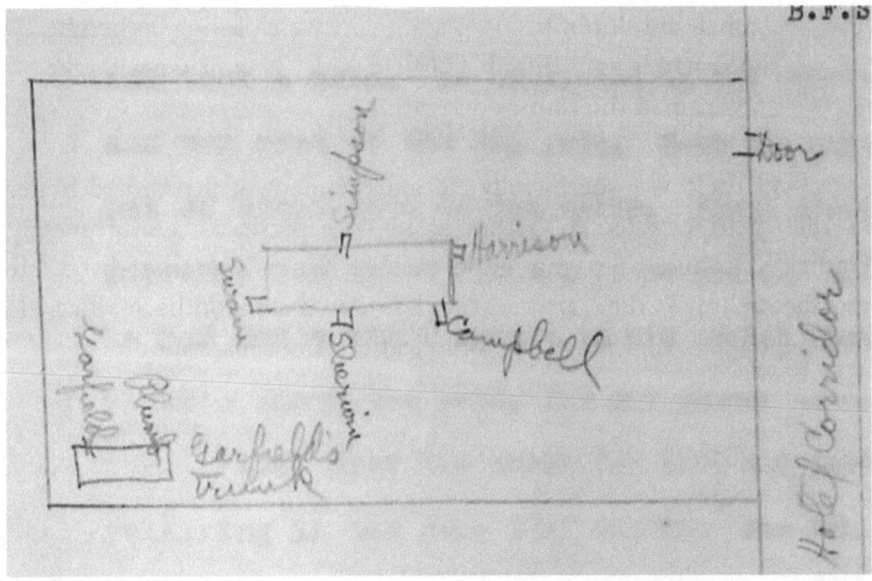

game about two hours and won most of the big pots. Near two o'clock there was a pot of about $400 on the table. Plumb seemed to be out of currency and asked Simpson if he had any money. Simpson said he had but a small amount in his pocket when the banker said Plumb's check was good, for any amount he wished to draw it for. Plumb drew his check for $500 and raised the last man remaining in the game that amount. The man said Plumb was bluffing, he believed, but was afraid to call him and threw down his hand. Someone said, "You made a pretty big winning in that game, Senator." Plumb replied, "Yes, but I made a bigger one than that tonight." In light of what happened later, Simpson believes this remark made by Plumb referred to another interview he had had with Garfield. Simpson never knew where Plumb had been after leaving him in the lobby of the hotel until he came into Merritt's room. He did not have an opportunity to talk with the Senator any more that night. When the delegation started to the Convention hall the next morning Plumb remarked to Simpson that they would finish the business that day, but did not say how it would be finished.

Simpson thinks Garfield was a willing recipient of the nomination but does not say that he was actively seeking it. After the nomination was made Plumb and Simpson went to Garfield's room to congratulate him. Garfield was standing in the hall in front of his door and many were passing. When he shook hands with Plumb, Garfield said, "Senator, we will take good care of the Kansas delegation."

Garfield was successfully elected President of the United States in 1880 with Chester A. Arthur as his vice president. Unfortunately, Garfield's promise of taking "good care" of Kansas was short-lived. He was shot on July 2, 1881, after serving less than three months in office. He died September 19, 1881, from complications from his wound.

Chapter 15

Greater Influence

Plumb quickly rose through the ranks of his fellow senators and made a reputation for himself as a man who was thoroughly informed on a variety of issues and a fierce debater. A.B. Browne, a lawyer who knew Plumb well described his mannerisms in the Senate to Connelley:

> Plumb made no pretensions to oratory, but was, nevertheless, a very effective speaker. He was constantly in action while speaking–bumbling his watch chain, thrusting his hands into his trousers' pockets, waving an arm in a sort of stiff thrust forward for emphasis, walking nervously to and fro, but you soon ceased to notice this and think only of the force and power of his argument. Browne said Plumb impressed him always as a rugged physiognomy, but that his square forehead always denoted power, force. He had not the classic face nor the delicately carved feature, but, rather, the face denoting immense strength of will and force of intellect–such a face as would brook no master, stop at no obstacle.
>
> It is the judgment of Browne that Plumb admired a fighter. He expected every man to contend vigorously for what he believed to be right. If Plumb attacked a man in debate he expected the man to come back at him. He had no respect for him if he failed to do so.
>
> Plumb was true blue. He was always willing to be convinced and was never stubborn or unreasonable in debate. But it took facts to convince him. He was not swayed or changed by persuasion.

Senator Shelby Cullom of Illinois was a friend of Plumb's and took notice of his ability to change the entire course of business in the Senate.

> Sometimes Plumb would seem to take little notice of some important matter that was engrossing the attention of the Senate and the Senators counted on his indifference to the

measure. But very frequently Plumb would unexpectedly rise in his place to make a few remarks and would make a speech that would overturn and upset everything and which would turn the bill as he wanted it. In these speeches, he surprised everybody with his knowledge of even the remotest effects of the bill and its history.

He made it a point to keep himself informed on all issues and was not shy about approaching others for information, or to get a job done. P.I. Bonebrake knew Plumb fairly well and described him thusly:

> He could get at the merits of any business matter quicker and more certainly and truly than any other man Bonebrake ever knew. He cut right into the heart of a matter and brushed aside all arguments and fallacies surrounding it. He just pushed his way into it and through it. Bonebrake illustrated what he meant to convey by saying that in any crowd that might gather on a street about a fire or other excitive matter, there would be many people who would be content to stand about the edges of the circle and get what secondhand information which might filter through the crowded ranks in front of them. Not so with Plumb–he came up with a rush and elbowed and see-sawed his way to the center, and saw for himself.

> Bonebrake says Plumb was the best informed man on political conditions both local and national, that he ever knew. He seemed to know everything that transpired in a political way. He was always first to know what Kansas would want to do, - knew it even before the people themselves would know. Plumb was a leader who followed the prevailing public sentiment as expressed by the great majority of people, being astute enough to foresee what this sentiment would be long before it was formulated and expressed. But he did not fall in with such sentiment because it was the majority opinion, but because in all political matters, almost, the feeling and attitude of the majority are usually just and correct. Plumb read the signs more readily and accurately than others. He was not a trimmer in politics, and he never surrendered his independence of thought and action.

Bonebrake relates an instance of the force of Plumb in business matters. It was the desire of the National bank with which Bonebrake was connected in Topeka to increase its capital stock. Bonebrake was sent to Washington by the directors to secure the necessary permission from the Secretary of the Treasury. Plumb went with him to see the Secretary–Hon. Lyman J. Gage. When they called at the Treasury Department some high flunky or functionary said the Secretary was very busy and could not be interrupted, and offered Plumb and Bonebrake seats while they waited. But Plumb was not awed by any such official etiquette. When told that the Secretary was busy, Plumb replied: "That's all right," and pushed by the attendant opened the Secretary's door and walked in and stated his business, got what Bonebrake desired, and was out in a few minutes. Plumb was not afraid of any man or official who ever walked.

Plumb did not speak unless he had something to say, and he had no qualms about raising his voice on a particular topic, even if that opinion was contrary to that of his party. Friend and fellow lawyer, George R. Peck described him, "When he made up his mind a thing was right he espoused and championed it with a vigor and power no other man of Peck's acquaintance ever possessed. It was only necessary to show him a thing was right to secure his support. And his support was worth that of a dozen ordinary men or a dozen ordinary senators."

Senator Pettigrew of South Dakota was a close friend of Plumb's and shared a number of stories with Connelley. He was fortunate to glimpse Plumb's sense of humor on more than one occasion.

> Senator Pettigrew says Plumb had a fine sense of humor but that he rarely indulged it. He saw the ridiculous quickly also. Once Pettigrew recommended a man from some land office in Dakota, and he was appointed. The matter of confirmation by the Senate came before the Senate Committee on Public Lands,–Plumb's committee. There was in Dakota then one Ordway, who had been sent out by Arthur as Territorial governor. Ordway was of the worst strips of carpetbaggers. He grafted in every way possible in his office–even selling county-seat locations for one of which he secured ten thousand dollars. Ordway opposed the

confirmation of Pettigrew's man, probably for the purpose of being bought off. At the hearing before the Committee Pettigrew told the candidate to go after Ordway roughshod–to tell everything bad about him he could in the time given. This the candidate did. When he had concluded Walker of Arkansas, one of the committee, said, "Mr. Chairman, I move that the Governor (Ordway) be acquitted and the candidate confirmed." Plumb (the Chairman) said, "You have heard the motion just made by Mr. Walker. All in favor of the motion say 'aye' those opposed say 'no.'" Everybody including bystanders, voted "Aye." With a smile, Plumb announced that the motion had carried unanimously and the candidate would be confirmed."

Plumb was a witty debater and often had sarcastic comments at the ready. The Congressional Record is full of his quips, and it would be impossible to share them all here. In one instance, the Senate discussed the creation of a permanent Census Bureau in 1891. A resolution was submitted by Senator Eugene Hale of Maine instructing the Secretary of the Interior to draft the Senate bill for the task. Plumb thought it poor that Hale was not going to write the bill himself, and made a point to bring it up during the proceedings.

> Mr. PLUMB: I wish to say, before the resolution passes from the consideration of the Senate, that it seems to me a little bit extraordinary to ask a Department to draw the framework of a bill.
> Mr. HALE: It will not hurt it any.
> Mr. PLUMB: I do not know that it will hurt it any, but it ought not to help it any. It is a little bit out of keeping, as I think; in fact, I know of some similar situations in which the Departments have been reflected upon because they did send draughts [drafts] of bills here.
> Mr. HALE: They can not be reflected upon in this case, if we ask them to do it.
> Mr. PLUMB: They ought not to be asked to do it.
> Mr. HALE: I should like to have half a dozen authorities draw such a bill.
> Mr. PLUMB: Of course, if the Senator himself is not familiar with the subject and desires the Secretary of the Interior, who

Illustration of Senator Preston B. Plumb addressing the Senate. Those unfamiliar with him thought that the papers he held in his hand while speaking were his notes, but he was known for reading his mail and giving speeches at the same time. He would become so engrossed and animated while arguing his case, that he often need to wipe the sweat from the back of his neck. This became a common mannerism of his. Drawing by Maria Rose Wimmer, author's collection.

may be a ready writer otherwise to draw up a bill, I have no objection.

Mr. HALE: I am not so familiar with this subject and all other subjects as the Senator from Kansas is.

Mr. PLUMB: That is an honest confession.

Another bill (H.R. 3967) that garnered strong debate in the Senate from Plumb was for the adoption of regulations concerning sick and diseased cattle. The summary of the bill states, "For the establishment of a Bureau of Animal Industry, to prevent the exportation of diseased cattle, and to provide means for the suppression and extirpation of pleuro-pneumonia and other contagious diseases among domestic animals." The American cattle industry was facing difficult competition in their export due to the lack of any regulations barring the sale of diseased cattle. Foreign countries not wishing to have diseased cattle cross their borders either refused to do business with the United States, or paid drastically less for American cattle than beef from other countries, such as Canada. Many senators opposed these regulations as undue requirements, and some opposed them because many in the cattle market did not care whether the cattle were diseased or not, as long as they could sell them undetected. The following exchange with Senator Coke from Texas illustrates Plumb's wit as well as his interest in this bill:

Mr. COKE: Will the Senator from Kansas permit me to ask him a question?

Mr. PLUMB: Yes, sir.

Mr. COKE: I propound this question to the Senator from Kansas: Do you find in the resolutions of the Legislature of any State or any body of stock-raisers or any assemblage interested in this question, that any demand has ever been made to Congress to include the so-called splenetic or Texas fever in any legislation that they have asked for?

Mr. PLUMB: I do not know that Texas fever has been dignified by mention, but it will get some before this debate is over that will be satisfactory I hope to the Senator from Texas.

Mr. COKE: I ask the Senator for a frank answer to my question.

Mr. PLUMB: The Legislature of the State of New York adopted a resolution calling upon Congress to pass a bill to carry out the recommendations of the Treasury Cattle Commission, which were to the effect that Texas cattle should not during six months in the year be permitted to go out of that State.

Mr. COKE: If the Senator will permit me, I have never heard of that resolution of the Legislature of the State of New York.

Mr. PLUMB: There has been a good deal of useful information abroad in this land which I presume the Senator from Texas has not heard of.

Mr. COKE: I will state that in all the resolutions of all the different bodies recited in the report of the committee of the other House, which reported this bill not a single one of them asked for legislation against the Texas or splenetic fever, but only against pleuro-pneumonia.

Mr. PLUMB: The bill does not mention Texas fever. It mentions "contagious, infectious, and communicable diseases," and if Texas fever is not a communicable disease nor a contagious disease then the bill does not apply to it. In addition to that, the Iowa Improved-Stock Breeders' Associations have petitioned for the passage of this bill. The Legislature of the State of Iowa have done the same thing. The Stock Growers' Association of the State of Kansas, embracing representatives located in every county in that State, thoroughly representative of the stock interests of that State and of as much importance to the people of that State as the interest of Texas cattle is to the people of Texas, have also petitioned for the passage of this bill. Now, who opposes the bill? I do not mean on constitutional grounds but on interested grounds. The Senator from Texas and a few men interested in the commission business in cattle, men who would just as soon sell a diseased animal as a sound one, because the commission is just the same, which is 12.5 cents a head. We have had here the spectacle of men who are interested in the selling of diseased cattle, or of cattle without reference to whether they are diseased or not, sending an attorney here, and I have a telegram from him on my desk in which he represents himself as being a sort of high joint commission; and he says he is arbitrating this question with somebody outside, and will I not please withhold this bill until he and the man he is conferring with have agreed upon something which they shall consent that Congress may pass. I have here a letter from the president of the

> stock-yard association of Kansas City, which I will put against the declaration of the stockmen of Chicago who have been quoted, and I may say for that body of men, represented by the manager of the association, that they do not want to sell diseased cattle to the people of this country or any other. They are interested in a trade which is legitimate; they are interested in maintaining it as a legitimate trade, and they handle as many Texas cattle as any other stock-yards in the world.

This bill was amended in the Senate and eventually passed and signed into law creating the Bureau of Animal Industry under the United States Department of Agriculture. It served to research animal diseases, protect against foreign animal diseases, and inspected livestock. This organization existed until 1953 when it was abolished under the Eisenhower administration and its functions were rolled into the newly created Agricultural Research Service.

As Plumb's influence in the Senate grew, so did his influence over Republican conventions, both statewide and nationally. His down-to-earth personality and ability to recall and remember people endeared him to his fellow representatives almost immediately. Captain Henry King, editor in chief of the *Globe Democrat* visited with Connelley about Plumb:

> The first time Captain King ever saw Senator Plumb was at the convention in Wichita which nominated Thomas Ryan for Congress. King was interested in the success of Ryan, and he noted the way in which Plumb controlled the convention. He used no force, no specious arguments, no bulldozing tactics. He knew personally almost every man in the convention. Many of them he had served with in the army, others he had met in the courts as fellow attorneys. Some of the delegates were new men whom he had aided in securing or retaining their homes on the public domain. He would walk up to a delegate, put an arm over his shoulder and talk a minute very earnestly, and then go on to another. To some old-time friend of early Kansas days he might say, "Hello John, I have not seen you since the border ruffians burned your cabin;' or, "Hello George, I have not seen you since we were mustered out;" or "Hello Jim, can you make as good time on foot now as you could from Indians in the Powder River Country?" Perhaps none of these were his exact words in

greeting his former acquaintances and companions, but something of this kind he used. He knew everybody and seemed on familiar terms with all the delegates. He controlled the convention in all its stages and did not make speeches, and, in fact, seemed not much in evidence, but he knew men and how to secure their cooperation.

Small Bills

Plumb's unceasing work ethic resulted in a nearly unheard-of amount of bills and resolutions. In the first and second sessions of the 47th Congress (1881 through 1883) he authored 97 bills and four joint resolutions. To put those numbers in perspective, most senators averaged about half that, with some authoring as few as four bills in the session.

Plumb's positions on the Appropriations Committee and as Chairman of the Public Lands Committee made him a force to be reckoned with in the various governmental departments. F.P. Metzger gave insight into his stature when he shared the following account with Connelley in 1910:

> I saw F.P. Metzger, President of the German-American State Bank of Topeka today. Metzger was formerly in the offices of the Geological Survey in Washington. Major J.W. Powell was Director of the Survey. Metzger was appointed from Kansas. He became a sort of protégé of Senator Plumb, as he was quite young. Once the money for payment of help ran low and the Director furloughed all the unmarried clerks until a new appropriation could be made. Among these furloughed clerks were Metzger and some young man from Arkansas, either the son, son-in-law, or proposed son-in-law of Senator Garland, then in Cleveland's Cabinet.
>
> Some two weeks after the clerks were furloughed young Metzger visited the offices of the Survey in a sort of idle mood to visit some friend or see what was going on. To his surprise, he found the Arkansas young man at his desk as though he had not been temporarily laid off. Metzger hastened to the Capitol and informed Plumb, saying that Kansas ought to be treated as well as Arkansas. Plumb took the same view, and when the Senate adjourned he and Metzger went to see Major Powell, whom

Plumb told that Metzger had to be reinstated at once or there would be no further appropriation for the Survey. Major Powell called in the Chief Clerk and directed him to put young Metzger to work.

Plumb became convinced that the Geological Survey was not accomplishing what it should for the money spent, and made a fight on it. He succeeded in cutting off most of its appropriation. Metzger remembers his speech on that occasion. Plumb had the Reports of the Survey brought in and piled by his desk. When he began his speech he turned through the first report and said that the only thing there was the description of a bird, the fossil of which had been discovered and mapped by the Survey, with teeth. The second volume had little of interest but did have the bird with teeth. And so of the third volume. And on an examination, he was able to announce that the old friend, the bird with teeth was still the main subject treated. When he took up the fifth volume he was happy to announce that an advance had been made. In that volume was an account of the discovery by the Survey of a second fossil bird with teeth. The Senate was convulsed with laughter during Plumb's address, and the appropriation was cut down to almost nothing.

Metzger says all the officials of the Departments feared Senator Plumb. He knew what they ought to accomplish and could not be deceived about what they did actually accomplish. Plumb had much influence in the Senate Committee on Appropriations, of which he was a member. He could cut down the appropriation for any Department he thought did not do enough work. Once Plumb sent Metzger to the Assistant Secretary of some Department to request that a Kansas man be given a place at $1200 a year. The assistant secretary said he would have the place, beginning at a certain time. Plumb took the applicant down and introduced him at the Department later and the time was fixed for him to go to work. When the man appeared to go to work he was told that there was no place for him. He went to see Plumb. Plumb was in no good humor about it. He went to the Department and gave the assistant secretary such a dressing down as few men ever got. The result was that the Kansas man was given at once a place at $2400 a year.

The "bird with teeth" story does not appear in the Congressional Record with Senator Plumb. A reference to it is made in the House of Representatives, but the Senate version is missing. As Metzger knew Plumb well it is likely that his memory of this story is correct, but it may have been removed from the Congressional Record. There are instances where entire spans of dialogue are "deleted" as long as the parties involved agree to have it removed. That would explain the absence of this story in the official record.

Plumb was serving as the chairman of the Committee on Public Lands when Senator James H. Berry of Arkansas was appointed to the committee. He recalled his time spent with Plumb on that committee very warmly.

> When he [Berry] took his seat, he was assigned, or appointed to the Committee on Public Lands. Senator Plumb was Chairman of that Committee. From the very first he found Senator Plumb especially kind to him. He always explained anything which came up and took particular care that Senator Berry should have all information about the public lands and the policy of the Government in their disposition. Plumb often requested Senator Berry to report bills which the Committee had agreed on. These courtesies Senator Berry, being a new member and without experience in Senatorial procedure, very much appreciated. Pleasant relations and friendship grew up between Plumb and Berry and these continued without any interruption until severed by the death of Senator Plumb.
>
> Senator Berry says that Senator Plumb was remarkably industrious and had the capacity for doing a very great deal of work—more so than any other man he ever knew. Plumb always knew all about any bill that was disposed of by the Committee of Public Lands. He was a member of several other Committees, and Senator Berry feels sure that he was familiar with the business of those, and also of the bills reported by them.

A simple thing that many people often take for granted are drinking fountains in public buildings. Nearly every government building across the country offers them, but that was not always the case. Plumb introduced and championed the bill that brought drinking fountains to the Capitol building. An unidentified man who worked in the building recalled to a *Washington Post* reporter how they came to be:

> 'It took Senator Plumb, of Kansas, nearly two years to get these water coolers placed in the corridors of the capitol,' said a gentleman as he quenched his thirst with ice water the other day. 'The senator was a fighter when he went into a fight, and it is said that some of his constituents who were visiting Washington for the first time called his attention to the fact that it was impossible for a stranger to get a drink of water in the big building. Of course, people who know the ropes can dodge into one of the numerous committee rooms and get a drink of water, and frequently something stronger, but before the coolers were placed in the main corridors the stranger stood little show. When the complaint was made to Senator Plumb he at once determined that there should be water for all who wished it. The senator went to work and introduced a bill, but this was lost in committee, and after repeated efforts lasting nearly two years, he managed to get it in as an amendment to an appropriation bill, with himself as one of the conferees. He was appealed to give up the effort, but announced that he would defeat the whole bill unless the amendment for coolers stuck. That settled it, and during the next recess, the coolers were placed in the walls. The water is kept cool by pipes through and around the storeroom in the basement of the building, where the ice for use in the building is stored.

When particular issues arose that provoked a strong personal interest from him, he could be counted upon to make a lengthy address to the Senate. These addresses were often well attended in the galleries, and his speech on Senate Bill 1448 on May 6, 1884, was no exception. The bill was about the American Merchant Marine with specific regard to shipbuilding and whether or not the United States should purchase foreign ships for commerce and the United States Navy. Plumb was thoroughly against the bill and argued that American industry and craftsmanship were at the head of the world. He presented hard numbers and laid out a strong argument for his case, harkening back to his career as a lawyer.

The argument was made by many Democratic senators that American Navy ships could simply be purchased from Great Britain and fly the American flag. That the cost of purchasing those ships would be lower than manufacturing them in the United States. Plumb offered facts and figures to argue that there would be no real cost savings, and then sought to humiliate them for even suggesting purchasing foreign ships to save money:

> There is no enterprise in the world beyond the ability of the American people to compass when once they address themselves to it. There is no problem their ingenuity cannot solve; there is no obstacle their courage will not overcome; there is no controversy in which they will ever engage from which they will not emerge triumphant...
>
> If this sentiment surrounding the American flag is to be held so cheaply we might hire the British government perhaps to exhibit it for us at so much an hour! If the flag is to stand for naught, if it is to represent nothing of American skill, no American investment, nothing that is material to the American people, let us emblazon it, like the sign of 'Cuticura' [a soap company] and 'St. Jacob's Oil [a liniment company],' at so much a yard, through the medium of some enterprising sign-painter, on the rocks and roofs, on the highways and in the byways, and on the temples of the Old World as an advertisement that there is such thing as the American Government. The cheaper this is done the better, for according to our Democratic brethren it is only the display of the bunting they are after.
>
> But Mr. President, the flag is nothing in itself. Unless it stands for something why float it? But the American people believe in it as a symbol, as representative of the power, the purposes of a great and free people. Wherever, therefore, it is spread to the breeze let it have underneath it all possible that bespeaks American labor, American genius, American courage, and American manhood.

Today, United States Navy ships are manufactured in the United States by American shipbuilders as they always have been. Plumb's fears of a foreign built United States Navy never came to pass.

Fellow Senators and Associates

Plumb had little time for high society events or showmanship, but he did enjoy spending time with his friends. His social circle consisted of a group of fellow senators, several of whom were democrats, as well as former soldiers and newspapermen.

In 1889, Plumb took a sightseeing trip with his friend Eugene Ware to Monticello. On the way back he purchased a newspaper before boarding the train, and as it rolled out he started to realize that all the news stories seemed rather familiar. He discovered that the "current" newspaper he'd bought was in fact a few days old. After the trip, Ware sent him the following letter:

> June 5, 1889 Wash. D.C.
> Dear Senator:
> While in Washington I have heard some little complaint as to the character of the umbrellas that you leave around in hat racks and hall-ways which comes from your pernicious habit of buying them by the pound.
>
> I send you one herewith with which you can sort of thicken up your former contributions to the general fund. I have put on the handle the date of May 10th which you will remember as the date we visited Monticello, as shown by the papers you bought of the newsboy.
> Yours, until we met again,
>   (Sd) E.F. Ware

He also occasionally found time to indulge in fishing with Senator Pettigrew in South Dakota at the home of Don Cameron. "They fished in a large trout pond but caught no trout. They could see one large trout in the pond but it did not bite. Cameron thought the pond was full of trout, but Pettigrew and Plumb said the big fellow they could see was the only trout there. Pettigrew had the Fish Commission put 10,000 trout into the pond that fall." It is not known if they had better luck the next time around.

Plumb's personality never changed to fit into the common ways of political operations in Washington. Many senators would sling harsh personal insults to further their agendas, which Plumb detested. He fought strongly for the causes he was passionate about, but did not resort to mudslinging or character assassination. Although these insults greatly upset him, he managed to take the high road and did not hold a grudge. Carrie Plumb told Connelley the stories below:

> Mrs. Plumb recalls one incident in which Senator Plumb was more enraged than she ever saw him before or afterwards. Senator Ingalls referred, in the Senate, to Plumb's plebeian birth. He never forgot or forgave that. When he came to his apartments at the hotel he was deathly pale, and Mrs. Plumb inquired if he was ill. He then told her of the incident.
>
> Plumb despised affectation and false pride. On one occasion he was going about with some army officers. One aristocratic officer could not go on without someone to carry his coat. No boy could be found, and Plumb took the coat off the officer's arm and carried it some distance, then handed it back to the snob.
>
> Plumb did not escape having bitter enemies. They misrepresented him and abused him shamefully. Once Mrs. Plumb asked him if he was not offended at a particularly vile slander. He said he was not; that we could not advance without enemies; that one should not be offended at what enemies said; that none could be perfect and what we said and our attitude might cause offense when none was intended. "He was very liberal with those who criticized him and reviewed his conduct to see if there could be any ground for it."
>
> "When we were in Washington we frequently met a certain gentleman and his wife. While the gentleman was very pleasant he was not particularly well informed and was rather snobbish, but my husband talked with him very freely whenever they were thrown together. One day I said to him, 'I don't see how you can find anything to interest you in that gentleman.' He replied we could learn something from everyone; that it was neither

becoming nor profitable to hold ourselves aloof from our fellow men.

Plumb's son, Dale, wrote Connelley the following letter describing an instance of Plumb's sense of humor, which he did not often exercise:

Washington, D.C.
January 19, 1911

To-day I met Mr. Alvord, of Ballard & Alvord, advertising agents, New York City. Mr. Alvord had charge of the Washington bureau of the New York Herald from 1890-1905, and said he remembered my father very well, that he met him a number of times around at Chamberlains, and he remembered that he was always full of fun. A man of abundance of dry American humor, that sometimes he would say nothing for a half an hour, and then would make some remark or tell a story which would convulse everyone in the room. He was a big hearted man, and while he was quick at repartee, amply able to hold his own with the best of them, he was a man of big heart and would not say cutting unkind things as Ingalls would. He remembers at one time a man was expatiating on the value of some mining property in Mexico, which he had to sell, and finally he turned to my father and said "Senator you have been in Mexico a number of times, you can bear out what I say." "Yes," was the reply, "I have been to Mexico a good many times, and all the tracks I saw there had their heels to the south," (people leaving the country). My father was a tireless worker, going everywhere, first to this Department and then that, doing something for his constituents. On one occasion Alvord heard him give one of the Secretaries of a Department a most vigorous dressing down, because he failed to keep some promise he had made.

Many Kansas constituents found reaching Plumb much easier than Senator Ingalls. Plumb understood the people and was a man of action. If someone approached him with an urgent matter, he had no trouble seeing to it himself. "Curley" Harrison, a longtime friend of Plumb's, recalled the following story about their mutual friend, Sam Benedict:

President Harrison issued an order directing the cattlemen who had leases in the Cherokee Strip to have their cattle out by a certain day. The time was short and the cattlemen found they could not comply with the order. They sent Benedict, who was interested in these cattle, or some of them, to Washington to secure a modification of the order. Benedict was a schoolmate of Senator Ingalls; they graduated together from Williams College. Benedict had always been one of the managers for Ingalls in Kansas. He always relied on Ingalls to do anything at Washington which had to be done, and which concerned him (Benedict) or his friends. Benedict knew Plumb well but did not ask any favors of him.

When Benedict called on Ingalls the Senator said he could not even talk about the matter until the next day at eleven o'clock. "This is no tomorrow or eleven o'clock job," said Benedict. "It must have immediate attention." But the Senator was obdurate and Benedict had to content himself with an appointment for eleven o'clock the next day. When he went to the Senator's office he was told that Ingalls had gone to the Senate Chamber. Benedict was a man whose wrath rose on occasion, and he went to the Senate in no good humor. He sent in his card, and it was returned containing the written notation that the Senator would see Mr. Benedict in the Cloak Room at four o'clock. This was too much for Benedict. He wrote on the card "Go to hell" and had it carried back to the Senator; and left the Capitol in high dudgeon. On the steps, he met Plumb, who was carrying a grip and had an overcoat across his arm. "Why, hello, Benedict," said Plumb, "What are you doing here?" "Trying to interview that 'blankety-blank' Ingalls, but without success." "What's up?" said Plumb, "Maybe I can help you." Benedict told his business. Before he had got half the story told Plumb seized him by the arm and said, "Come on, I will go and see the President with you." They walked, and Benedict said he had to trot to keep pace with Plumb. Plumb burst in on the President without much ceremony and told what Benedict wanted. "But," said the President, "I have a Cabinet meeting in a few minutes and cannot attend to this today." But Plumb said the matter could not wait another day. "Well, then, write out the essentials of the modification you desire, and I will attend to it today." Plumb hurriedly wrote the order, looked it over, read it to the President, who approved it, and taking Benedict by the arm bid the President good day as he was disappearing towards his Cabinet, and said, "Come on, Sam, everything is all right now. I must hurry to the Senate. I have just returned from (some place Harrison had forgotten). Come around to my office this evening. I want to talk to you about Kansas." From that day Benedict was the friend and champion of Plumb. And Benedict never thought much of Ingalls after that.

Kansas Supreme Court Justice A.W. Benson was aided by Plumb and told his story to Connelley:

> Some citizens of Ottawa [Kansas] were on the official bond of a Federal office holder who defaulted for a considerable sum. Of the sureties, but one had any property which could be reached by execution, and he thought it a hardship to have to pay the whole defalcation, so sent Benson to Washington to secure a compromise if possible. The matter was in the hands of a Solicitor for the Treasury Department. Benson found it very difficult to reach this official, as he was fenced in and hedged about by doorkeepers and attendants and was very difficult to access. He was a portly and courtly old gentleman, a Whig from the South, and of the antebellum days. And his reserve was hard to break through. He set a time when he would see Benson, who felt that he had not reached any satisfactory status in the official's estimation, and he went to see Plumb about the matter that evening.
>
> The next morning Plumb went with Benson to see the Solicitor, and was not in the least hindered by the doorkeepers and lackeys, but brushed them aside and went in. His introduction of Benson made a vast difference in the standing of the Kansas lawyer, and a satisfactory adjustment of the claim was reached.

That evening Benson again called on Plumb to report the conclusion of the matter and to tell how satisfactorily everything then stood, thinking it was finally disposed of except the payment of the money, which he was to send on when he returned to Kansas. But Plumb told him there were many slips in the settlements of such matters, and that this one ought to be closed up at once. Benson said he could not get the money from Kansas for several days by the ordinary methods of transmission. Plumb told him to draw a sight draft on his client, known to be good for any such amount. Benson did so. Plumb endorsed the draft and went with Benson to a bank, where the money was advanced on the draft, with which Benson immediately completed the settlement and made a final disposition of the matter the same day.

"Plumb's whole term of public service was full of just such acts," said Benson. "He sought every opportunity to be of service to Kansas and her people."

Plumb had served on the Military Affairs Committee when he first became a Senator, and as a veteran himself, he was always eager to help fellow veterans and friends if he could. Judge Tom Ryan told Connelley the following story, which illustrates that part of his personality:

As a friend Senator Plumb was one of the most loyal I ever knew. In the interest of a friend it was not unusual for him to exert his powers forcefully to secure a given object and yet the friend would never know anything about it. It was, I may say, a habit with him while he was really doing all in his power to promote the interest of another his manner and conversation were much as to impress the interested party that he was not taking very much interest in the matter whereas, in fact, he was vigorously faithful from start to finish. He seemed to be acting upon the theory that it was better to keep the mind of his friend prepared for defeat than to fill him with high hopes which possibly might not be realized. However the wisdom of this was questionable, for in case he did not succeed this would have the effect to produce the impression upon the mind of the interested party that failure was due to the Senator's indifference and inattention, but on the other hand, in case of success it was likely to have the effect of increasing gratitude, but fortunately for Plumb, he generally succeeded.

A good illustration of this characteristic of Plumb was the case of a court-martialed army officer who had appealed to him for assistance. The officer had been deeply wronged and Plumb, with a keen sense of the injustice the officer had suffered by court-martial, appealed to the War Department for his relief. The officer was most worthy in every respect. He was accomplished, brave, highly educated, had a fine sense of honor, and was a thorough gentleman. I became acquainted with him and assisted Plumb what little I could, on his behalf. He had strong opposition in the War Department and the matter dragged along for a considerable time without action, although Plumb was making a persistent fight and had his whole heart in it because of the wrong the officer had suffered and because also he had come to like him very much. As success under all circumstances was doubtful, he was, if anything, more than usually careful not to give the officer much encouragement. The result was that the officer himself became discouraged and became impressed with a doubt as to whether Plumb was taking much interest in the matter anyhow and in that frame of mind came to my office one morning to tell me that he had concluded to abandon the fight and go home and to thank me for my kindness in his matter.

Knowing Plumb's disposition in such matters I suspected at once that he had lost confidence in Plumb, so I asked him why he was going home. He said that he had become satisfied that the War Department would do nothing and that he did not feel warranted in troubling his friends any more in the matter. I told him it would be a pleasure to his friends that were interesting themselves in his behalf to continue to do all in their power and that I did not regard the case as so hopeless as to justify an abandonment of the contest. I then said to him you are mistaken about Plumb, and you must not go home. Plumb is your main support in this matter and not myself and unless something has happened since I last saw the Senator. I do not hesitate to tell you that you are doing him injustice. He replied that he had had a talk with him that morning and his impression was the result. I then said to him, you stay right here Captain and I will go up and see the Senator.

I found Plumb in his office and after a moments conversation I said, "By the way, how is Captain _____'s matter getting along? Seems to me it drags a little too much."

"So it does," said Plumb, and turned loose a torrent of sulfurous criticism against the Department and some of its officials. He then said, "let's go up and see the President about it." I said all right and we went.

In his conversation with the President, he became excited and while he did not transcend the limits of decorum, his manner, his vigor of speech, his intensity of feeling, his vehement gesticulation, and his almost savage characterization of the wrong inflicted upon the officer evidently produced a profound impression upon the President. I shall never forget that most extraordinary scene. The President said the matter should have early consideration and we left.

When I returned to my office the captain was there and I told him exactly what had transpired. Tears came into his eyes and he said, "I am sorry I said anything. I will stay." It was but a few days after that when the Department took favorable action in the matter. It is needless to say that ever after, that officer was one of the most devoted friends Plumb ever had.

Plumb was keen to help those who had shown promise and who he thought would succeed in certain departments. Philip Campbell was just such a man and recalled how Plumb had changed his life:

Philip P. Campbell, Pittsburg, Kansas, Representative Third District, today told me that his success in life so far was due in large degree to the friendship for him of Senator Plumb. In the campaign of 1888 Campbell worked hard for the Republican ticket in Kansas. He made speeches in most parts of the state. He met Senator Plumb there for the first time to become at all acquainted with him and was with Plumb at many meetings. Plumb became attached to him, and when the campaign was closed and Harrison elected there was a meeting of the leaders at Topeka. The disposition of patronage was discussed. Plumb requested that the place for Campbell be left to him and asked that no objection be made by anyone entitled to patronage to the plan he might give Campbell, and this was agreed to. Senator Plumb came home for the holidays. From Chicago, he telegraphed Campbell to meet him at Emporia. When Campbell got there, he found Plumb's office full to overflowing of friends and public men from all parts of the state. He could not get into the room for some time. When Plumb saw him he came over to him and shook hands with him cordially and told him to go back to the hotel and wait for him–that at six o'clock he would be at the hotel and they would have dinner together. Plumb came and at the dinner, he told Campbell he had a place for him which would pay $2500.00 per annum and $3.00 per day and railroad fare–the $3.00 being for sustenance. This was good news for Campbell, for he had never had more than $15.00 a month for his labor in his life. It seemed too good to be true.

When Plumb had told him of the place and assured him of it, he added, "but if you were my son I would not permit you to have this place for anything on earth."

"Why?" asked Campbell, surprised.

"For this reason," replied Plumb, "I observed you closely during the campaign. You say you are studying law–have been since your graduation from Baker University. I know you can make a lawyer and build up a good business and become independent. If you take this place you will be sure of it for four years. But you will then be less capable of starting in life for yourself than you are now. We may be successful in the next national campaign, and in that case, you would have the place or some other four years more, at the end of which you would be still less able and inclined to go into any business for yourself. I have seen so many young men of promise ruined by getting into the service of the Government that I thought I ought to say this to you. But I have the place for you. Think over what I have said and talk it over with your mother. If you decide to take the place, pack your trunk and come to Washington the last week of February and be there to see the inauguration. There are no strings to the place and it is yours if you want it."

Campbell came down off of the mountain of exultation he had been placed on by the announcement that he was to have the place. But he was convinced that Senator Plumb had his interest at heart and knew what he was talking about. He agreed to think it over well and try to come to the right conclusion. When he told his mother what Senator Plumb had said she was both glad and sad,–glad that Senator Plumb had encouraged her son to think he could succeed in his chosen profession, and sorry to give up the sure thing of $2500.00 a year. Campbell decided to try to work up a practice and declined the position. At the end of a year and a half, he wrote Senator Plumb thanking him for the advice he had given him and proudly reporting to him that he had done well in the law and had just closed one case that netted him a fee of six thousand dollars. Senator Plumb wrote him a letter of congratulations the night before his death– perhaps the last letter the Senator ever wrote, and Campbell has it now at home.

Chapter 16

Family and Business

By 1881, the Plumb family was complete with the birth of their son, Preston Jr. Caroline had been born only a few years earlier in 1879. Caring for five children with a husband often away from home in Washington D.C. undoubtedly exasperated Carrie Plumb's already fragile health. She spent nearly as much time away from home as her husband, traveling to sanitariums and various doctors back east seeking treatment for her ailment. Although the exact medical condition is unknown, it did leave her bedridden and weak quite often. A subject that concerned her husband a great deal.

> Thomas S. Krutz told me today that Senator Plumb was a tender and anxious husband. Mrs. Plumb's health was very bad, and the Emporia physician had said she could not get well at all. In New York, there was a physician who had recommended a meat diet exclusively for certain ailments. Senator Plumb took Mrs. Plumb there and the treatment was beneficial to her. Senator Plumb did not fail to spend Sunday with Mrs. Plumb returning to Washington early Monday mornings. Senator Plumb wished to have his son Preston, then but a child, cared for by his aunt in Ohio, so that Mrs. Plumb would be relieved of any care while regaining her health. Krutz took the boy to Ohio to the aunt. The Senator had Krutz attend to much business for him. Some men in business with Senator Plumb got an enterprise into bad condition, and he had Krutz straighten it out. Mrs. Plumb saw that the matter was worrying Senator Plumb and she desired to know what the condition of the property was, but her husband put her off. She inquired then of Krutz who told her the property was first class in many ways and would turn out all right. Some days later Senator Plumb took Krutz by the hand and with a tear in his eye and a voice choking with emotion thanked him for his talk to Mrs. Plumb, saying it had relieved her of worry. This is the only time Krutz saw him so deeply moved, and it was all for his wife's happiness.

Plumb's tenderness and care towards his wife showed a far different side of him than what one would see on the Senate floor. Longtime friend, Walter Stevens recalled:

> The gentleness and tenderness toward the invalid wife were beautiful. The Senator was of powerful mold. He had biceps like a blacksmith's. Sometimes when he went out in a hurry he slammed the door so that it could be heard from basement to attic. But in the presence of the frail wife and mother, the great strong man was another character. His voice took on a tone unusual to those who only knew him in public life. His movements were subdued, and his manner indescribably delicate.

While Carrie was away at sanitariums in New York and elsewhere resting, Plumb would often visit her whenever he could. Carrie told Connelley:

> Once when Mrs. Plumb was ill the Senator had her taken to a Sanitarium in New York City. He went there to see her every Saturday. He always took with him, a valise full of letters to read on Sunday. Many of these he read to Mrs. Plumb. Once he received a letter from an old soldier who was being wronged in a business transaction and who had written about it. The letter seemed to impress Plumb much. He told Mrs. Plumb that he knew the man—that he was a good man, and he would have helped him. Plumb threw himself on a lounge. Mrs. Plumb said: "Preston, you have never forgotten that you were a poor boy, have you?" Plumb held up his hands and said he had not—he hoped he never would—that sometimes he feared he might, but he struggled against it. The newspaper correspondents noticed that Plumb went to New York every Saturday, and knowing nothing of why he went, some paper said he was going there to consult with Wall Street speculators. That offended Plumb and wounded him deeply, for he was going to visit Mrs. Plumb, then in the Sanitarium there.

Carrie's near constant trips to hospitals, doctors, and sanitariums took her away from Plumb and her children. It was very difficult for her to go through as evidenced in her writing. In a letter to Preston Jr. From New

Portrait of Carrie Plumb taken June 1880. Image courtesy the Plumb family.

York sent in April 1889, she wrote, "I hope Papa will be over this week. It is two weeks now since I have seen him....Remember Mama always loves her darling boy." Carrie underwent various treatments and therapies for her chronic illnesses–many of which were difficult. She wrote in another letter to Preston Jr., "The Dr. has me do some things I don't like to do one bit. But then I think of my little boy and the others I want to live for. And no one knows, but I like to do them…Remember Mama thinks of you often and would like to know just that minute what her little boy is doing." Plumb wrote in a letter to Preston Jr. that Carrie had recovered some strength finally and could sit up in bed.

Senator James Berry of Arkansas told a heartwarming story of Plumb's generosity regardless of political affiliation. Senator Berry was a democratic senator from Arkansas whose daughter had seemed to come down with the same health issue as Carrie. When Carrie discovered this, she asked her husband to inquire of the senator the nature of his daughter's illness, and if the treatment she had received at Salisbury and Moore in New York that had benefited her, might also be of help to the young girl.

> One day Plumb inquired of Berry if his daughter was not ill from a nervous disease, saying that Mrs. Plumb had spoken to him about it. When Senator Berry had told him of the nature of the illness of his daughter, Plumb requested permission to call and see what resemblance there might be in her illness to that of Mrs. Plumb, which permission Senator Berry was very glad to give him. Plumb and one of his daughters came soon to see Miss Berry. When Plumb saw Berry, after that visit, he said that her trouble was similar to that of Mrs. Plumb, and which Salisbury and Moore had cured. He strongly urged Senator Berry to send his daughter to those physicians for treatment.
>
> Senator Berry replied that he had already had his daughter treated by the best physicians in the West and that he had just brought her home from treatment by Dr. Mitchell of Philadelphia, who had told him there was very little hope for her. He said that he really had lost hope for his daughter, and having no faith that she could be benefited and not a rich man he hesitated to go to the further expense, for the expense would

be large—that if he had hope that she could be helped he would manage to send her.

Plumb then said that it seemed too bad that she should not have the benefit of this medical treatment, which, from its success with Mrs. Plumb, he felt sure would help her much and perhaps cure her. And he said to Senator Berry, "Do not allow money to stand in the way. I am much interested in this matter. Draw a check on me for one thousand dollars and send the girl to New York. If you ever feel able to pay me the money, all right, and if you are never able to pay it, I will never ask you for it."

This revealed to Senator Berry how deeply in earnest Plumb was. He told Plumb he could not take the money, for he might not be able to pay it back, but as he was sure of beneficial results he would find the means to send his daughter to New York. He thanked Plumb for his kindness, and he sent his daughter to New York, and she was very much benefited. Her health was practically restored. She married and died ten years later. "And," said Senator Berry, "Senator Plumb never asked me a favor in his life. He never asked me to vote for nor against any bill in the Senate. There was no favor he wanted of me and there was none I could have rendered him. His action was entirely disinterested and from friendship alone."

The value of that offer equates to roughly $25,000 in today's money. Plumb was a keen investor and over the years had done well in mining and real estate. Although he was certainly in a position to benefit personally as a U.S. Senator, he was very clear not to get involved in any business dealings that could be seen as a conflict of interest. He always paid his railroad fare and did not invest in any dealings that he was connected with in the Senate.

Children

Due to his wife's health issues, she was often unable to care for their children. Plumb usually accompanied her to doctor's visits and live-in treatments or he was in Washington D.C. away from them. The children were often sent to live with Carrie's family in Ohio, or were taken in by Mary Perley in Emporia. As was customary at the time for well-to-do families, the children attended boarding schools to receive the best possible education. Their youngest child, Preston Jr., attended Nazareth Hall in Nazareth, Pennsylvania. The school was founded in 1754 as a military cadet school, and by the time of the Civil War, had become a premier school in the nation. Plumb's letters to young Preston give excellent insight into what he wanted them to achieve, and also offer a glimpse into a more personal side of the man.

The following letter, written in December of 1887, was sent to Preston Jr., from Washington D.C. back home to Emporia, when he was just six years old:

> My dear Boy,
> I have had so many things to do that I could only think about you, as I do so very often, but not write to you. Mamma sent me the letter you wrote her, and I was very much surprised to see how good a letter you could write. You have learned much since you went to Mr. Perley's. I hope you will learn more. You are old enough to know to read and write very well. Your papa could read when he was only four years old—but I think it is just as well for boys to wait until they are six or seven before learning to read and write, but <u>then</u> they ought to hurry up, as I hope you will do.
>
> The ground is covered with snow here, and this afternoon I saw many children rolling over and over in the snow in the parks. They were very glad the snow came but as there are no hills in town they cannot ride down hill on their sleds; but they race each other on their sleds in the streets as you and Carrie [sister Caroline] did in Emporia. The birds, too, seem to enjoy it, for they fly around in flocks and alight in the snow, wash themselves and fly away only to alight somewhere else and hop around as if they were having heaps of fun. I wonder their feet don't get cold. But nobody has proposed to make shoes for them…
> Good bye my boy God bless you
> From your Father

Plumb saw value in the children learning music and encouraged them all to take lessons. Daughters Ruth and Caroline both played the piano, and in the following letter from March 1890, he is happy to hear that young Preston wishes to learn the violin:

> My dear Preston—
> Your letter of the 2d came duly to hand and I was very glad to hear from you. I am willing that you should take lessons on the violin, and I am glad you wish to do so. Music is the source of pleasure to those who practice it and to nearly all those who hear it. The person who is a musician has, therefore, the means of pleasure for himself and also of conferring pleasure upon others—and no one ought to overlook in getting knowledge of any kind the value of which he may thereby confer upon others. No one should live for himself alone—but also that he may confer benefit on others. So I hope if you have taste for it you will take lessons on the violin…
> With the greatest love.
> Always your Father

In September of 1891 when Preston Jr. was 10 years old, Plumb wrote:

> Dear Preston—
> Your letter of August 18th has remained unanswered for a long time, but I think of you very often, and I hope it will not be long until the family will be united in our home. Still while children are getting an education it is often necessary that they go away from home, and while they are away they should be careful to learn those things which make them better men and women and more useful. I have no doubt you had a pleasant vacation, and now you are down to your books again. I hope you will do your best to be the head of your class. Though it often happens that those who are at the head of their class are not the best scholars. But it is a good idea to do one's very best at school as well as elsewhere.

Although Plumb's work often took him away from home, he tried to maintain involvement in his children's lives through letters and visits. Carrie and Plumb often traveled to New York, Pennsylvania, and

Washington D.C. for medical treatment and Plumb's work, which made visiting the children much easier.

Business

Plumb maintained the presidency of the Emporia National Bank for some time after his election to the Senate. He also took portions of the money he earned and invested them in various business ventures. These ranged from railroads, to mines in Colorado, and to inventions. Jesse McDonald, an early pioneer of Emporia, recalled that Plumb had once told him, "whenever you do make money salt part of it in something else that you consider perfectly safe." Colonel O.E. Learnard recalled, "Plumb was in business of all kinds, buying, selling, developing, and was remarkably successful in almost all his ventures. He lost money in some of them, but made enough in others to more than offset these. Learnard once met Senator Vest and another gentleman in New York looking for Plumb. They were anxious to find what he was buying so they could buy the same, knowing that Plumb did not deal in anything that was likely to fail."

The work of tracking down exactly which mines and businesses Plumb invested in is nearly impossible today. He seemed to purchase interests, sell them, and use the proceeds to purchase new shares in other businesses. This was a carryover from his early days in Emporia. While he managed the *Kanzas News* he also sold real estate, insurance, and practiced law. Noyes Spicer worked for Plumb during the majority of his Senate career dealing with several mines he was invested in. From his account, it is possible to catch a glimpse into what Plumb was working on:

> Spicer became associated with Plumb in 1879. Plumb sent him to Leadville to superintend a mine he was interested in there. People were dying rapidly there with a throat trouble. Spicer got Mountain Fever, had the throat trouble and developed erysipelas [a skin infection], and was about to die. People dying so fast that about a hundred feet of a trench was kept open all the time in which to bury them. Plumb came, and Spicer told him to have a carriage ready the next morning to take him to the railroad alive or dead. Plumb did so, Spicer got to Denver and recovered. Doctors told him he would die if he went back to Leadville. Plumb did not think so and wanted him to go back, but Spicer

refused absolutely and would not return. He was not with
Plumb in Small Hopes Mine on that account.

He next went to Washington mining camp for Plumb, about 74
miles south of Tucson, Arizona. Was there for about six months,
and the mine was sold.

Then he went to New Mexico to look after some mines for
Plumb, but these did not amount to much, and were disposed of,
and he did not remain there long.

On a trip to Colorado to look over some of his mining interests, Plumb ran into A.B. Browne, a lawyer from Washington D.C.

> Browne said Plumb was a combination of brusqueness, force, and tenderness of heart. He saw Plumb, soon after their acquaintance, in Colorado, where he was on some business connected with some mining business. Plumb saw him first as he was starting up the mountains in a stage or coach, which was not a public conveyance. He wished to know how Browne was going up and was told he would get up in some sort of conveyance. "Nothing of the kind", said Plumb, "you will go up in my carriage" and he took Browne in. Browne remembers that when they got well up the mountains frequent stops were necessary. The lightness of the atmosphere made it impossible for the horses to go far without stopping to rest. When a halt was made Plumb would get out and go on ahead. He would go out of the way and look over the country. Even when the horses could not go more than a hundred feet without resting, Plumb would walk rapidly up and around the mountain apparently without the least inconvenience. He would cut across curves in the road and have a fine look at the mountains before the carriage came up. The altitude seemed to have no effect on him. Long afterwards he would joke Browne about finding him when he was lost in Colorado.

Helping Others

While Connelley was conducting interviews with politicians who knew Plumb, a chance meeting introduced him to John Roberts of the Government Printing Office. Roberts offered several stories giving a rare insight into Plumb's personality while a Senator, as well as that of his wife, Carrie.

> Roberts is a Welshman, and lived formerly at Emporia, where he became acquainted with Senator Plumb. He recalls that Plumb once came into the office of the newspaper on which he worked, sat down at a table, and wrote a long editorial on the subject of the sugar beet. Plumb was greatly interested in the cultivation of the sugar beet and believed that Kansas could raise it in immense quantities. He believed the sugar problem could be largely solved by the cultivation of the beet. The editorial was along this line Roberts believes.
>
> It was late when Plumb came in to write the editorial–after midnight. He wrote so long that the foremen believed the whole editorial could not be set up and put in the paper with time left to get the paper into the mails for the morning trains. But Plumb took off his coat, secured a "stick", went to a "case" and set type for an hour or two, and this enabled the paper to come out on time.
>
> Roberts said that a printer was once put off the train at Emporia because he was dying of consumption and could not stand the trip further. His wife was with him. The printers of the town took him to a hotel, where it was found that he had no money. Mrs. Plumb heard of the matter. She rented a room for the printer and his wife, paid all their expenses, and when the printer died bought his casket and a ticket for the widow and her dead husband, paid all bills, and sent them home. This she did for the reason that Senator Plumb had told her never to see a printer suffer for lack of money.
>
> Roberts left Emporia and went to Kansas City where he got work on the *Kansas City Journal*. He had but three day's work each week, which was not enough to support himself and his family. He slept at the fire station and got most of his food at free lunch counters in order to send his wages to his wife at Emporia.

Just at this time, there was a Senatorial Committee at Kansas City to investigate the charges filed by shippers against the Kansas City Stockyards management. Senator Plumb was a member of the Committee, and he had rooms at the Midland Hotel. The weather was extremely cold. Roberts was suffering from lung trouble and was having hemorrhages from the lungs every day, almost, and never fewer than three a week.

One night after a severe hemorrhage, in a saloon, he started to the fire station to sleep on the hay there. He was weak and a terrific storm of snow and sleet was blowing down the streets. The bartender had given him a glass of brandy to make him strong enough to get to the station. He had his head down, facing the storm, and making what progress he could through the snow drifts. He did not look ahead and he ran into someone. On looking up he saw it was Senator Plumb, who recognized him at once, and who wished to know what he was doing there. Roberts told him his story. Plumb took him to his apartments in the hotel. There he told Roberts that he must return home at once and gave him the money with which to do so. He told Roberts he should have a place in the Government Printing Office at Washington and that he must wait at Emporia until sent for. In a short time, Plumb sent him a telegram to come to Washington and go to work which he did, and excepting a few vacations, he has been in that place ever since.

Roberts was often at Plumb's offices. He said Plumb, at that time, always went to work on his mail at a quarter to five in the morning. He had a gentleman and his daughter, both stenographers, come at that hour. He dictated his letters to them. At that time, he was receiving about six hundred letters daily, as Roberts believes. These were on all subjects—pensions, politics, public land, all sorts of public affairs. Many of them required trips to [federal] departments. He usually got through his mail about nine o'clock. Then he would send out for a glass of milk, drinking which, he would start out for his daily round of the Departments. He usually arrived at the Capitol about a quarter to twelve, where he was busy until adjournment. Then he would usually eat a hearty dinner–and being hungry usually ate too much, this being the only meal in fact, that he ate during the day. He would sometimes eat nothing for a whole day–and occasionally he would go without food for two days if very busy and much occupied.

Plumb's sister, Ellen, owned and operated a bookstore in Emporia for several decades. While home from Washington D.C., he could sometimes be found helping her. Mabel Edwards, a niece of Plumb's, recalled the following instance told to her by Laura Thomas who had been a clerk in Ellen's store for many years. "Miss Thomas also told me about the time when Miss Ellen Plumb was sick and had to go away. Miss Thomas was left in charge; the holiday goods were coming in to be unpacked and then sold and she worked very hard to make things go right. Senator Plumb came in and helped her and when it was over he said to her, "Laura if you ever want a position; if you are ever out of work, let me know and I will get you something."

Plumb never allowed himself much time to indulge in personal pursuits that weren't somehow related to work, but he was an avid reader. Emma Lane-Randolph gave a speech on Plumb and remarked, "Senator Plumb was a lover of literature, fond of poetry. A member of his family told me that when he traveled he frequently put in his traveling bag a copy of Longfellow or of Whittier, and he read as he journeyed. W.B. Stevens in the *Globe Democrat* said of his reading: "He bought more books than any other member of the Senate. One of the largest book dealing houses in New York sent him monthly, or oftener, a descriptive list of everything received in stock since the former report. On this list, the senator checked all that aroused his interest. The list was returned to the dealer and the box of books came. He went through the books in the same steam engine-like way he did everything."

Although Carrie Plumb was often very ill and spent much of her time nearly bedridden, she was passionate about improving her community. Reading was a lifelong passion of both her and her husband, and Carrie was heavily involved with the creation of the first public library in Emporia.

A group of women met at the Plumb family home in October of 1883 to discuss the creation of a library. These women, in many cases, were early settlers to Emporia, such as Mary Perley, Abigail Morse, and Mrs. C.S. Cross. Their plan was to raise the needed funds to create a public library in the reading room of the *Emporia News* building, and the ladies organized themselves into committees to accomplish the work. Carrie formed a committee with Mrs. L.A. Platt to visit the library in Topeka in order to study its operation and management, to more effectively establish a library in Emporia. The women continued to hold their meetings at the Plumb residence, and in 1884 they were successful in organizing hundreds of volumes of books scattered from previously unsuccessful attempts at a library. In addition, Carrie championed an effort to raise funds to purchase an additional 1,000 books for the new library. It was then turned over to the city for management while some of the women remained involved in an advisory capacity.

Carrie was also involved in charity and social functions of the Congregational church. She was a member of the Old Settlers organization and attended reunions around the state. In 1877 she served as treasurer of the ladies auxiliary of the "Home of the Friendless," an organization for the benefit of poor and destitute women. Like her husband, Carrie also had a strong interest in helping others whenever and however she could.

Chapter 17

Senator of the West

During Plumb's time in office, many of the western territories were not states yet. Citizens in the territories of Washington, Oregon, New Mexico, Arizona, and Wyoming often appealed to Plumb for help in the Senate. These territories had no representation in the Senate and Plumb was all too keen to help however he could.

An incident arose in New Mexico territory involving lands held by poor families who had been there for generations. "Judge Sluss was a member of the Court which passed on many of the land grants in New Mexico. It developed that there were hundreds of poor people, mostly New Mexicans of Spanish extraction, who held small tracts of land fronting on streams and running back to cliff or mesa. They had no titles to their lands save that of possession. Their ancestors had lived on these tracts, neglected and undisturbed by the Spanish government. Plumb was particularly anxious that the poor people should be confirmed in their rights to this land. He often said to Sluss that his chief concern was that they should be taken care of. And they were given their lands with a good title." Plumb was a strong advocate for them to remain on their lands during Senate debates during the 1883-1885 session.

Senator James H. Berry of Arkansas remarked to Connelley:

> "I think," said Senator Berry, "that Plumb's association with the Southern Senators had somewhat modified his views in regard to the Southern people. And I believe that he had some ambition that the South and West might become united in political action, as their interests lay in the same direction. I know he was pulling the West away from the New England influences in the Senate. His sympathies were strong for the West. He was always ready and anxious to stand for the people of the West whenever the interests of the East and West came into conflict."

Senator Henry Blair of New Hampshire echoed Senator Berry's statements on Plumb's service to the West:

> The Index of the Congressional Record will show his name takes up more space than that of any other Senator, except, Blaine. He

did an immense amount of business for his people in Kansas,—all sorts of business for all sorts of people. I think three-fourths of the Kansas Senatorial work was done by Plumb—perhaps more than that. The West did not then have so many Senators and it had much public land. Plumb was Chairman of the Senate Committee on Public Lands, and this made him a kind of general Senator from the West – he acted for all the West. No other man ever had so large a constituency, and never will have, for all the West now has Senators – or almost all.

Although the Civil War had ended a dozen years prior to Plumb's entrance into the Senate, old wounds are difficult to heal, and the scars from that conflict were ever present in Congress. Senator Charles F. Manderson of Nebraska entered the Senate in 1883 and sent the following statement to Connelley describing Plumb, as well as the political divisions within the Senate as a result of the late war:

> No man of greater physical vigor, or more virile mental force, than Preston B. Plumb, United States Senator from Kansas, served in the Congress. His personality was like his vigorous young state, and with Ingalls and Plumb as Senators, no state presented, in the National councils, a more winning and aggressive force. A combat with either, or both combined, was a conflict well worth witnessing. One was the polished orator, the other the sturdy debater. Ingalls fought with the rapier, and the quick flashing of the pointed blade brought wounds to his adversary. Plumb dealt with the battle-ax, which he wielded with such force and power as to bring incurable injury to his opponent. Plumb was powerful in Committee work and immensely strong on the floor.
>
> You could always depend upon him. He would ever be for you or against you. He was friend or foe, and the evidence of what he was came either by favor freely granted, or opposition forcibly bestowed. Kansas has never had such prominence in national affairs, and was such an aggressive and winning power as when these differing types represented her in the Senate.
> During my twelve years service in the United States Senate, I was a member of many important Committees, but the

committee that was most to my taste and upon which I performed the greatest amount of duty was the Committee on Military Affairs, of which Gen. John A. Logan and afterwards General Joseph R. Hawley, were chairmen. This committee was composed of men who had served in both the Federal and Confederate armies during the war of the Rebellion, and our intimate association on that committee led to mutual regard and esteem, and, I might properly say, affection.

During the twelve years that I served in the Senate, I became acquainted with a large number of senators who had had military service, and at one time a matter occurred showing the feeling that existed between those that had fought against each other in the great war. The Senate was Republican in majority and it became necessary to elect the president of the body. It was well understood that the two men who would be balloted for at the caucus were Senator Hoar of Massachusetts and Senator Frye of Maine. A few days before the caucus was to be held, Senator Plumb of Kansas, an able vigorous, and aggressive man, came to me and said, "Will you accept the Presidency of the Senate?"

[I said,] "No man would refuse so distinguished an honor, but the next President will be Senator Frye or Senator Hoar."

He replied, "Perhaps not, for a large number of us want you."

"Well," I said, "the mere suggestion is compliment enough, but I favor the election of Senator Frye and propose to vote for him." The caucus was held and to my surprise I received a large vote, the ballots being equally distributed between Frye, Hoar, and myself. As the balloting continued, to my astonishment there was a constant gain in the Manderson vote, and finally, I was elected.

I was greatly surprised, indeed overwhelmed, with this complimentary honor, and went to my committee room to be followed in a short time by Senator Sherman, who told me a very distinguished honor was to be mine. I replied, "I appreciate that, Mr. Sherman, and am really surprised at what has occurred." He said, "I do not mean your selection by the Republican caucus, but, after the caucus adjourned I met Senator Gorman of Maryland and he wanted to know the result of our deliberations, and when I told him, he said, that is what we have been waiting to hear. There are a lot of old Confederate enemies, now friends of Senator Manderson, and their insistence is that if he should be elected by the Republican caucus that we shall make no nomination against him and elect him by the unanimous vote of the Senate."

I have been told that this was the first instance in the history of the Senate, at least for many years, that the minority party of the Senate made no nomination for the presidency of that body. I served as president of the Senate for several years, until there was a change in the political complexion, and the Democrats obtained a majority, when Senator Harris was elected my successor.

Land Rights and Civil War Pensions

Plumb was always aware of even the smallest details within bills. One such bill dealt with the former Kaw Native American lands in the area of Council Grove. When lands were first opened up for settlement, squatters often arrived and quickly left if they were unable to start a homestead or if the land did not prove worth investing in. A short time later, settlers arrived and invested the time and energy into tending the land and building homes. A bill was introduced that would have given the rights to the land to the first squatters (who had since abandoned the land in many cases) rather than those currently living on it who had built homes on the property. John Maloy of Council Grove, Kansas was concerned with this language and wrote to Judge Thomas Ryan, the representative for that district. He asked him to:

> take out the clause in the bill giving first squatters authority to assign their rights to anyone. When Ryan received Maloy's communication the bill had already passed the House, but he turned the letter and telegram over to Plumb. Plumb inserted in the bill the clause, "those now on the land and in possession." This clause gave it to the settlers then on the land–those rightly

entitled to buy it. If squatters had been given the right indiscriminately to assign their rights men who had squatted for a short time there years before could have assigned their claims, and the real settlers would have had much trouble to perfect their titles, and in many cases would have lost their land altogether. "Plumb always stood for the people. He was alert on their behalf. He was a hard worker, and the people loved him."

Many of Plumb's Senate bills were pension requests for aged Civil War soldiers and their dependents. Some of them had been killed in the war, and their families had not been given the pensions which they were entitled to. Plumb seemingly took on every request made of him by a veteran or their families. Mabel Edwards, a niece of Plumb, recalled the following stories to Connelley:

> Miss Laura Thomas who for a long time clerked in Miss Ellen Plumb's bookstore, while at Mrs. Wibley's in September 1910, told me of an incident that came under her notice. A Mrs. Williams who lived out in the country, and whose husband had deserved a pension but never received one, through the efforts of Senator Plumb received the pension and considerable back pay. Her husband had been sick for a long time before his death. Mrs. Williams was also sick and had cataracts on both eyes and was almost blind. They had had to put a mortgage on their farm and were having a very hard time. It was difficult to get the pension on account of the loss of some papers but finally Senator Plumb pushed the matter through. Not long after, he was in the bookstore one day talking with some friends. Mrs. Williams was in the store and recognized his voice. She had had her eyes operated on and could see faintly. She turned and looked at him and said, "Oh, Mr. Plumb I want to thank you for the pension you got for me—you don't know how much it meant to me; it has raised the mortgage from the farm, clothed my children, and helped me to regain my health and my eyesight." And then she said it over again, "You don't know what it was to me." It is seldom that gratitude is ever expressed as it was by that woman. I can see Senator Plumb's face now as it lighted up with pleasure. The tears came to his eyes and choking

them back, he said, "I am very glad I was able to do something for you."

Miss Thomas also told me that Senator Plumb secured a pension for her mother after considerable effort. Her brother had been killed in the war but they found a letter in which he said he wanted his mother to have what was coming to him and to get certain things. Miss Thomas says she remembers when she received the letter from Senator Plumb saying he had secured the pension for her mother. She was at the store and broke down and cried so Miss Plumb told her she better go home. Mrs. Thomas was so pleased over getting the pension and said now she was not dependent on her daughters, her son had provided for her support.

Public Lands

During the time of westward expansion in the 19th century, the Committee on Public Lands was one of the most powerful Senate committees to serve on. It controlled which lands would open up for the building of new railroads, where commerce would flow, where new ports might open, which lands would be freed for settlement, and the management of the natural resources on those lands (timber, precious metals, oil, etc.). Not only was Plumb a member of this committee, but he served as its chairman from 1881 to 1891.

During this time there was no U.S. Forest Service as there is in modern America. Stewardship of the land was in many ways a new principle and laws were just being set to preserve those resources. Plumb's work with Senator Pettigrew of South Dakota laid the groundwork for the nation's forestry laws and also paved the way for the later introduction of forestry reserves.

> Senator Pettigrew was on the Senate Committee on Public Lands with Plumb. He had been a surveyor by contract of public lands in the Dakota Territory and had had much to do with public lands. Holman of the House, got passed in that body a brief bill, repealing the timber grabbing law, by which railroads and others had secured much of the timber of the Pacific Coast. This law had been designed to aid bona fide settlers to get timber for the development of their farms, but had been

perverted and distorted by the timber corporations. When Holman's bill came to the Senate, it was referred to the Senate Committee on Public Lands. Plumb, Pettigrew, and Walthall, of Mississippi, upon its consideration, became convinced that it was a just measure. They also saw that the whole public land system had arrived at a period when it should be revised throughout. A revision, was, accordingly made. The bill consisted of twenty-four sections—the twenty-fourth being the provision which empowers the President to withdraw forest lands or other lands from entry at his discretion. Under this law all the great forest reserves of the country have been made—most of them by Roosevelt. Holman's law was made one of the sections of the bill.

Senator Pettigrew said he and Senator Plumb formulated and passed the present Forestry Law, and he said that Senator Plumb's views on the public domain were always right. He understood the whole matter from top to bottom. Plumb believed the time had come, even in his day, when all public lands should be withdrawn and held for disposition under strict conditions and in small tracts to aid settlers. He also advocated the withdrawal of all coal, oil, and gilsonite lands, and the leasing of these to corporations who should pay the government a royalty on the product mined. He recommended that this be done in Utah, but Lacy, Chairman of the House Committee on Public Lands would not consent and the law was lost. It was Plumb's intention to make the Utah law the general government policy.

Plumb also championed bills in the Senate to preserve the lands and forests that would later become Yosemite National Park and Sequoia National Park. Plumb's goal was to prevent deforestation and development of those areas and to regulate industries that could have stripped those natural landscapes.

Women's Suffrage
Women's Suffrage was a national issue and Kansas was no exception to the fervor. Plumb's record on the subject shows that at the 1858 constitutional convention he served as a delegate to, he was in favor of it.

By the time of his service in the State Legislature in the 1860s, he was against it, and actively campaigned against it. A convention was held regarding women's suffrage in Emporia in 1867 and Plumb headlined the opposition gathering held the following day. Mary Perley of Emporia was for women's suffrage and told the following story:

> At one time they were going to have a suffrage meeting here and had decided they would like to have someone make a speech in opposition to it and then have someone answer it. Mrs. Sterry and I went to Senator Plumb to know if he would make the answer to the opposition speech. He said no he did not care to go on record that way. Mrs. Sterry said, "Senator Plumb why are you opposed to woman's suffrage?" He said, "I will tell you in a few moments. If we had woman's suffrage every woman would be voting for the best man and that would disorganize politics."

Plumb's reversal on the issue in 1867 may have been for pragmatic reasons. Plumb supported suffrage for both women and African Americans at the Kansas constitutional convention of 1858, although women's suffrage did not pass the vote. In 1867, efforts were being made to grant African Americans the right to vote and many in politics felt that it would be impossible to grant both women and African Americans the right to vote simultaneously. It would be easier to get one through and then the other. This would explain why he spoke against women's suffrage in 1867, and again reversed his position after 1870 when African Americans were granted suffrage with the 15th Amendment. His senate record shows him consistently in favor of women's rights and women's suffrage.

In his first session of Congress (the 45th Congress), Plumb presented a petition from the citizens of Kansas urging for an amendment to the constitution to prohibit citizens from being disenfranchised from voting based on their sex. In 1884 he presented a petition in the Senate signed by many citizens of Kansas urging for the passage of a constitutional amendment allowing women the right to vote. The issue came to the forefront again when the state of Washington was admitted to the Union in 1889. As a territory, Washington had permitted women to vote and Plumb was one of only twenty-two senators who believed that women should retain the right to vote once it was admitted as a state. Plumb was always keenly aware of the concepts of fairness and justice. To him, it would have been unfair to take the right of voting away from women in order for Washington to become a state, when they had already been given while it was a territory.

Department of Agriculture

Today, the federal government consists of numerous ancillary departments, such as the Department of the Treasury, Department of Labor, Department of Energy, etc. In Plumb's time, there were far fewer departments. Department heads were given regular access to the president and became part of his inner circle of advisers. Federal departments were given more authority to shape policies and agendas of administrations, which allowed for them to have a larger impact. Kansas as an agricultural state was especially impacted by this. In essence, without a separate Department of Agriculture, agricultural concerns did not have a strong voice within the federal government. Plumb created a bill to remedy this in 1882 and introduced it in 1883. Unfortunately, it failed in the Senate. In 1888, another bill was introduced to make the Department of Agriculture its own executive department, this time in the House of Representatives by Representative William Henry Hatch of Missouri. This was a significant change as it would have elevated the department dramatically. For this, and other political reasons, the change was met with resistance in both the House and the Senate. The bill, H.R. 8191, arrived in the Senate in March of 1888 and was sent to the Committee on Agriculture and Forestry, of which Plumb was a member. His committee worked on the bill and reported it back to the Senate on August 7, 1888, with amendments. The bill spent several days in debate in the Senate with Plumb being its strongest advocate. He knew that this would elevate the industry of agriculture within the federal government and have far-reaching effects, not just on Kansas, but other states and territories with strong agricultural interests. After much debate, the bill was eventually passed and signed into law by President Grover Cleveland on February 9, 1889.

Sorghum

Another agricultural interest of Plumb's was the sorghum industry. In the 19th Century, sorghum was a well-known grain used to make flour. It could also be used to make a sweet syrup similar to molasses and a granular sugar, which could rival the sugar beet and sugar cane. Research in this field was relatively new, and Plumb was at the forefront of funding it. In 1884, he secured $40,000 in funding from the federal government for Kansas to test using sorghum cane to make sugar.

H.W. Wiley described his work with sorghum to William Connelley in a letter:

> I knew Senator Plumb quite intimately from 1885 to 1889 during the time that I was engaged in experimenting in Kansas in the production of sugar from sorghum. Senator Plumb was the one who secured the appropriations, and they were of a generous nature. The sorghum industry never had a better nor more active friend than Senator Plumb. It was through him that the money was given with which to carry on the experiments at Fort Scott, at Ottawa, at Medicine Lodge, and in other localities in Kansas. All together, in the course of six or seven years the Department expended on these experiments probably between a quarter and a half million dollars, a large part of which was spent at Fort Scott and Medicine Lodge. In connection with these manufacturing experiments, cultural experiments were carried on in Kansas with the collaboration of the late A.A. Denton. Senator Plumb also took a lively interest in this part of the work. The appropriation bill for many years carried the specific appropriations for these experimental investigations and while others in Congress were interested in the matter, Senator Plumb was always the leader. You can give him full credit for being the leading man in securing the legislation which made these experimental investigations possible.

Eventually, the push to use sorghum to produce refined sugar died out. Alternative sugars received serious pushback from the large established sugar manufacturers, and the equipment of the time proved too costly to make the business profitable. Today, Kansas is still a leader in sorghum production.

Reelections

Plumb was reelected twice as U.S. Senator. After his last reelection in 1889, Henry Booth wrote him a congratulatory letter. Booth served with Plumb in the 11th Kansas Volunteer Cavalry and was later elected to the state legislature. At the time of this reelection vote, Booth was Speaker of the House, and Plumb received a record vote. The Democratic party did not have a candidate to run against Plumb, and the Republican Party did not wish to run a candidate against Plumb. The other political parties also did not have candidates, and those who would have voted against Plumb based on party lines, simply did not attend the session. This granted Plumb the unique experience of being the only U.S. Senator from Kansas to be elected unanimously.

> Topeka, January 24, 1889
> Hon. P.B. Plumb
> Dear Col.
> You no doubt get letters enough from parties here, keeping you posted, and clamoring for positions without being bored by any from me, but the happy result of the Senatorial election, electing you your own successor without a dissenting vote prompts me to write a few words. The democrats were all willing to vote for you but the fusion members would not agree to it, especially the man Campbell from Stafford Co. so the democrats agreed to stay out if the fusion members would, so they did not go into the House and Ed Carroll withdrew from the Senate. In the House, 118 members voted every one for P.B. Plumb. Swenson from McPherson was unavoidably absent, but he had his vote recorded in the Journal the next day in Joint Convention as voting for you. You do not feel any prouder Colonel than I do. Nothing could have been more gratifying to me than to sit in the Speaker's chair and hear the roll called and every man announced his vote for P.B. Plumb. I could but contrast the scene with that of 12 years ago when we had such a struggle to elect you, and I was proud of the fact that the prediction I then made had proven true, that you would make the most useful and most acceptable member of the U.S. Senate Kansas had ever had. Your hold on the people of Kansas is without a parallel I believe in any State and is as deserved as it is gratifying to you and your friends.

McKinley Tariff

In 1890, Senator Plumb came up against a force he couldn't match. Long an advocate for fair trade and honest business, he was against the system of tariffs that let manufacturers and importers set the rates on duties, giving themselves the most favorable rates possible. In the matter of wool tariffs, Plumb had a more personal connection. His brother,

Portrait of Senator Preston B. Plumb taken around the mid-1880s. Image courtesy author's collection.

George, ran a successful sheep farm in the Emporia area and was very involved in the wool growers association.

> I remember a conversation I had with Preston just before he went to Washington for the session of Congress that passed the McKinley tariff bill. I joshed him a little about looking after my interests,—I was a wool grower. He laughed it off. After we got thru supper and went into the other room, I said, "I expected to come down to Washington this winter." He said, "Don't you do it, George." I said, "Don't you want to see me?" He said, "Yes, I would like to have you come to see me but don't come about the wool schedule; that has been fixed."
>
> I was one of the Executive Committee of the National Wool Growers Association who were expected to look after the wool schedule before the House Committee. Preston told me the Importers and manufacturers of wool had put up a large fund for the election of McKinley and that they were to have what they wanted. I said, "Do you mean to tell me that this thing is all settled when you fellows have been going around here saying we were all going to be treated right when the tariff was revised?" He said, "You did not hear me say that." I replied I had gone with others to Junction City and heard Ingalls make a speech in which he said it." He said, "Well I did not say it. I know better than that." He said, "George, I tell you there is no use in your spending any time on the matter; they are going to have just what they want."
>
> W.H. Wallace was on this Committee and W.H. Lawrence Ex-Congressman from Ohio. They kept writing me to come on and go to Washington with them. Of course, after this talk with my brother, I did not intend to go but could not tell them why, so kept putting them off. Wallace wrote me on a certain date the thing was to come up before the Committee and for me to be sure and be there, and he sent me transportation thinking I presume that that was what had kept me from coming before for the wool growers were pretty poor in those days. I returned the transportation and said something had come up and that I could

not leave here then. The house committee and the wool growers fixed up a schedule but the manufacturers refused to accept it. The Ways and Means Committee of the House and the wool growers finally patched up an agreement which was the best they could do. Wallace sent me a petition addressed to the Senate which he wanted me to circulate; it was getting late and some of the wool growers were holding their wool in hopes that a better rate would go into effect. I had talked with a few of the wool growers here about it when I got a telegram saying not to circulate the petition; to wait for a letter. This letter from Mr. Wallace told me just what my brother had told me so long before. The next thing I had from Mr. Wallace was a card with his compliments showing that he was being sent to Australia as a special minister of some kind. They were getting him out of the country for fear he would tell what he knew.

This made me lose all interest or faith in the tariff and when the McKinley bill passed I sold my sheep. Preston did not believe in the way they were making their schedules.

Senator Richard Pettigrew described the fundamental issues with the McKinley Tariff Bill:

They [Senators Plumb, Paddock, and Pettigrew] had seen the protected interests come to McKinley and demand that unjust, unfair, and burdensome duties be levied in their favor. And McKinley had allowed these interests to name the several schedules and rates in which they were interested. The wool men had named the rate of duty on wool. The weavers had been permitted to name the rate on cloth, McKinley did not fix the amount of duty in any great number of instances, but accepted the rates admitted by the manufacturers; sometimes the latter seeing that they had everything their own way, returned to demand an increase of the rates they themselves had submitted a week before.

Senator Pettigrew of South Dakota was one of the Senators who joined with Plumb to vote against the bill. He described the methods of bribery used by party officials, which worked with some of the senators, but not with him, Senator Algernon Paddock, or Plumb.

Pettigrew said the protected interests always operated along the same lines. They, in that instance, made up an immense slush fund. The man having the fund in charge–the agent of the trusts or protected interests–saw those Senators it was desired to influence and swing back to the party. He would say "Does not your Central Committee need some money to carry the State this fall?" This was said to Pettigrew who said it might be well if the Committee could have Two Thousand Dollars for postage, etc. "How would Twenty Thousand Dollars do?" asked the liberal agent. "That might be all right," said Pettigrew, "but I am of the opinion that the Committee does not need so much." "Well", said the generous agent, "I will send out Twenty Thousand. And, by the way, you understand that those interests expect to be taken care of when the vote is called on the final passage of this tariff bill, and expect the people they help to help them." "If that is why you are putting up this money, you need not send a dollar to South Dakota. If you do send it I shall report the whole proceeding in the open Senate. I shall vote against the bill on its final passage," said Senator Pettigrew.

Sometimes the agent would hand the amount suggested to the Senator to be by him carried out and handed to the Committee, or put in his pocket. The agent cared nothing of what became of the money as long as the Senator voted for the interests…Some of them returned the third time, each time increasing the rates over former figures they had submitted. The whole proceeding was a disgusting revel of crime against the people—a base betrayal of the people by their representatives. The three saw the outrages imposed on the people by the corrupt system of fixing tariff duties, and they determined to make an effort to correct the system.

As the time came closer to vote on the McKinley Tariff Bill, Plumb was one of only a handful of Republican senators against it.

> Senator Plumb, Senator Paddock, and myself [Senator Pettigrew] voted against the conference on the McKinley tariff bill. The bill as it came from the House, contained every possible objectionable feature conceivable in a tariff bill, and was framed

purely in the interests of property and of the exploiting classes, rather than of the people. Several western senators, eight I think, joined together in very materially amending the bill reducing the rates in very many instances, and placing binding twine and other articles which were known to be controlled by the trusts, upon the free list. We also secured an amendment for a tariff commission to thoroughly investigate the cost of production at home and abroad, and thus determine more clearly what rate of duty to be fairly protective, would be required, and not allow the capitalization of an excessive duty for the purpose of plundering the American people.

After the bill passed the Senate and was in conference, a meeting of the eight Republican senators who had secured, with the assistance of the Democrats, the decided and important amendments to the McKinley Tariff Act, was held, for the purpose of insisting that our amendments be agreed to by the House. The Senators present at this meeting were Plumb and Ingalls of Kansas, Wilson of Iowa, Davis of Minnesota, myself and Moody of South Dakota, and Paddock of Nebraska. Mr. Ingalls and myself were selected by the eight to inform the Conference Committee that we eight would vote against the conference report unless our amendments were retained. This declaration on our part led to the calling of a Republican caucus in the Senate for the purpose of compelling the eight Senators to recede from their position and vote for the conference report, even after it was stripped of the amendments which we considered essential. Great pressure was brought to bear by Harrison's administration upon all of us, with the result that five of the eight were whipped into line. Senators Plumb, Paddock, and myself held out and voted against the conference report.

I do not know what the result was particularly with regard to Senator Plumb, but as far as I was concerned, I was told by President Harrison that I had chosen to be a Republican and therefore could have nothing further to say with regard to the patronage, which was regarded by him as purely a party asset.

The same fight with regard to the tariff finally after twenty years, has resulted in dividing the Republican party, and must ultimately cause its overthrow if the warning we gave then had been heeded, if the prediction which Senator Plumb made then with regard to the future had been believed, there is no doubt but that the Republican party might have continued to be the champion of human rights rather than the champion of the rights of property.

The McKinley Tariff Bill is one of the only specific political issues where documentation survives between Plumb and his wife, Carrie. Although minimal, this further solidifies the statements from those who knew the Plumbs that he often discussed politics with her and that he valued her advice.

On the day of the vote on the bill, Plumb received the following telegram from Carrie:

> WESTERN UNION TELEGRAPH CO.
>
> Sept. 28, 1890, Emporia, Kansas
>
> Sen. P.B. Plumb,
> Washington
>
> Remember I would rather you vote with the few and be <u>right</u>, than with the majority.
>
> Carrie S. Plumb

The story goes that he had that very telegram on his desk when he cast his vote against the bill on September 30, 1890, and was one of only three Republican senators to do so. He was vilified in some newspapers for his stance, but those who knew Plumb were not surprised by it. He was no stranger to splitting from his party if he felt differently on an issue than they did. He did not simply toe the party line and was not one to shy away from standing up for himself. A few days following the vote, he responded to Carrie with this letter:

> Washington, D.C. Oct. 2, 1890
> Dear Wife:
>
> Your dispatch came and I was ever so glad to receive it on account of the interest you manifested in those things which

have been the subject of so much controversy and about which there is a great criticism. Hope the vote I cast met your views. It represented my conviction of duty to my own people.
Mrs. Pomeroy has returned. Have not yet seen her but she dropped me a note. Mr. P. has been sick.

I am just getting over a nap which was much needed at the close of the session. Go to N.Y. tonight–shall be back here in a couple of days and then start for home, except for something unforeseen.
Always your
Preston

Senator Jonathan P. Dolliver of Iowa came into the Senate years after the McKinley Tariff had been debated but he had followed its course when it was contested.

He was a believer in the protective tariff, as his party has ever been, but he saw that our manner of treating it, especially in the enactment of its schedules, would ultimately break it down and perhaps destroy it. In theory, Congress is supposed to determine the tariff schedules. The practice is to allow the beneficiaries of the tariff – the manufacturers–to write the schedules. This Senator Plumb believed to be scandalous and immoral–if, indeed, not criminal. He believed it wholly indefensible even from a party standpoint, for in our form of government–by parties–anything which injures a party injures the country.

Having in mind these principles and the good of his country at heart he sought to remedy the evil of which he was convinced. He believed the gravest consequences would follow upon the continuance of our methods. To avert these he devised a complete system to supplant our old scheme. His plan consisted of a commission, non-partisan in character, which should have charge of the tariff and arrange its schedules in the interest of the government and the people as a people. He made an exhaustive study of the matter and was completely informed. His plan was comprehensive–the work of a patriotic statesman. He introduced it into the Senate as an amendment to the Mills bill. So masterly was his support of it that it was unanimously adopted by the Senate. But the interests benefited by the unjust schedules were able to prevent its final enactment into law. Last year [1909], in the discussion of the tariff matter, I cast about for what had been done in the enactment of previous bills and fell upon Plumb's plan. At first, I thought it had been the work of Allison, Iowa's great Senator, but found that it was the conception of Plumb. I introduced it in the Senate and it became within three votes of being adopted. Had it been adopted we, as a people, would now be enjoying complete prosperity, and our party would not have been placed in the impossible and impracticable condition in which we find it. In my remarks introducing this measure, I paid a tribute to Senator Plumb which may be found in the Congressional Record.

This was the highest point attained by Plumb in his long and useful career in the Senate. His fame as a statesman will finally rest on it. His plan will have to be adopted and will be someday. The thing which we got in the Payne Bill in lieu of it is practically of little benefit, and it does not partake of the strong and perfect institution devised by Plumb.

Senator Pettigrew also supported Plumb's tariff plan:

Senator Plumb had been working on a tariff commission plan for some years prior to this time and had offered it in the Senate. He had given the matter much thought and hard study. He was familiar with the workings of the whole scheme of our government. He had adjusted his tariff commission to all the government needs. It was a scientific plan to raise the revenues necessary for the support of the government, accurately adjusted to all needs of the government. Plumb, Pettigrew, and Paddock studied the McKinley bill with care and worked long and hard to correct its evils by the formation of a tariff commission along lines worked out by Plumb. Failing to secure the authority for this commission by a provision in the bill; they considered it their duty to vote against the bill with its monstrous crimes against the people and they did vote against it.

This vote was the supreme test of the loyalty of Senator Plumb to the interests of the people, as, indeed, it was to all of the three. But Plumb was a pretty strict party man and when it was possible for him to do so, he voted for the measures and policies of his party. He had great influence in the Senate and stood high in the councils of his party. But none of these, nor all of them, counted when his duty to the people was put into the balance. Plumb was an honest man.

Senator Pettigrew introduced the Plumb tariff-commission plan as an amendment to the Wilson tariff bill, but the same influences controlled the Democratic party that had controlled the Republican party, and it was defeated.

Chapter 18

"The Senator"

By the late 1880s, Plumb was a national figure within the Republican Party and a powerhouse within the senate. He had become the archetype of a new type of senator, a man of the west with a sometimes blunt manner but unflinching honesty. In 1889, Plumb served as the inspiration for the titular character of "The Senator" in the comedic play by David D. Lloyd.

Although the plot was fictional, the mannerisms of the main character were based upon Plumb. The play went on to great critical and popular success and was made into a silent film in 1915, which has sadly been lost to time. The renowned stage actor William H. Crane played the role of the Senator in the play. He dictated the entire story of his experience with Plumb and the play to William Connelley in 1912, which is included, unedited, below.

> So in the Fall of 1889 Mr. Joseph Brooks, the well-known manager with whom I am again associated in business, became my individual manager and we opened negotiations with Mr. David D. Lloyd of New York, a well-known writer and who at this time also was the Tribune correspondent at Washington, for a play on Washington life to be called "The Senator."
>
> Previous to this time a play had been written on this subject by Mr. Benjamin E. Wolf of Boston, called "The Mighty Dollar", in which Mr. W. J. Florence played the senator, an Hon. Bodwell Slote; but this senator by Mr. Florence was broadly farcical and a caricature of the character of the senator, who was supposed to be open to all sorts of bribery and corruption. When Mr. Lloyd and I first met to discuss the character and the story of the proposed play of "The Senator," he mentioned this play of Mr. Florence's to me. I told him I was glad he did so as I thought Mr. Florence's play was splendid and I was glad he thought of that, as it was diametrically opposite of what I wanted.
>
> We discussed the type of man to be the central figure of the proposed play, and my instructions to Mr. Lloyd were to the

effect that I wanted to portray a character who was absolutely honest, thoroughly in earnest, those being the fundamental principles of his character; then to put in as much comedy as he possibly could. He agreed with this and then in talking over the possible type we settled unanimously upon Senator Preston B. Plumb as the type of man we wished to convey in this play. Mr. Lloyd then proceeded to make a scenario of the proposed play, grafting his story and founding it upon the well-known Armstrong Claim (General Armstrong Fayal), the theme of the play being the pressing of the Armstrong claim and its being brought to a successful issue by the Senator. But during the progress of the play was also the story of the self-sacrifice of the Senator, who, falling in love with the daughter of the claimant, believes her to be in love with an attaché of the Austrian Embassy and to ensure her happiness he gives up his chances of success to bring the other affair to a successful termination. But discovering the perfidy of the attaché, he defeats his plan to elope with the young wife of the old Secretary of State, exposes him to save the girl, and then discovers that she really is in love with him.

Before this play was produced, after the first copy was made, during a visit to Washington, I received a letter from Mr. Lloyd, the author, saying that as Congress was in session, he would like very much if I could go into the Spectator's Gallery in the Senate Chamber, see Mr. Plumb upon the floor, hear him talk and possibly become familiar with his manner, style of delivery, etc. Mr. Charles Reed, who at that time was the Assistant Sergeant at Arms of the United States Senate, was an old personal friend. When I mentioned this desire on my part to Mr. Reed, he asked me how I would like to meet the Senator personally. I assured him that I would be delighted if it could be brought about without annoying or bothering the Senator in any way, as I would like very much to talk with him personally to become more familiar with his general manner. So I met Mr. Reed one day by appointment at the Capitol, we went to the door of the Senate Chamber, Mr. Reed went on to the Floor of the Senate and fortunately found Mr. Plumb at liberty.

Mentioning the fact that Mr. Crane would like to speak with him, he came out at once, I was presented and we had a most agreeable and charming conversation for at least fifteen or twenty minutes.

When I am interested I have been accused of not knowing when to stop talking, but on this occasion, though intensely interested I had sufficient wit to talk just enough to start Mr. Preston B. Plumb talking, and I can truthfully say that I have never had a more interesting twenty minutes in my career. We reminisced, he asking me many questions about my experiences with Mr. Robson in the "Two Dromeos", which he stated that he had witnessed several times with great pleasure, and he seemed much amused at the little stories that I related to him of things that transpired during our experiences with this play. But when Mr. Plumb had really warmed up, his talk and gesticulations and manners which I were observing closely, interested me greatly. I never told him at this time of my intention to produce a play called "The Senator" in which he was supposed to be the central figure.

I did not see him again until after the play was produced. During the first engagement in Washington, a luncheon was tendered to me which took place in the Committee Room on Military Affairs in the United States Capitol, the third act of our play being located in this very room, the scene being an exact reproduction of a corner of this room. At the luncheon when my health was proposed, I gave my experiences up to that time regarding the production of the play of "The Senator." I related to the senators present how I had met Mr. Plumb, how we had talked together and how he had become quite pleasantly excited in talking over the plays he had seen, etc., but he had no idea at that time, as I explained to them that during all of his talk I was sizing him up for reproduction. In making up for "The Senator" I never aimed to be an exact likeness of Senator Plumb, but a resemblance, and I evidently succeeded well enough to cause the press and people who knew of Senator Plumb to remark upon this resemblance.

On our way back from this luncheon, which began at one o'clock in the day, we arose from the table about seven in the evening, I had to hurry to get to the theatre in time for the evening performance. I went back to the hotel in a carriage with Senator Blackburn and his secretary and Senator Plumb. When we reached the hotel, Senator Blackburn took me to one side and said, "Mr. Crane, there is one little trait of Mr. Plumb's personality that you have not yet gotten hold of. Whenever he makes a speech on the floor and becomes a little excited or warmed up in his subject, he invariably pulls a handkerchief out of his back pocket and mops the back of his neck. This is well known to all the members of the Senate. If you will do that tonight, I have a splendid silk bandana handkerchief that was given to me by some friends in the South and which I will give you as a souvenir of this occasion."

I assured him that I would do this. That night all of the lower boxes had been taken by the senators who were thoroughly familiar with Mr. Plumb's peculiarities. So at the right moment in the scene where the Armstrong claim is passed, after an impassioned speech I pulled out my handkerchief and mopped the back of my neck, with the startling effect that twenty four men laughed uproariously while the balance of the audience saw nothing funny in the action whatever.

I might say in this connection that it was fifteen years after this occurrence, sitting in the Metropolitan Club one night I met the former secretary of Senator Blackburn who had driven home with us on the day of the luncheon from the Capitol. He had just been talking with the Senator from Kentucky, who recalled the incident and said:

"I have never given Mr. Crane that bandanna handkerchief." The next day it was sent to me with a beautiful letter, and I am very happy to say that I still have it in my possession.

The friendship that began at the door of the Senate Chamber continued during the life of Senator Plumb. Later, when the play was produced in New York where it ran on its first engagement

This cover to the program for "The Senator" features a photograph of William H. Crane in costume. Crane grew the same style of beard as Plumb and wore the same style of clothing. Image courtesy author's collection.

for twenty-three weeks and then being reproduced in the Fall for seventeen weeks more, it was the custom of Senator Plumb, who was called to New York very frequently on business or affairs of State, to go after his dinner and when his business was concluded, directly to the sleeping car at about half past nine or ten, then going back to Washington on the midnight train, thus ensuring a good night's rest. But while our play was in progress, Senator Plumb very frequently came to the theatre and would come around to my dressing room and spend the time between the acts chatting and talking over the play and various subjects of mutual interest. I know that Mr. Plumb was pleased with the idea that this play was founded upon his personal individuality, as the character was that of a straightforward, energetic, hustling type of a thoroughly honest Western man.

I shall never forget one night Senator Plumb came to my dressing room with a Mr. [Judge Thomas] Ryan, who had just been appointed Minister to Mexico. The Senator had allowed his chin beard to grow rather long—much longer than he usually wore it. So as we sat smoking our cigars between the acts and chatting, I said to him:

"Mr. Senator, will you pardon me if I make a comment on your personal appearance?"

He looked at me a little startled and commenced brushing his clothes.

"Why, certainly Mr. Crane. What's the trouble?"

I said: "It is not your clothing, but I notice that you have let your beard grow much longer than usual. You will have to trim that down or you won't look a bit like me."

The impertinence of this remark tickled Senator Plumb immensely, and when I got to Washington I think I heard that story repeated to me a dozen times by those to whom Senator Plumb had related it.

The last time that I saw Mr. Plumb was in New York. I had asked him to be sure and call on me whenever I should play in Washington again, and Mr. Reed, who has since died, told me that about ten days or two weeks before my engagement in Washington, he had met Senator Plumb who spoke to him of my coming engagement in Washington asking Mr. Reed if he would meet him on my opening night and go with him to my dressing room, Senator Plumb saying that he didn't like to go alone but would rather go with somebody who knew Mr. Crane better than he did. He was so diffident about coming in to see a person that he thought would be intensely occupied or very busy. However, Mr. Reed assured the Senator that he would meet him on my opening night—he would call for him—and that they together should come to my dressing room to see me, and if my memory serves me right, Senator Plumb was dead within three days of that time.

My only meeting with Mr. Plumb took place, as I have described, either in the theatre or when I met him casually, but I was always impressed by his earnestness. I could understand why Mr. Plumb, if he had lived, would have become a great force. He always impressed me as having a great deal of tenacity, that he would stick to anything he started. He acted on the David Crocket motto: Be sure you are right and then go ahead. But he had a most charming democratic manner that made him a delightful person to meet and talk with, and intensely interesting in this conversation. He was rather brusque but impulsive, energetic and he struck you as a man who was a great hustler and of great determination.

I had never seen him in my life until he walked out of the door of the Senate Chamber with his plain, unassuming manner. He was one of the most unassuming men I ever saw and so absolutely genial that when he shook hands with me it was as though he was shaking hands with a friend whom he had known for years or at least of forming an acquaintance he was desirous of keeping all his life. He took great interest in talking about plays he had seen. Shakespeare's "Comedy of Errors" interested him intensely and he wanted to talk about that all the time. He met some of my company just casually. I introduced him to Mrs. Georgia Drew Barrymore. He never would walk on the stage or stand on the stage behind the scenes. He would sit in my dressing room, smoking a cigar and chat with me between the acts. He was a splendid storyteller. I don't remember the stories he told, but he had a fund of them and was also a magnificent listener. In other words, he was interested in the events of the stage and would ask me questions about any little experiences that I had had, and they would amuse him tremendously as, of course, it was an entirely new field for him.

Did he have that inquiring manner?

Yes, always asking questions.

He would come to the front of the house and as the manager and all the attachés of the theatre knew him, they would simply take Mr. Plumb around to my dressing room. Why, many times I have come off the stage without ever knowing he was in the city and see Senator Plumb smoking a cigar in my dressing room. He impressed me as a man I would like to know better, as a man whose friendship I would like to have. I felt that he liked me personally the same as I felt toward him—a mutual sort of intimate feeling that one could not help but obtain with a man of his personality.

There is a very singular thing in connection with Senator Plumb's death. After he died, the *Philadelphia Inquirer* having no portrait of Senator Plumb, published a picture of me as the Senator, explaining the fact that they had no picture of the Senator but this makeup of mine was supposed to be a likeness or a resemblance. I never claimed to make a likeness of the Senator, but aimed to produce a resemblance that would be recognized, and it was his gesticulations that I endeavored to copy in order to make Senator Plumb recognizable. His actions were not the labored gesticulations of the would-be orator, but entirely natural. His disposition obtained vent through his gestures.

Crane told the following story to the *New York Times* in January 1891:

> It is well known to the crowds that have witnessed the performance of "The Senator" at the Star that W.H. Crane, the comedian, "makes up" to represent as nearly as possible Senator Plumb of Kansas. Mr. Crane, until quite recently, had flattered himself that he had succeeded in reproducing the figure and personal appearance of the Kansas statesman almost to perfection, and he was encouraged in the notion by his hosts of friends, all of whom were unanimous in declaring the "The Senator" of the Star and Mr. Plumb were "as alike as two peas." If the comparison was not original it was at least emphatic, and was accepted as decisive on the question of Mr. Crane's make-up.
>
> But the comedian has been subjected to a complete disillusion on this subject, and by the only person in the world who was thoroughly competent to criticize his "make up"–Senator Plumb himself. Mr. Plumb, in company with the Hon. Thomas Ryan, United States minister to Mexico, recently visited the Star and watched the performance of "The Senator." They laughed and applauded as vigorously as anybody in the large audience, but it was noticed that whenever the "business" of the play required Mr. Crane to display his "stovepipe" hat Senator Plumb moved wearily in his seat and whispered to his companion. When the curtain finally dropped on the last act, Senator Plumb and Minister Ryan visited Mr. Crane in his dressing room. Mr. Plumb's first greeting as he stepped inside the door and grasped the comedian's hand was, "Crane, where did you get that hat?"
>
> "Hat! That hat!" stammered the comedian, picking up the object which had been thus flippantly referred to and holding it admirably at arm's length. "That hat! What's the matter with that hat?"
>
> "Oh, the hat's all right," laughed Senator Plumb. "Only I never wore a silk hat in my life, and my creditors wouldn't know me for myself in a head piece like that."
>
> Crane, who had been flattering himself that his counterfeit presentment of Senator Plumb was little short of perfection,

dropped into his chair and fairly gasped. He threw the offending hat into the corner and declared that he would never wear it again. "But I have worn it, and I shall again," said the comedian, in relating the story. "People in New York would not recognize 'the senator' now without his stovepipe. I shall make plumb wear that hat in spite of himself till the end of my season here. Then, when I go to Washington, 'the senator' will appear in a plain, round felt hat, the only kind Mr. Plumb was ever known to wear, and he will wear it so long as he breathes the breath of life."

Chapter 19

His Last Campaign

As busy as Plumb was with his Senate work, he was also often on the campaign trail speaking at local fairs and events throughout Kansas, as well as traveling to other Republican states to endorse candidates there. He was invited to speak in Maine multiple times at Republican events and shared the platform with Frederick Douglass, James Blaine, and other New England senators.

On the campaign trail, Plumb's photographic memory and ability to recall facts and information made him an excellent speaker and popular with guests. He was regularly able to recall names of those he'd met only briefly, much to their amazement.

Plumb was a regular fixture at county fairs, Grand Army of the Republic reunions, and many other public events where he could speak and meet with the citizens of Kansas. His schedule was often tight between business and political meetings, and in one humorous story, his train to give a speech in Newton, Kansas was running late. Judge Bowman said, "Just east of Newton there was a steep grade in the track of the railroad and trains climbed it with difficulty and sometimes moved slowly there, which was the case with this one. Senator Plumb jumped off when the train slowed up and then walked across the fields to the fairgrounds. He made a good speech and was enthusiastically received by the people. The people of southwest Kansas regarded Plumb as their personal representative. They always appealed to him when any matter was to have attention."

Plumb made his speaking engagements against all odds. When others might have quit, he came up with a solution and forged ahead. Judge W.A. Johnston of the Kansas Supreme Court told Connelley:

> Plumb was always expected to do the hard work in State campaigns. And he did it. He never missed an appointment. Bad roads, foul weather, and poor conveyances were all overcome by him. He would break down one team after another to make his appointments. Johnston recalls that Plumb once came to Minneapolis (Johnston's home then) to speak. It was late in October. It was stormy and cold. The next morning it was blowing a gale and the air was filled with a half-sleet, half-rain.

Plumb had an appointment at Lincoln that night. Johnston remonstrated with him for the intention of trying to get there. It was necessary to drive. Plumb said the people would expect him and he must go—that he could make it all right. He got the best team he could at Minneapolis [Kansas], and then enquired where he might find farmers who had good teams. He would exhaust one team, then drive up to a farmhouse and explain the situation and get another team. This was kept up all day through mud and rain and sleet, but he got in on time and kept his appointment at Lincoln.

And this he did all over western Kansas where there were few railroads. And he did it for a generation, in his law business and as Senator.

Plumb was especially known for traveling to the rural areas other speakers wanted to avoid.

When Bonebrake was Chairman of the State Central Committee of the Republican party of Kansas he found Plumb his main reliance for addresses to audiences in the larger towns of the state. He was the only man who could be depended on to be always on hand. Plumb was prompt at any and all his engagements, no matter what might come up. Bonebrake always felt safe and secure when Plumb was on the circuit. And he did not confine himself to the larger cities or more thickly populated counties. He often made pilgrimages into the frontier counties. In fact, he liked to do so. He had lived on the frontier and felt the charm of pioneer life. Bonebrake once sent Plumb on a hard trip into the southwest part of Kansas. There was a meeting to address at one point and a drive of ninety miles to be made to address another meeting the following evening. The meetings had not been at first arranged that way, but some speaker had fallen down in his tour, and Plumb said he would try to fill all dates. And he did speak at one place one evening and then drive ninety miles and speak at the other point the next evening.

Beyond just being one of the few people of his stature willing to travel to the remotest locations to speak, Plumb also knew what topics would be of interest to his audience and found it easy to work his political beliefs into talks of a more practical nature. Former Kansas Lt. Governor George Finney recalled to Connelley:

> Sometimes Plumb was called on to make the principal address at the Fair held annually there [Neosho Falls, Kansas], which was the largest in the State for some years. He could talk on any subject and his addresses often dealt with the practical things the farmers had to deal with, such as cattle-feeding and general farming. He was well informed on these matters, and urged farmers to study to get the most out of their business, which he said, was their duty. But he never failed to discuss national affairs and he did this in such a way that everyone understood the questions under consideration. He talked rapidly, earnestly, and well. He was always going about the grounds meeting people and becoming acquainted with those he had not before known. Men, women, children—all were met and greeted in a free and cordial way, and he did this because he loved the people and wanted to meet them. It would have been the same with him if he had not been in public life. There was nothing affected or assumed in Plumb's bearing or attitude. His actions were always the result of feelings. There was nothing of the hypocrite or demagogue about him. He was always intensely earnest and sincere. As this was always perfectly apparent, he was very popular with the people. They loved him. He talked to each man about what interested him banking, railroad-building, cattle-raising, politics, national affairs, breaking sod or building barns, houses or towns–anywhere or on any topic he was at home.

The following story told to Connelley in 1910 by W.F. Shamneffer perfectly illustrates the appeal Plumb had across the political spectrum in Kansas. Although a Republican, there were many Democrats who had personally been helped by Plumb and therefore were staunch supporters. Plumb's last reelection was further proof of that support as not a single Democrat cast a vote against him, allowing him to be reelected unanimously.

> "Today I saw W.F. Shamneffer, Mayor of Council Grove [Kansas]. He knew Senator Plumb well. He laid out the town of Augusta, in Butler County, or was in the company that laid it

out. In that matter, he had to have the sum of $3000 once in a hurry. He went to Plumb and told him his situation and Plumb took his note and let him have the money. He could not have secured the money of any other person. He was always the friend of Plumb after that, and, although a Democrat, he always worked for his reelection.

He remembers that Plumb was at the banquet at Council Grove when the M.K. & T. Railroad was completed to the town. Plumb made one of the best speeches of his life at this banquet. He was an enthusiastic man anyway and always dwelling on the riches and inexhaustibility of the resources of Kansas and picturing the future glory and power of the state. That was his theme that night.

Plumb made one of the last speeches he ever made in Kansas in the yard of Shamneffer. The Republicans could not find a suitable place in town and went to Shamneffer to get his grove for the speech. They did not at first say who was to speak, and he refused the use of the grove. When they said Plumb was the man to speak Shamneffer said Plumb might stand on his front porch and abuse the Democrats all he wanted to, and told the committee to use his grove.

Plumb was hearty and cordial. Shamneffer says he was such a man as it did one good to talk to. He says Plumb has often slapped him on the back or thigh, while talking, with such force that he has felt the effects of the slaps for a week, but that he felt good every time he felt the twinge of pain, for it brought to mind the goodwill and hearty cordiality of Plumb. He could not have suffered any other man to slap him that way. But with Plumb, it was all right.

Senator Joseph Bristow of Kansas was a newspaper editor at the time Plumb was in office and had been critical of him in his paper. He traveled to Salina, Kansas with Plumb and was shocked to find that he did not behave as other senators he had met.

> In Salina, there were three hotels then–two good ones and one not very good. The poor one was the Old Pacific House, down near the depot–the first one built there. In the early days Plumb had stopped there, and now he did not pass it by. Bristow went out to look for Plumb and found him down at the Pacific House. He was surrounded by an enthusiastic crowd of pioneers whom he had known from the first settlement of Kansas. Bristow there got a new idea of the man. He saw that he was one of the people; that he loved the people—the farmer, the settler, the pioneer, the stock-man. And they, one and all, loved him. Bristow believes that Plumb was the most loved public man Kansas ever had. The people had a genuine affection for him. This was because he was one of them—not affected, not stuck up, but just his natural self.

Plumb's popularity revolved around his relatability with the common people and his lack of affectation and false pride. He was down to earth and cared little for the pretentious aspects of being a U.S. Senator, as many senators did.

Amos Wilson of McPherson, Kansas first met Plumb after he had been a senator for quite some time.

> About 1890 he [Wilson] desired the appointment of bank commissioner and had some correspondence with Senator Plumb about that matter. This must have been early in 1890, possibly in 1889. Senator Plumb made an appointment for him at Emporia. Wilson, Jim Simpson, and A.W. Smith went to Emporia in the spring of 1890 to see Senator Plumb at the time which had been fixed. Wilson had never seen Plumb before and it was about an hour that he saw him at this time. About a year later Wilson was on a Santa Fe train coming east through Great Bend about dusk. Plumb was out making campaign speeches and boarded the train at that place. He had a grip in his hand, and was coming thru the car and stopped at Wilson's seat and put down his grip saying, "Take care of this Wilson. I will be back after a little while." Wilson was greatly surprised that Plumb should remember him at all, and that he did so in the darkness was a remarkable instance of memory as Wilson believes. Wilson remembers how Plumb went down the aisle after putting down his grip; he went in a great hurry, into

another car to see some other parties and talk with them. Plumb had not seen Wilson except the one time and he remembers that Plumb came back and sat down and talked with him for a few minutes but got off soon at some place where he was to make a speech that night.

Plumb was always a strong supporter of Benjamin Harrison and had helped to bring about his presidential nomination in 1888. He was still a supporter of President Harrison for the 1892 election but worried about the growing strength of the People's Party within the state of Kansas. About 60% of the counties were leaning towards the People's Party with only 40% of the counties in Republican hands. In March of 1891, fellow Republican Senator Ingalls had been replaced by Populist candidate William Peffer. Plumb approached Ingalls to help him canvass the state of Kansas, but Ingalls refused, "saying that it was an off year and that the Constitution intended that in off years the people should do what they damned pleased and raise all the hell they could. He went off to Colorado." Plumb understood politics better than most and knew that the Republican Party would need to regain control of the political arena in the state to set the stage for the campaign of 1892. For this reason, Plumb chose to set out alone on a massive campaign all over Kansas for the Republican Party.

Plumb's campaign of 1891 was the most strenuous he had ever done. He was successful in his efforts and kept to a grueling schedule to accomplish it all. "Curley" Harrison recalled:

> He [Harrison] wanted Plumb to speak at Ottawa [Kansas] and was chairman of the Central Committee of Franklin County. Plumb was making many of his own dates, speaking in many small places about the larger towns to which he was sent by the State Committee. He telegraphed Harrison that it would be impossible to make Ottawa under the route marked out for him by the Committee, but that he would try to make it anyway. And he did. Here is how he did it.
>
> He spoke at Parker, a small town in Linn County, at night. The next morning he drove eighteen miles to Osawatomie and addressed a large meeting; after which he got a train for Ottawa on the Missouri Pacific Railroad, arriving at Ottawa a little

before two o'clock. He had not eaten breakfast nor dinner, but he did not hesitate to begin his address at two o'clock.

He had a magnificent audience, fully ten thousand people being present. After speaking an hour he called Harrison aside and directed him to have a carriage at the platform at four o'clock and to have a lunch in the carriage. Then he resumed his speech and closed after four. It was five before he could enter the carriage. He drove to Paola, about twenty-five miles, eating lunch on the way. He spoke to a large audience at Paola and finished near midnight. Then he had the dizzy spell told of by Barney Sheridan. The next day he and Harrison went by train to Olathe, where he addressed a large audience, after which they went by train to Holliday. Plumb had to speak at Bonner Springs (some say Edwardsville) that night and no train could be had that would get them to that town in time. Harrison got a boat and Plumb rowed it across the Kansas River at Holliday, and they walked to Bonner Springs and got in after dark, and Plumb made a speech, closing late at night. The next day Harrison left him and returned home, but Plumb kept up that pace to the end of the campaign.

Plumb kept a tireless pace traveling from one town to the next. He was always friendly and social with those he had just met and old friends alike—often partaking in a hair-raising cocktail of a pint of oysters mixed with a pint of whiskey at the local watering hole. Justice A.W. Benson of the Kansas Supreme Court often met Plumb on the campaign trail and saw him in his element numerous times.

That Plumb was a hard worker everyone knew. As a campaigner, he had no equal in his day. He loved the people, loved to meet them, mix with them and talk with them. At Ottawa in 1891 Benson was present and on the platform when Plumb spoke there. It was a warm day. Plumb took off his coat while speaking, and when he had finished was wringing wet with perspiration. He did not stop to change his clothing, however, but got into a carriage after four o'clock and was driven to Paola to address a meeting there in the evening; and the distance was about twenty-five miles. "I did not understand how he could hold up under such work in such weather by such methods. He never permitted anything to interfere with his appointments; and he never cut a speech short because of heat or cold; he always finished his arguments."

Unfortunately, Plumb's tireless work on the campaign trail caused irreversible damage to his health.

Plumb's Health

Plumb was what we would call in today's vernacular a "workaholic." He was intensely dedicated to the people of Kansas, the Republican Party, and his friends and family. He worked tirelessly on their behalf and never took time for himself. This was a fact that he was well aware of, but for all of his wisdom in business, politics, and the affairs of state, he did not seem to see how his work ethic was slowly physically destroying him.

Colonel O. E. Learned met Plumb in his youth when he was a young printer at the *Herald of Freedom* in Lawrence, Kansas, and remained his friend throughout his life. He remarked:

> Learnard stopped at the Riggs House and for some time Plumb took his meals there, always seating himself at the same table with Learnard. He always brought letters and papers to the table with him to be read while he was eating. He held and handled these letters and papers with one hand and ate with the other. He seemed to eat mechanically and to pay no attention to what or how much he was eating when engrossed with his papers and correspondence.
>
> Learnard says he once found Plumb sick in his apartments. This was about three years before Plumb's death. Plumb had been very busy about something and had not eaten or slept much for several days. Learnard says Plumb would have died at that time but for his (Learnard's) interference. He took Plumb to a hotel and called a physician to see him and had him supplied with proper food, and in a few days, Plumb was all right. This, Learnard says, was a peculiarity of Plumb–he would become so engrossed with a matter that he would forget or neglect to eat for several days, working in the meantime as no other man could work–speaking in the Senate, digging into archives and papers for facts, examining records in the Departments, writing letters,

going through law books and public documents. Then when the matter was disposed of and relaxation from the intense strain came, nature asserted herself and he sometimes overate or ate injudiciously. Learnard thinks this habit had much to do with this death in the fullness of his strength.

Plumb's disregard for his health and his health was noticed by his fellow Senators. Senator Pettigrew remarked:

> Pettigrew says Plumb had been in very poor health for some time before his death. About two weeks before Plumb's death Pettigrew went to his apartments and found him lying on a couch quite ill. Plumb must have felt then that his end was near. He told Pettigrew that he did not care to live beyond the time when his powers became impaired. He said he wished to die in the harness, as had Senator Beck, who dropped dead in the railroad station at Washington. The mere matter of existence without the ability to work did not appeal to him. He told Pettigrew that the physicians had urged him to spend months in sanitariums, in travel, in doing this and doing that, but that he could not bring himself to follow their advice. He abhorred a sanitarium or any place where he could not work hard.
> Either on the visit above described, or another within a day or two, Plumb requested Pettigrew to take from his hand a roll of money and put it in his (Plumb's) pocket for him, saying, "My right hand refuses to respond to my will."

Plumb's Death

The following is a letter from Linson de F. Jennings, included in its entirety, describing the details of Plumb's death. Plumb rented a furnished apartment from Jennings, which also served as his office. This letter was sent to Carrie Plumb:

> Dear Madam:
> I desire to express to you my deep sympathy in your bereavement, this sympathy in my case is most heartfelt as in your departed husband I lose the staunchest, truest, friend man ever had.

This is one of the last known photographs taken of Senator Preston B. Plumb. It was likely taken in honor of his second reelection to the United States Senate around 1890. Image courtesy Library of Congress.

In the more than four years that Senator Plumb had been an inmate of my home, I had conceived for him a deep affection. As the time passed, and we became better acquainted his relationship changed from that of our lodger to a member, (and one beloved by all) of our family.

From the standpoint from which I viewed the senator's daily life, I have felt that for two years past he has been in serious danger. On a number of occasions he has sent for me and his complaint was uniformly that he suffered from headaches, and inability to sleep. I never till this last occasion felt that he was in immediate danger, and his trouble always yielded to such simple home remedies as we ourselves applied. The soaking of his feet in hot mustard water, the application of cold cloths to his head, and often the laying of my hands on his head induced the quiet sleep he so much needed. At exactly, two o'clock Sunday morning Dec. 20, Senator Plumb shook the knob of my bedroom door and upon my saying, "Who's there?" He replied, "Jennings I am a very sick man, I wish you would hurry down and look at me." I was at his bedside almost as soon as he reached it. I asked him what his trouble was and he said, "Oh! I have an excruciating headache." He was extremely nervous, and tossed his head, and arms. Mrs. Jennings came downstairs, and I deemed it best to instantly go for his physician, Dr. Whales, which I did. During my absence, Mrs. Jennings had placed hot irons at his feet, and gave him aromatic spirits of ammonia to inhale, and on my return from Mr. Whales the senator was apparently sleeping. The doctor reached the house at two forty-five. He roused the Senator, and in reply to his questions reiterated his complaint of his head. I stood beside the senator near the foot of his bed, his face was perfectly natural, his voice strong, and his articulation as usual. There was no indication that I could see of anything beyond an unusually severe headache.

The doctor gave me a prescription for some morphine (1/16 grain) with atropia (1/120 grain) which I procured at the druggists, and on my return, the doctor administered a hypodermic injection. It acted promptly and the senator fell into a natural sleep. The doctor, Mrs. Jennings, and myself sat in the front room till half past four when Mrs. J. retired. The doctor remained till six thirty. All this time the senator slept peacefully. Just before Dr. Whales left, he went to the bed and examined the senator. I asked him as he was going out if the morphine would not in all probability cause nausea and vomiting when the Senator wakened, the doctor said it probably would. Then I said, "I suppose the usual antidote black coffee should be given him." The doctor said, "Yes give it to him weak." I then said if this is not successful in relieving the nausea what then? His reply was give him aromatic spirits of ammonia. I said, "How much?–half a teaspoonful?" and the doctor said yes that will do. He then left the house saying that he would be back during the forenoon. You may think it strange I did not send for Mr. Flenniken, but in the first place I did not know where he lived, and secondly, I was used to watching with the senator and was so anxious regarding his [health] that I thought of nothing but him and it. I sat in a chair between the folding doors facing the senator's bed two gas jets were burning and I could plainly see him. Suddenly at 6:45 just fifteen minutes after the doctor left the senator sprang from his bed, and stepped quickly to the corner where the slop jar was. I was there in time to place my hands on his head to support it. He vomited quite freely. I wiped his face and mouth, and he said, "Don't press my head so hard, it is so sore." Then as I took my right hand from the back of his head he vomited again. He now sat down on a chair that stood beside him and after three or four minutes seemed inclined to doze, so I said, "Senator don't sit here, get up and let me help you to bed, I fear you may take cold." He instantly rose and I assisted him to his bed, and upon lying down he spoke his last words, he rolled his head and pressed his left hand to his forehead, and said, "Oh! My head, my head." Then I said, "Senator put your hand down, let me hold your head possibly I can help quiet the pain." He did as I asked him and I held his head gently between my hands, and in four or five minutes he began to breathe deeply and naturally, and sank into a peaceful sleep. I sat and watched him from this time (7 o'clock) till 10:10 when Mr. Flenniken walked into the room. I told him the story, and said if the senator wakes he may be sick to his stomach and if he is, send up for me at once as the doctor has told me what remedies to give him.

I had breakfast, dressed, and then went up to my room and lay down to read the paper. At 11:30 my son, Harold, came running upstairs and said, "Papa, the doctor has just come and you can hear [the] Senator's breath all over the halls." I sprang downstairs and went up to the bedside. The doctor sat there holding [the] Senator's pulse. He said, "This is apoplexy–the senator is a very sick man, have you any whiskey?" I said no but I will get some in a moment. I ran over to the Ebbit house and procured the liquor and was back in three minutes. As I came in the doctor said, "Put it on the table it is too late." The senator was breathing with great difficulty, the doctor held his right hand in his, and I sat on the foot of the bed. Mr. Flenniken standing behind me. In a few moments there came that most dreadful rattle in the senator's throat and he ceased to breathe. I took out my watch and it was exactly ten minutes of twelve. The shock to us was almost stunning, tears fell from our eyes, while our hearts bled for our country and his dear ones. About ten minutes after the senator passed away the doctor began the various tests for death. I was an eyewitness to his thoroughness and care. I have seen many dead persons, and have been at many deathbeds, and I saw all the symptoms and heard that ominous sound that is always the precursor of the end. The rest, my dear Madame, you know from Frank.

In the death of the senator you have lost a noble husband, I a true dear friend, and our country a statesman, patriot, and soldier, of whom may be spoken those words uttered by President Lincoln, as he died "With charity for all, with malice toward none." I know our Heavenly Father welcomed him to his everlasting home with the words of the scripture "Well done thou good and faithful servant, enter thou into the joys of your Lord."

Carrie had been bedridden for some time and finally felt well enough to attend church. It was there that she was notified via telegram of her husband's illness. She immediately fell into hysterics and collapsed. She had to be carried out of the church and taken home in a carriage. Upon arriving home, she received a second telegram informing her of his death. Newspaper reports described her as "completely prostrated." Her relationship with her husband was an extremely close one, and losing him so suddenly was an overwhelming amount of grief that she never fully recovered from.

Plumb's body laid in state in the Capitol Building on December 21st and a funeral service attended by President and Mrs. Harrison, members of Congress, Supreme Court Justices, and countless friends and associates was held. The body was then transported to Topeka, Kansas where a funeral procession transported it to the state capitol where it laid in state again. Over 15,000 mourners came to Topeka to attend the procession and view the body. After that, the body was brought to the Plumb home in Emporia and guarded by members of the Grand Army of the Republic which included many of his former soldiers of the 11th Kansas. Thomas Barber of Emporia, who had served closely with Plumb during the war, was among those who stood guard outside the Plumb home in the bitter cold. Approximately 3,000 people paid their respects to the funeral train when it arrived in Emporia, nearly all of them would have personally met or been connected to Plumb in some way. A private service was held at the family home and then a public service at the Congregational Church was held later that afternoon. Plumb was interred in the family plot at Maplewood Cemetery in Emporia. Plumb's funeral was with full military and Masonic honors. He had been the first to join the Emporia Lodge and had remained a Freemason throughout his life as a member of the Knights Templar. Plumb had been a member of the Military Order of the Loyal Legion of the United States since 1884, and many members of that organization were also present.

Walter Stevens, a friend of Plumb's, described some instances in the aftermath of his death, when the family and friends came to pack up his apartment in Washington D.C.:

> When the people with whom the senator lived put things in order a couple of days ago, after the funeral, they found in a drawer a bundle of crochet work for the holidays. They were mystified at first. Then they remembered that they had seen an old lady at the door with a basket of these articles trying to sell some of her handiwork. They remembered that on that same morning, the Senator had come to them and got a quantity of

change. Since then the old lady has come again, and she has told of her talk with the kind senator and of his promise to buy all of the crochet work she could make up to Christmas time.

There was another discovery which brought moisture to the eyes. In the senator's room, after the removal of the remains, was found a collection of holiday presents. The Senator had planned to have his boy [Preston Jr.] come down from school in Pennsylvania to spend the holidays with him, and he had found time in the midst of his public engagements to lay in a stock of surprises. Can a man who loved all children, as Senator Plumb did, be said to have no "pathos," no "sentimentalism." He did much of the work which came to him from the pure enjoyment it gave him to be helpful to others and without selfishness of motive.

Right: The funeral procession for Plumb was attended by approximately 15,000 mourners. It was one of the largest funeral events in Topeka. Image courtesy Kansas Memory, Kansas State Historical Society. Above: Funeral dais in Emporia. Below: Funeral procession in Emporia attended by 3,000 mourners. Images courtesy Plumb family.

Above: The hearse carrying the body of Senator Plumb to the cemetery. Below: The decorated grave of Senator Preston B. Plumb in Maplewood Cemetery, Emporia. Images courtesy Plumb family.

PRESTON B. PLUMB

Oh, man of strong, indomitable will,

Oh, friend of earnest, sympathetic heart,

Oh, statesman, void of politician's art,

Oh, patriot, mid the unfaithful, loyal still,

Who now his honored place can take and fill?

In country, or in city's busy mart,

Can any where be found his counterpart?

A man thro whose great spirit went a thrill

At tale of woe, whose very life was spent

For good of all; who with an open hand

His kindly benefactions ever lent.

The hearts and homes of many thro the land

For him are with an unfeigned sorrow rent,

Whose name will o'er his compeers ever stand.

J.M. Cavaness

Chapter 20

Legacy

Memorial Addresses

The Senate and House held many memorial addresses after Plumb's death. In his memorial, Congressman Horace F. Bartine of Nevada said this of him:

> Senator Plumb was a tireless worker. His mind was ever active and full of plans for the improvement of society. His ideas were broad, national, and thoroughly American. He made no claim to perfection; his friends made no such claims for him. Had he been perfect he would not have been human. His life was a lesson that should never be lost upon the youth of our land. Born with the love of liberty in his heart, that sentiment grew and blossomed and ripened upon the plains of Kansas. In the midst of stormy, turbulent scenes, frequently ending in strife and bloodshed, as a mere boy he helped lay the foundations of one of the greatest and grandest states of the American Union. That same love of liberty combined with patriotism, made him a soldier of the Union, and upon the battlefield he displayed the same resolution and determined courage that distinguished him in civil life. His career in the senate was in the highest degree honorable both to himself and the people whom he represented. He was a strikingly conspicuous figure in that body. A close student, a thorough investigator, familiar with nearly every detail of governmental administration, a clear, incisive, and ready debater, he shrank from no encounter. His lance was ever couched, and it seldom failed to reach the object at which it was aimed. But he always struck in a spirit of kindness and never intentionally gave pain. Associated with some of the strongest intellects of the age, he grew and strengthened by the association. His tremendous physical energy and mental activity enabled him to transact an amount of work that is almost incredible, and the impress of his sturdy and practical mind has been left upon many a page of statute books of the country.

Mr. Plumb was a Republican and deeply imbued with the fundamental principles of that party. He realized, however, that no political organization can be uniformly right and upon matters of detail, not going to the principles upon which the party was founded, he was boldly and sometimes aggressively independent. More than once he drew upon himself the censure of his party associates. But it was political censure only. He was a brave and honorable opponent, never lurking in darkness, never firing from ambush, but always in the clear light of day, fighting upon open ground, and he held the respect and esteem of this brother senators to the last. As a member of the body in which it is generally believed that patrician ideas have to some extent found a lodgment, Mr. Plumb was essentially a tribune of the people.

Former Kansas Governor John St. John summed up Plumb well when he said:

> Plumb was a very useful senator. He was a man Kansas should be proud of. He was simple, plain, straightforward. He worked for the people of Kansas. In fact, he killed himself doing hard work. He wrote a reply to every letter he received. It did not matter who wrote him nor on what subject, he always replied and I understood that for years he wrote his replies with his own hand. If you asked a favor of him he would grant it if possible, and if he could not grant it he would write you a letter telling why he could not do it and when he could do it, if he ever could. He knew almost all the Kansas people personally or by reputation, and he kept himself informed of what was going on in the state. He was a good senator and a good man.

Perhaps one of the most moving stories to be told following Plumb's sudden death came not from a lofty politician but from a man who, for a time, was a bitter enemy of Plumb's.

> A man lay in a dazed condition in a Leadville [Colorado] boarding house. It was during the rush for fortunes when that city was only a mining camp. Mountain pneumonia caught its victims and carried them over the divide like a whiff. This man's

condition was that critical stage when a few hours continuance at the 10,100 feet altitude meant pneumonia and death. Plumb, who was fortune-seeking in the camp, heard of the sick man. Twenty-five years before, the two had been friends and business associates in Kansas. Twenty years before they had differed and quarreled. They had not spoken to each other in all that interim, though their paths had crossed and recrossed. Perhaps hard words had been spoken to mutual friends. Into the sick man's room at early morning came Plumb, without a word of previous intimation to pave the way. "You must get out of this," he said, after a look. A couple of hours later the sick man, wrapped in blankets, was lifted downstairs and into a four-horse ambulance, which was worth money in those days. Over and down the mountain went the outfit to Park City, then the terminus of the railroad. The sick man was lifted into a special car. Plumb was still by his side. He did not leave him until he saw him in a hotel in Denver and in the hands of people who would nurse him through. Then, with a, "You'll be all right now." He was off. The two did not meet again for years. But the story explains why on Sunday night Richard J. Hinton walked the streets of Washington weeping like a child. The news of Senator Plumb's death had just reached him.

"A strong man was Plumb," said he whose life had been saved as described, and his voice shook with emotion, "in all senses and ways except taking care of himself. He gave generously of his vital forces, and never balanced the spending. It was his ambition to serve well, and as he was conscious of ability to do so on a generous scale he was ambitious of a large place. Under a brusque but never a rude exterior he veiled one of the kindest of dispositions. He was a man of simple courage; he never could have known how to avoid or evade a danger or duty, physical or mental. No man despised mere conventionalism more than he did, and so he was at war with the faction—that the United States Senate is the finest of clubs. He made it a forceful arena, and always held it in honor as a lofty forum. He was a man not afraid of his valet, for he never dreamed of being a hero. He only strove to be a fully equipped, honest workman—the noblest human in our daily life. I had noticed in him of late a milder judgment; less of the Berserker, a more genial balancing of will and action."

Legacy

It can be difficult to measure the legacy of one life, but there were many people impacted by Preston Plumb's life at the time of his death. From the thousands of veterans who received their pensions through his efforts as a senator, to innumerable businesses and charities started and sustained through his generous donations. His tireless efforts in the Senate resulted in the U.S. Department of Agriculture finally gaining stature in the government, the creation of forestry laws that evolved into the current U.S. Forestry Service, and the creation of Yosemite and Sequoia National Parks. He was very forward-thinking and many of his ideas that failed in his time, eventually gained new life in the decades to come.

One can only imagine the things Plumb may have accomplished had he lived longer. There were rumors that he may have received the Republican presidential nomination, however, it is difficult to say that he would have accepted it. Plumb detested pomp and circumstance and preferred to work hard and accomplish things. Had he accepted a cabinet position or presidential nomination, he would have been forced into the bureaucracy that he detested. At the time of his sudden death, he was at the height of his political influence and no doubt would have accomplished far more in the years to come.

On a local level, he had been working on creating a new library for Emporia which would have been similar to what would be called a community center today. Due to his death, this was never accomplished. Mary Perley, a close friend of the family, had been conversing with Plumb about this project for some time:

> Mr. Plumb had an idea of building a library and endowing it in this way. He intended to put up a large building on a corner lot centrally located and have a store on the first floor in the front part. There was to be a room at the back with an entrance on the side and the library was to be upstairs. The room downstairs was to be a lounging and reading room for the poor people of Emporia who would not like to go, with their muddy boots and clothes upstairs. He wanted someone in charge they would have enough respect for to make them behave. He thought if it was

practical he would like a lunch room in connection with this room. He asked me if I would not present it to the mayor. He wanted the city to buy the lots and he would put up the building; the revenue from the building was to be used as an endowment for the library. Mr. Weaver was Mayor at that time and he brought it up before the council. A man by the name of Sexton, I think, who lived in the southeast part of town, and who called himself a socialist (I called him an anarchist) worked against it; did not think it a good thing to have the library in that way. Mr. Plumb had his arrangements all made and wanted to do it. I gave Mrs. Plumb the letter which he wrote me about the matter in the first place. His suggestion was that they buy fifty feet on the corner where the Government building now stands [this location is likely incorrect as the Government already owned that land prior to Plumb's death], but that was merely a suggestion he did not intend to dictate the location, but he happened to know that that corner was probably available. Mr. Weaver thought it could probably be managed another year, but in another year Plumb was gone and it was too late.

Plumb's sudden death plunged Carrie and the children into a world of chaos. Carrie and their son, Dale, were named executors of the estate and former business associates and scammers soon tried to stake a claim to the large estate.

Some of Plumb's closest associates turned on the family and brought suits. Major Hood was one of them, and resorted to blackmail in an attempt to get Carrie to pay him what he thought he was owed. In a letter she wrote to Dale, she told of the blackmailing and said that she had talked it over with Preston's brother, George. He was of the mind that she should pay, while she believed that if she paid Hood once, she would be paying him forever. Hood threatened to release information to the newspapers that her husband had been having affairs around Washington. Carrie refused to pay Hood and countersued him, and the matter was settled out of court. In the settlement, the Plumb family retained ownership of what they were entitled to, and it seems Hood remained bitter towards them after that incident.

Plumb's death also caused a rift between the family and his personal secretary, Benjamin Flenniken. He had been with Plumb for the vast majority of his senate career and managed many of his personal affairs. Upon Plumb's death, the family dismissed Flenniken and let Dale manage all of the business affairs. The reason for this was likely twofold: the first being that Dale was perfectly capable of managing the affairs, and secondly, the family was embroiled in so many lawsuits that they had very few people they could trust. In fact, things were so bad, that Dale and Carrie communicated by code in their letters and telegrams while fighting the many lawsuits. The suits dragged on for five years after Plumb's death. For a time, Carrie could not travel to certain states back east for fear of being served papers. They dealt with solicitors at the family home in Emporia harassing them to settle and pay claims. In the end, the Plumb estate was victorious in every single court case brought against them. Carrie and the children were much like Plumb, they did not back down from a fight, no matter how difficult.

Dale continued to manage the family's business affairs from Emporia which had diversified into a wide variety of ventures, one of which was the Massachusetts Avenue Heights housing development in Washington D.C. Today, this neighborhood is near the Naval Observatory and the location of premium homes of ambassadors and other high society people. When Plumb bought the land, there was nothing out there at all. Dale partnered with others to create a subdivision of luxury homes and made a small fortune through his endeavors.

In 1893, Carrie began remodeling the Victorian mansion that she had lived in together with her husband. The construction went on for a few years and resulted in one of the most preeminent mansions in Emporia when it was completed in 1895. For her, the renovation work was likely a distraction from the grief over the loss of her husband. She wrote to her daughter Ruth in 1899 on the eve of the eight-year anniversary of his death:

> My dear Ruth,
>
> I have been asleep and wakened to think of you and these hours eight years ago. I did want you to go to school so much. To advance. To grow but I thought I could not bear to have you away from me. I have tried it and found I could do it. Yes and be happy with you, and happy because I am sure it is as your father would have me do.
>
> That is my life to bring into the lives of my children all that (so far as I can) he would have done for them. I have failed many times. Sometimes because of want of judgement [sic].

Sometimes because I am not well enough to see clearly all that I ought to do. I wish you with the others might feel my heart has been right at all times.

This is a time of rejoicing for all. At first I thought I could not bear the brightness at the same time of my sorrow. But that feeling has passed. I think now I would not change it if I could. It has put a new meaning to the season. For was it not the birthday of the one dearest to me into a new life. A new existence. And I can think of him now as growing, expanding beyond me to be sure. But I take comfort in his faith "We shall know eachother [sic] there better than we have ever known eachother [sic] here." And his words rang out clear. They have followed me all these years.

Dear Child, no Christmas I can make for you can ever express my love for you.

Mother.

It is clear that Carrie was very devoted to her husband and mourned his death for some time. His grave in Emporia remained bereft of any sort of headstone or marker for several years. He had requested in his will a specific type of granite boulder, which took Carrie some time to procure. Those who were not well acquainted with the family supposed that the lack of a marker was because she did not like him. No doubt, these beliefs were fueled by Hood's stories from his blackmail threats. In reality, Carrie special ordered a variety of flowers and foliage to be planted on his grave until she could locate the stone he wanted. She ordered clematis, roses, and ivy, which in Victorian flower language mean "soul mates," "eternal love," "happy love," "marriage," and "mourning."

In addition, Carrie commissioned a bust of her husband by R.P. Bringhurst in 1895. The bust was completed and presented to the state of Kansas to be placed in the state capitol. It was later moved to the governor's office, and Carrie would make time to sit and spend time with it alone, whenever she was in Topeka.

The 11th Kansas continued to hold reunions each year, and Carrie remained as involved as ever. She gave the men books she thought they would enjoy and was active in supporting them and helping them however she could, just as her husband had done. For her efforts, she was named "Mother of the Regiment" in 1893. That same year, members of the 79th Ohio Volunteer Infantry held a reunion in Emporia and were received at the Plumb home by Carrie and Dale. She presented each of the men with a large photograph of her husband as a keepsake, which they were very pleased with.

In 1910, she sent Lt. George Walker in Iowa a gift of William Connelley's book on Quantrill's Raid. Walker was a member of the 11th Kansas, and had served as an aide to Plumb during the war. The thoughtfulness of the gesture inspired him to write her a kind letter, illustrating that nearly twenty years after her husband's death, she was still very much appreciated by the men of her husband's regiment. He wrote:

> On last evening the agent of Wells-Fargo Express Co. delivered a pkg. from Emporia, Kans. On opening it I found it to be a copy of a very valuable and interesting book *Quantrill and the Border Wars* and on further examination found it was from you. To say that I was surprised and pleased is stating the fact mildly. I was delighted. The book is valuable in itself; but coming as it did from the life Companion of my friend and Commander greatly increases its value to me…I appreciate the book very highly and thank you not only for the book but for remembering me.

Following Carrie's death in 1919, their three daughters gifted the Plumb mansion to the Young Women's Christian Association as a community center. Their sons contributed money at the same time in order to facilitate its transformation into a community center more quickly. That generous gift from all of the Plumb children served that function and as a home for women for nearly 100 years before closing in December 2020.

The legacy of the Plumb family is far reaching. From senate bills and laws, to small pensions for disabled veterans; from his leadership in the Civil War to her charity work with libraries in Emporia–the impact of the Plumbs cannot be overstated. Today, the town of Emporia, Kansas has over 25,000 residents and has grown to be an important city within the state. Without Plumb's determination and tenacity, it may never have gotten off the ground in 1857. Throughout his life, Plumb remained unpretentious and sought only to help and serve others. He instilled that same drive in his children, and his wife carried on with causes that were dear to him, despite her ill health. He embodied the true spirit of a westerner and built strong foundations of towns, businesses, and legislation wherever he went. He was a man who came from humble beginnings and rose to become one of the most respected and beloved men of his time. Kansas, and indeed, all of America could take a lesson from Plumb's life. His qualities of charity, kindness, strength, and justice combined with an unflinching work ethic carried him to great heights.

But if one were to ask Plumb what accomplishment he was most proud of, he would say his children. In the following letter written to his friend, E.N. Morrill, only a few short months before his death, he stated exactly that:

> Ruth and Carrie are with their mother and Dale at Clifton Springs, New York. Mrs. Plumb has had a somewhat serious attack of heart trouble, but is better at the present time. Amos [Dale] is better than he has been for some time, and I think is doing very well indeed, although he has a long road before him which he must travel before he can come to anything like recovery. Ruth had very strong regrets at not going with your party to California. I must tell the truth about her, which I get from a letter which she wrote to her mother. She put up another excuse to me, but she wrote to her mother that it had occurred to her at the last moment that I was coming back, and that if she went away I should have no home to come to, and so she concluded that her duty was to stay; and so made believe, of course, that this was her pleasure as well.
>
> If I were called on to say what I thought was my chief title to consideration on the part of my fellow men, I should say it was the children which I have brought into the world.

Mary Plumb

1868-1940

Amos "Dale" Plumb

1869-1939

Ruth Plumb Brewster

1874-1976

Caroline Plumb Griffith

1879-1973

Preston B. Plumb

1881-1955

Dale Plumb's picture courtesy John Meredith. All other portraits of the Plumb children courtesy the Plumb family, Carrie Clarke and Jody Wolf.

Notes

The following Notes are limited to direct quotations and paraphrasing of quotations, largely from William Elsey Connelley's interviews. The Bibliography includes a more comprehensive list of sources consulted for this book, however, it would be impossible to list all the sources the author has gathered for this work. For the sake of conciseness, the Bibliography is limited to sources that were heavily referenced or quoted in the book.

Chapter 1

Early Years in Ohio

"Around the age of six": *PFC: Connelley Book 4*, 100

"Ellen recalled that she came out of the house": Ibid., 100

"Plumb had his own encounter with serious injury": *PFC Connelley Book 3*, 377.7

"By 1849, Plumb had attended all of the schools": Connelley, *Life of Preston B. Plumb*, 12

"Kenyon College had a reputation as a strict school": Ibid., 13

"While at Gambier working in the office": *PFC Connelley Book 24*, 159

"On his return to Marysville, Ohio": Connelley, *Life of Preston B. Plumb*, 14

"Not long after Plumb began working": Ibid., 15

Xenia News

"Also at this time, Plumb added": "Senator Plumb had No Middle Name" *Topeka Daily Capitol*, November 19, 1909

"By all accounts, The *Xenia News*": Connelley, *Life of Preston B. Plumb*, 20

"He [Plumb] was a good printer": *PFC Connelley Book 2*, 213-215

"In 1856 Dumble sold his interest": Ibid., 214

"In March of 1856, Jacob Stotler": Connelley, *Life of Preston B. Plumb*, 21

The Sacking of Lawrence

"He [Parrott] confirmed all the reports": *PFC Connelley Book 9*, 34-35

"It is impossible to fully detail the impact": *PFC Connelley Book 3*, 377.10

"The Xenia News – Friday, July 18, 1856" *PFC Connelley Book 9*, 46-62

Chapter 2

Kansas Settlement

"Pierce arrived at Iowa City": *PFC Connelley Book 2*, 4-12

"On the trip across Iowa": Connelley, *Life of Preston B. Plumb*, 46

"The party remained in Topeka some days": *PFC Connelley Book 2*, 12-15

"The Xenia News Friday, Oct. 24, 1856": *PFC Connelley Book 9*, 89-92

"The Xenia News Friday, Nov. 14, 1856": Ibid., 101-108

"The first time Harris saw Plumb": *PFC Connelley Book 2*, 41

"Colonel O.E. Learnard also": *PFC Connelley Book 6*, 76

"A day or two after Harris": *PFC Connelley Book 2*, 41-44

"The Xenia News Friday, Dec. 12, 1856": *PFC Connelley Book 9*, 109-111

"The Smoky Hill": *PFC Connelley Book 24*, 71-73

"The Xenia News Friday, January 23, 1857": *PFC Connelley Book 9*, 112-117

"The Xenia News Friday, Feb. 20, 1857": Ibid., 124-134

"One night when [Pierce's] party was building": *PFC Connelly Book 2*, 17-20

"Plumb returned to Ohio": *PFC Connelley Book 4*, 109

"After Preston came back from his first": Ibid., 110

Chapter 3

Founding Emporia

"He took a boat at Kansas City": *PFC Connelley Book 1*, 173-174

"He did not know how to get money ": *PFC Connelley Book 4*, 110-112

"Father and I were crossing Sixth Avenue": William Hammond, *Emporia Centennial Booklet*, 25-28

"We stopped in front of the hotel": *PFC Connelley Book 2*, 74-75

"She remembers that when the people": – Ibid., 70-71

"In the fall, he [John Brown]": *PFC Connelley Book 4*, page 85

"Warrants continued to issue from": Tanner, *Kansas Historical Collections, Volume XIV, 1915-1918*, 230

"Plumb was always an independent": *PFC Connelley Book 6*, 1

"We decided not to follow the Santa Fe Trail": *PFC Connelley Book 3*, 377.17-19

"A man by the name of Wright": *PFC Connelley Book 4*, 91-92

"In 1859 Plumb decided to pursue": *Kansas News*, January 15, 1859

"He left Emporia in October 1859": *The Weekly News Democrat*, Oct 29, 1859

"He is accompanied by Mr. H.G. Plantz": *PFC Connelley Book 24*, 176

"During this time, Plumb worked and resided": – *PFC Connelley Book 4*, 83

Chapter 4

War Breaks Out

"During this time the Emporia Normal School": *PFC Connelley Book 2*, 28

"After a question had been debated": *PFC Connelley Book 18*, 93

"In January 1862 a committee of five": *PFC Connelley Book 13*, 113-114

"By August 1862 another regiment of troops": *PFC Connelley Book 24*, 191

"About 300 people had congregated": Ibid., 191-192

"There were 140 total enlisted, of this number": *PFC Connelley Book 18*, 96

"he'd suffered two hemorrhages": *PFC Connelley Book 3*, 377.15

Chapter 5

Off to War

"We have been furnished by Lieut. Gregg, Sergeant Taber" – *Buck & Ball*

"Owing to the space required for the details": Ibid.

"At Cane Hill the Eleventh was charging": *PFC Connelley Book 6*, 51-52

"Broke camp as usual. Marched to": Bodwell, *Bodwell Diary*, 50-51

"The 11th received its baptism"; *Saint Louis Globe-Democrat*, 22 March, 1888, page 6

Chapter 6

Battle of Prairie Grove and Aftermath

"At Prairie Grove Plumb was in command": *PFC Connelley Book 6*, 51

"Sunday Dec. 7th": Bodwell, *Bodwell Diary* 53-54

"In the battle of Prairie Grove the Eleventh": *PFC Connelley Book 7*, 152-153

"After the battle, Plumb": The Osage County Chronicle, Aug 24, 1882, 5

"Fairfield was in the march": Ibid., 153-155

"On the 8th (Barber thinks)": *PFC Connelley Book 6*, 52

"Colonel Weir, Tenth Kansas was trying": Ibid., 53

"We had marched all night": *PFC Connelley Book 24*, 81

"Fairfield was regimental postmaster": *PFC Connelley Book 7*, 152

"Shot through the lungs": *PFC Connelley Book 13*, 24

"Plumb's younger brother": (Report of the Adjutant General of the State of Kansas, Vol. 1. - 1861-1865. Leavenworth, Kansas: Bulletin Co-operative Printing Company, Chicago. 1867)

"Ewing had practically no cavalry": *PFC Connelley Book 7*, 155

"It took some time for the orders": Bodwell, *Bodwell Diary*, 106

Chapter 7

Quantrill's Raid

"It was sometime in the fore part of August": *PFC Connelley Book 4*, 94-95

Lawrence Raid

"[Corporal]Fairfield says General Ewing": *PFC Connelley Book 7*, 155-156

Pursuit of Quantrill

"I left Emporia the day before": *PFC Connelley Book 4*, 102-106

"Plumb kept sending dispatches": *PFC Connelley Book 6*, 59-60

"I am now seeing that in order": Ibid., 60

"General Order No. 11": Wikipedia

"West Point, N.Y., Jan. 25, 1877": *PFC Connelley Book 5*, 52-56

"Colonel Van Horn did not see Plumb": *PFC Connelley Book 7*, 131-132

"Before the Quantrill raid": *PFC Connelley Book 6*, 58-59

Chapter 8

Bushwhackers

Fall of 1863

"George Plumb continued to be on": *PFC Connelley Book 4*, 87

"Saturday 26th Sept. [1863]": Bodwell, *Bodwell Diary*, 124-125

"Thursday Oct. 1st/63": Ibid., 126

"Sabbath Oct. 4th": Ibid, 127-128

"Walker does not remember what": *PFC Connelley Book 6*, 8-11

1864

"During the war": *PFC Connelley Book 5*, 43-44

"I knew Senator Plumb before he went": *PFC Connelley Book 3*, 16-17

"Independence, Mo. 28th Sept. 1863": – National Archives, Plumb Personnel Military File

"I remember well when a detachment": PFC Connelley Book 1, 181

"Plumb was with a scouting party": Stevens, "Wherein Plumb was Great," The Kansas City Times, Monday, 28 Dec 1891, page 5

Chapter 9

Price Raid

Second Battle of Lexington

"February 22, 1864, at Pleasant Ridge": *PFC Connelley Book 18*, 80

"When it was known": *PFC Connelley Book 7*, 163-164

"Simpson says that the battle with Price": *PFC Connelley Book 25*, 174-176

"Tuesday, 18th": Bodwell, *Bodwell Diary* 173-177

"Sabbath, October 23rd, 1864": Ibid., 178

"In the battles to check Price": *PFC Connelley Book 18*, 80-81

"Then came the real battles": *PFC Connelley Book 7*, 164-165

"Monday, Oct. 24/64": Bodwell, *Bodwell Diary*, 179

"Twenty-two years ago today": PFC Connelley Book 18, 36

"Capt. Pierce of the Eleventh Kansas": *The Leavenworth Times*, March 21, 1865 – Page 3

Chapter 10

Headed West

Winter of 1864-65

"In the winter of 1864-5": *PFC Connelley Book 2*, 88

"On this march the Regiment": *PFC Connelley Book 18*, 81-82

"Monday, February 20, 1865": Plumb, *Plumb Diary*

"Captain Palmer married Betty Houck": *PFC Connelley Book 7*, 126-127

"Only a brief stop was made": *PFC Connelley Book 18*, 82

"The following is a letter written": *PFC Connelley Book 6*, 61-65

"Their destination of Platte Bridge Station": Wickman, *Lost Forts of Casper*, 39

"Warm, with wind northerly but light": Bodwell, *Bodwell Diary*, 214

"While thus engaged they camped": Stevens, "Wherein Plumb was Great." *Kansas City Times*, December 27, 1891, 5

"Then came the hazardous task": *PFC Connelley Book 6*, 65-66

"Thomas Barber was in the Powder River Expedition": *PFC Connelley Book 24*, 126-128

"This expedition spelled the end": *PFC Connelley Book 7*, 123

"This is one of my lonely": Bonwell, *Bonwell letter to his mother*, Fort Caspar Museum

"Headquarters Eleventh Kans. Cav. – Lt. Col. Plumb": Plumb letter to Lt. Ira Tabor – National Archives Letter

"Here [at Platte Bridge Station]": *PFC Connelley Book 24*, 128-129

"Monday June 5, 1865": Plumb, *Plumb Diary*

"Dear Sir: You are Undoubtedly": PFC Connelley Book 25, 186-187

"Dear Sir: I notice that": "From the Plains – 11th Kansas," *The Leavenworth Times*, June 29, 1865, 2

"Sunday, June 11, 1865": Plumb, *Plumb Diary*

"Friday, September 29, 1865": Ibid.

Chapter 11

Back to Civilian Life

"Before we left the army": *PFC Connelley Book 4*, 113-114

"In 1866 Plumb was re-elected to the State Legislature": Connelley, *Life of Preston B. Plumb*, 210

"At the close of the Legislature in 1866": *Osage County Chronicle*, June 3, 1886, Page 1

"Mr. and Mrs. Plumb, aged 29 and 20": – *Carrie Plumb letter to Preston Plumb Jr.*, April 2, 1889, Plumb Family Collection

"and lived in "a one-story, three-roomed house": *PFC Connelley Book 24*, 155

"He [Plumb] was a believer in thorough": *PFC Connelley Book 2*, 139

"Mrs. Morse relates that once": Ibid., 138-139

"The firm of Ruggles and Plumb": *PFC Connelley Book 1*, 80

"When Plumb was in El Dorado": *The Ellsworth Populist*, January 11, 1896, page 2

"Even though his law firm was at the head": *PFC Connelley Book 1*, 180

"Plumb's work as a lawyer required him to travel": *PFC Connelley Book 24*, 155-156

"Mr. Plumb was very kind to the Welsh people": *PFC Connelley Book 2*, 47-49

"Mr. Newman came to Kansas in 1867": Ibid., 128-129

"Lewis took a homestead near the present town": Ibid., 51

"Plumb was always alert for the people": *PFC Connelley Book 5*, 73

Chapter 12

Mr. Plumb Goes to Washington

"The fact is, Perry,": - Preston B. Plumb, *Letter to Leslie J. Perry*, January 4, 1876, LCHC, Plumb Correspondence Folder 4

"I knew Senator Plumb from 1866 on": PFC Connelley Book 1, 115-117

"In '77 there were four candidates for Senator": *PFC Connelley Book 4*, 48-50

"Plumb was a man who was not very much disposed": *PFC Connelley Book 1*, 117-118

"I was in hopes that someone of the": Connelley, *Life of Preston B. Plumb*, 235

"When Learnard first went to Washington": *PFC Connelley Book 6*, 78-79

"In all public affairs, he was active, well-informed": *PFC Connelley Book 1*, 118-119

"The election of Plumb to the Senate": *PFC Connelley Book 24*, 155

Chapter 13

A Thorough Kansan

"Plumb spoke the Kansas language": *PFC Connelley Book 3*, 366.4

Once a Newsman, Always a Newsman

"I had occasion to call on Senator Plumb": *PFC Connelley Book 24*, 115-116

"Mr. Scott said he was the correspondent": *PFC Connelley Book 1*, 22

"He says Plumb was a favorite with the": Ibid., 35-36

"It has never been definitively determined": Ibid., 70

"Lawyer A.B. Brown once met with Plumb": Ibid., 77

Plumb's Connection to the People

"On the 29th of May, I called to see": *PFC Connelley Book 2*, 131

"Despite now being on the national stage": *PFC Connelley Book 25*, 178

"I learned as the years went by": *PFC Connelley Book 2*, 89-90

"Yesterday afternoon I was introduced": *PFC Connelley Book 1*, 44-45

"My acquaintance with Senator Plumb": *PFC Connelley Book 2*, 57-59

"He got all the Eleventh Kansas": *PFC Connelley Book 7*, 12-13

"Plumb was generous by heart": *Cedar County Republican*, January 8, 1892, page 3

"Judge Graves said General J.K. Hudson": *PFC Connelley Book 2*, 111

"Nobody who witnessed the evident pleasure": Stevens, "Wherein Plumb was Great," *Kansas City Times*, December 28, 1891

Gifts and Charity

"Plumb was very thoughtful of his family": *PFC Connelley Book 6*, 78

"Nov. 28, 1886": Plumb letter to Mary Jane Perley, *PFC Connelley Book 2*, 125-126

"Mr. Plumb always gave double": *PFC Connelley Book 4*, 79

"United States Senate": Preston .B. Plumb Letter to Cavaness, Ibid., 40

"There was a merchant at Chanute": Ibid., 67-68

"Washington, April 7, 1889": President Benjamin Harrison to Plumb, *PFC Connelley Book 18*, 132

Personality

"Senator Plumb had a great many enemies": PFC Connelley Book 1, 121-123

"Plumb was a man of courage": Ibid., 145-147

"A central figure of the scene": "A Round up of Our Heavy Weight Politicians," *The Weekly News Democrat*, October 10, 1889, 1

"It [the conversation] related to the": Stevens, "Wherein Plumb was Great" – *Globe Democrat*, *Kansas City Times*, 28 Dec 1891, 3

"There are not many people in Washington": Ibid., 3

"Barney Sheridan tells this political story": *PFC Connelly Book 3*, 377.19-20

Appointments

"Many of Plumb's friends": *PFC Connelley Book 1*, 61

"While on a trip to Muskogee": *PFC Connelley Book 4*, 117-118

Chapter 14

A Big Winning

Garfield Presidential Nomination

"About the nomination of Garfield": *PFC Connelley Book 25*, 167-173

Chapter 15

Greater Influence

"Plumb made no pretensions to oratory": *PFC Connelley Book 1*, 77-78

"Sometimes Plumb would seem to take": Ibid., 151

"He could get at the merits of any business": Ibid., 101, 103

"Plumb did not speak unless": Ibid., 93

"Senator Pettigrew says Plumb": Ibid., 192-193

"MR. PLUMB: I wish to say": Congressional Record, February 16, 1891, 2722

"MR. COKE: Will the Senator from Kansas": Congressional Record April 24, 1884, 3341-3342

"The first time Captain King": *PFC Connelley Book 1*, 83-84

Small Bills

"Plumb's unceasing work ethic": Bills and Joint Resolutions in the US Senate: 47th Congress, 107-113

"I saw F.P. Metzger": *PFC Connelley Book 1*, 108-110

"When he took his seat, he was assigned": Ibid., 131

"It took Senator Plumb, of Kansas": "Friend of the Thirsty," *Emporia Republican*, May 29, 1902, 4

"There is no enterprise in the world": Plumb, *American Merchant Marine Senate Speech*, May 6, 1884, 7 and 11

Fellow Senators and Associates

"June 5, 1889 Wash. D.C.": *PFC Connelley Book 18*, 142

"He also occasionally found time to": *PFC Connelley Book 1*, 191-192

"Mrs. Plumb recalls one incident": *PFC Connelley Book 24*, 154, 159

"Washington, D.C.": Ibid., 201

"President Harrison issued an order": *PFC Connelley Book 3*, 366.2-4

"Some citizens of Ottawa [Kansas]": – Ibid., 376.2-3

"As a friend of Senator Plumb": *PFC Connelley Book 1*, 123-125

"Philip P. Campbell, Pittsburg, Kansas": Ibid., 37-39

Chapter 16

Family & Business

"Thomas S. Krutz told me today": *PFC Connelley Book 1*, 74

"The gentleness and tenderness toward the invalid wife": Stevens, "Memories of Plumb, *Cedar County Republican*, 8 Jan 1892, 3

"Once when Mrs. Plumb was ill": *PFC Connelley Book 24*, 153

"I hope Papa will be over this week": Carrie Plumb, Letter to Preston Jr., April 2, 1889, Plumb Family Collection

"The Dr. has me do some things": Carrie Plumb, Letter to Preston Jr., No date, Plumb Family Collection

"One day Plumb inquired of Berry": *PFC Connelley Book 1*, 133-134

"My dear Boy": Plumb, Letter to Preston Jr., December 18, 1887, Plumb Family Collection

"My dear Preston": Plumb, Letter to Preston Jr., March 12, 1890, Plumb Family Collection

"Dear Preston": Plumb, Letter to Preston Jr., Sept. 24, 1891, Plumb Family Collection

Business

"Plumb maintained the presidency": *PFC Connelley Book 4*, 79

"Colonel O.E. Learnard recalled": *PFC Connelley Book 6*, 78

"Spicer became associated with Plumb": *PFC Connelley Book 2*, 112

"Browne said Plumb was a combination": *PFC Connelley Book 1*, 76-77

Helping Others

"Roberts is a Welshman, and lived formerly at Emporia": *PFC Connelley Book 2*, 117-120

"Plumb's sister, Ellen, owned and operated": Ibid., 195

"Plumb never allowed himself": Lane-Randolph, "Life of P.B. Plumb," *PFC Connelley Book 3*, 374.9

"A group of women met at the Plumb": "The Emporia Library", *Weekly News Democrat,* October 23, 1884, 2

"Carrie was also involved in charity": *Weekly News Democrat,* June 15, 1877, 3

Chapter 17

Senator of the West

"An incident arose in New Mexico": *PFC Connelley Book 1*, 55

"I think," said Senator Berry": Ibid., 132

"The Index of the Congressional Record": Ibid., 145

"No man of greater physical vigor": Ibid., 140-143

Land Rights and Civil War Pensions

"Plumb was always aware of even the smallest": *PFC Connelley Book 5*, 73-74

"Miss Laura Thomas who for a long time": *PFC Connelley Book 2*, 194-195

Public Lands

"Senator Pettigrew was on the Senate Committee": *PFC Connelley Book 1*, 189-190

Women's Suffrage

"At one time they were going": *PFC Connelley Book 4*, 82

"Plumb's reversal on the issue": "Women Suffrage," *Manhattan Republic*, October 13, 1887, 2

"In his first session of Congress": – *Journal of the Senate Second Session of the 45th Congress*, 72

"The issue came to the forefront again": Congressional Record, February 3, 1889

Department of Agriculture

Sorghum

"I knew Senator Plumb quite intimately": *PFC Connelley Book 3*, 388

Reelections

"Topeka, January 24, 1889": *PFC Connelley Book 18*, 78

McKinley Tariff

"I remember a conversation I had": *PFC Connelley Book 4*, 144-116

"They [Senators Plumb, Paddock, and Pettigrew]": *PFC Connelley Book 1*, 186

"Pettigrew said the protected interests": Ibid, 185, 186

"Senator Plumb, Senator Paddock, and myself": Ibid., 195-197

"WESTERN UNION TELEGRAPH CO.": Carrie Plumb to Preston Plumb, *Connelley Book 18*, 153

"He was a believer in the protective tariff": *PFC Connelley Book 1*, 137-138

"Senator Plumb had been working on a tariff": Ibid. 1, 186-187

Chapter 18

"The Senator"

"So in the Fall of 1889": *PFC Connelley Book 3*, 373.2-10

"It is well known to the": *The Anaconda Standard*, January 20, 1891, 11

Chapter 19

His Last Campaign

"As busy as Plumb was": *Bangor Daily Whig and Courier,* July 14, 1882, 2

"Plumb was a regular fixture": *PFC Connelley Book 1,* 49

"Plumb was always expected to do the hard work": Ibid., 81-82

"When Bonebrake was Chairman": Ibid., 101-102

"Sometimes Plumb was called on": Ibid., 62-63

"Today I saw W.F. Shamneffer": Ibid., 65-66

"In Salina, there were three hotels": Ibid., 170-171

"About 1890 he desired the appointment": *PFC Connelley Book 18,* 95

"Plumb was always a strong supporter": *PFC Connelley Book 3,* 372.1-2

"He [Harrison] wanted Plumb": Ibid., 366.1-2

"Plumb kept a tireless pace traveling": Narratives on P.B. Plumb. KSHS, Collection 16, Box 43, Folder 404. March 6, 1913.

"That Plumb was a hard worker": *PFC Connelley Book 3,* 376.1-2

Plumb's Health

"Leanard stopped at the Riggs House": *PFC Connelley Book 6,* 77

"Pettigrew says Plumb had been in very": *PFC Connelley Book 1,* 190-191

Plumb's Death

"Dear Madam": *PFC Connelley Book 13,* 19-23

"Carrie had been bedridden": "Mrs. Plumb Completely Prostrated," *Democrat and Chronicle,* December 21, 1891, 1

"When the people with whom the Senator": Stevens, "Senator Plumb" *Globe-Democrat,* December 27, 1891, 6

Chapter 20

Legacy

Memorial Addresses

"Senator Plumb was a tireless worker – Lane-Randolph, Connelley Book 3, 374.10-12

"Plumb was a very useful Senator – St. John – Connelley Book 1, 67

"A man lay in a dazed condition – Stevens – "Senator Plumb" *Globe-Democrat*, 27 Dec 1891, Sunday page 6

Legacy

"Oh, man of strong, indomitable will": *PFC Connelley Book 4*, 39

"Mr. Plumb had an idea of building a library": *PFC Connelly Book 4*, 79-80

"Some of Plumb's closest": *Letterpress Book 94*, page 146, Plumb Correspondence

"Plumb's death also caused a rift": "Plumb Estate Wins," *Emporia Republican*, August 27, 1896, 3

"In 1893, Carrie began remodeling": *Holton Signal*, March 15, 1893, 4

"My dear Ruth": Carrie Plumb Letter to Ruth, Wolf Plumb Family Collection, December 19, 1889

"It is clear that Carrie": *Plumb Family Collection Book 61*, 271

"In addition, Carrie commissioned a bust": *Emporia Gazette*, February 22, 1895, 1

"The 11th Kansas continued to hold": *Emporia Daily Republican*, December 9, 1893, 4

"That same year, members of the": "Seventy-Ninth OVI Reunion" *Emporia Gazette*, March 30, 1893, 4

"On last evening the agent of Wells-Fargo Express Co.": *PFC Connelley Book 24*, 80, 82

"Ruth and Carrie are with their mother": Preston B. Plumb letter to Morrill, Wolf Plumb Family Collection, 1891

Bibliography

Primary Sources

Unpublished

<u>Author's Collection</u>
Preston B. Plumb Letter to E.N. Morrill, August 1891.
"Soldiers of the Republic." Speech by Preston B. Plumb, 1862.

<u>Carrie Clarke</u>
Carrie Plumb letter to Ruth Plumb, December 19, 1889.

<u>Fort Caspar Museum</u>
William T. Bonwell Letter to Mother. May 28, 1865.

<u>Lyon County History Center</u>
Plumb Family Collection
Plumb Correspondence, *Letterpress Book 61*, 271.
Plumb Correspondence, *Letterpress Book 94*, 146.
Preston B. Plumb letter to Leslie J. Perry. Plumb Correspondence, Folder 4. January 4, 1876.

William E. Connelley Notebooks
Connelley, William E. *Book 1*. 1910-1913.
Connelley, William E. *Book 2*. 1910-1913.
Connelley, William E. *Book 3*. 1910-1913.
Connelley, William E. *Book 4*. 1910-1913.
Connelley, William E. *Book 5*. 1910-1913.
Connelley, William E. *Book 6*. 1910-1913.
Connelley, William E. *Book 7*. 1910-1913.
Connelley, William E. *Book 9*. 1910-1913.
Connelley, William E. *Book 13*. 1910-1913.
Connelley, William E. *Book 18*. 1910-1913.
Connelley, William E. *Book 24*. 1910-1913.
Connelley, William E. *Book 25*. 1910-1913.

<u>Kansas State Historical Society</u>
Bodwell, Sherman. *Bodwell Diary*. 1862-1865.

Connelley Collection
Narratives on P.B. Plumb. Collection 16, Box 43, Folder 404. March 6, 1913.

National Archives Records
Preston B. Plumb. Military Personnel File, 1861-1865.
Preston B. Plumb Letter to Lt. Ira Tabor. June 4, 1865.

Plumb Family Collection
Carrie Plumb letter to Preston Plumb Jr., April 2, 1889.
Carrie Plumb letter to Preston Plumb Jr., No date, from The Dakota, NY
Plumb, Preston B. *Plumb Diary*. February 1865 through September 1865.
Preston B. Plumb letter to Preston Plumb Jr., December 18, 1887.
Preston B. Plumb letter to Preston Plumb Jr., March 12, 1890.
Preston B. Plumb letter to Preston Plumb Jr., September 24, 1891.

Robert and Lesa Reves
11th Kansas Cavalry Descriptive Roll, Company K, May 1865.

Published

Books

Blaine, James G. *Twenty Years of Congress 1861-1881, Vol. II*. Henry Bill Publishing Company, 1886.

Britton, Wiley. *Memoirs of the Rebellion on the Border: 1863*. University of Nebraska Press, 1993.

Dewolf, C.W.; Eakin, Monnett, Schnetzer. *The Splendors and Horrors of a Battlefield: A Yankee Cavalryman, C.W. Dewolf, Views the Battle of Prairie Grove and Afterwards*. Two Trails Publishing, 1999.

Plumb, Preston B. *American Merchant Marine Speech*. Government Printing Office, 1884.

Ponce, Pearl. *Kansas's War: The Civil War in Documents (Civil War in the Great Interior)*. Ohio University Press, 2011.

Simpson, Benjamin F. *An Eulogy: Preston B. Plumb, Delivered at Emporia, Kansas, May 30, 1892*. Geo. W. Crane, Printer, 1892.

Stotler, Jacob. *Annals of Emporia and Lyon County: Historical Incidents of the First Quarter Century, 1857-1882*. Emporia, Kansas.

United States Congress. *Bills and Joint Resolutions in the U.S. Senate: 47th Congress*. Government Printing Office, 1883.

United States Congress. *The Congressional Record*. Washington, D.C.: Congressional Research Service, April 24, 1884. ProQuest Congressional.

United States Congress. *The Congressional Record*. Washington, D.C.: Congressional Research Service, February 3, 1889. ProQuest Congressional.

United States Congress. *The Congressional Record*. Washington, D.C.: Congressional Research Service, February 16, 1891. ProQuest Congressional.

United States Congress. *Journal of the Senate of the United States of America, Second Session of the Forty Fifth Congress Begun and Held at the City of Washington December 3, 1877*. Government Printing Office, 1877.

United States Congress. *Journal of the Senate of the United States of America, First Session of the Forty Sixth Congress Begun and Held at the City of Washington March 18, 1879*. Government Printing Office, 1879.

United States Congress. *Journal of the Senate of the United States of America, Second Session of the Forty Ninth Congress Begun and Held at the City of Washington December 6, 1886*. Government Printing Office, 1887.

United States Congress. *Memorial Addresses on the Life and Character of Preston B. Plumb, Feb. 20 and March 19, 1892*. Government Printing Office, 1892.

Newspapers

The Anaconda Standard. January 20, 1891.

Bangor Daily Whig and Courier. July 14, 1882.

Buck & Ball. December 7, 1862.

E. "From the Plains--11th Kansas." *The Leavenworth Times*, June 29, 1865.

Emporia Daily Republican, December 9, 1893

Emporia Gazette. February 22, 1895

"The Emporia Library." *The Weekly News Democrat*, October 23, 1884.

Holton Signal. March 15, 1893.

Kansas News. January 15, 1859.

The Leavenworth Times. March 21, 1865.

"Mrs. Plumb Completely Prostrated." *Democrat and Chronicle*, December 21, 1891.

"Plumb Estate Wins." *Emporia Republican*, August 27, 1896.

"Seventy-Ninth OVI Reunion." *Emporia Gazette*, March 30, 1893.

The Weekly News Democrat. October 29, 1859.

The Weekly News Democrat. June 15, 1877.

The Weekly News Democrat. "A Round up of Our Heavyweight Politicians," October 10, 1889.

"Women Suffrage." *Manhattan Republic*, October 13, 1887.

Secondary Sources

<u>Books</u>

William Ralston Balch. *The Life of James Abram Garfield*. Hubbard Bros., 1881.

Burke, W. S. *Official Military History of Kansas Regiments: During the War for the Suppression of the Great Rebellion*. Kansas Heritage Press.

Connelley, William Elsey. "The Lane Trail." *Collections of the Kansas State Historical Society, 1913-1914*, 1915.

Connelley, William. *The Life of Preston B. Plumb, 1837-1891: United States Senator from Kansas for the Fourteen Years from 1877 to 1891*. Browne & Howell Company, 1913.

Dietz, Theresa. *The Complete Language of Flowers: A Definitive and Illustrated History (Volume 3) (Complete Illustrated Encyclopedia, 3)*. Illustrated. Wellfleet Press, 2020.

Frank Leslie's Popular Monthly, Volume XXIX, January to June 1890. Frank Leslie's Publishing House, 1890.

Hinton, Richard. *American Reformers: John Brown and His Men, With Some Account of the Roads They Traveled to Reach Harper's Ferry*. Funk & Wagnalls Company, 1894.

Hinton, Richard. *Rebel Invasion of Missouri And Kansas, And The Campaign Of The Army Of The Border Against General Sterling Price (1865)*. Kansas Heritage Press, 1994.

Hunt, R. D. *Colonels in Blue: Missouri and the Western States and Territories.* McFarland & Company, 2019

Lee, Fred L. *The Battle for Westport*. Westport Historical Society, 1982.

Report of the Adjutant General of the State of Kansas 1861-1865. Vol. 1. Chicago: Bulletin Co-operative Printing Company, 1867.

Scott, Kim Allen. *The Fighting Printers of Company E*. Kinally Press, 1987.

Tanner, Alpheus Hiram. *Kansas Historical Collections, Volume XIV, 1915-1918*. Kansas State Historical Society, 230.

The Battle of Prairie Grove. Prairie Grove Battlefield Historic State Park.

Wickman, Johanna. *Lost Forts of Casper*. History Press, 2016.

Magazines

Hall, Tony. "Plumb Helped Emporia Get Started." *The Emporia Journal* 3, no. 3 (February 1992): 3–7.

Triplett, Roger. "1857—Emporia—1957." *Centennial Emporia Kansas Historical Booklet*. 1957: 25-28.

Newspapers

Cedar County Republican, January 8, 1892.

The Ellsworth Populist, January 11, 1896.

The Osage County Chronicle, August 24, 1882.

The Osage County Chronicle, June 3, 1886.

Saint Louis Globe-Democrat, March 22, 1888.

Stevens. "Memories of Plumb." *Cedar County Republican*, January 8, 1892.

Stevens. "Senator Plumb." *Globe-Democrat*, December 27, 1891.

Stevens. "Wherein Plumb Was Great." *The Kansas City Times*, December 21, 1891.

"Senator Plumb Had No Middle Name." Topeka Daily Capital, November 19, 1909.

www.ingramcontent.com/pod-product-compliance
Lightning Source LLC
Chambersburg PA
CBHW021335230426
43666CB00006B/296